NON-FORMAL EDUCATION

NON-FORMAL EDUCATION

Dr. Rajesh Verma
Lecturer, School of Education,
Nalanda Open University,
Patna

CENTRUM PRESS
NEW DELHI-110002 (INDIA)

CENTRUM PRESS
H.O.: 4360/4, Ansari Road, Daryaganj,
New Delhi-110 002 (India)
Ph.: 23278000, 23261597

B.O.: No. 1015, Ist Main Road, BSK IIIrd Stage
IIIrd Phase, IIIrd Block,
Bangalore - 560 085 (India)
Tel.: 080-41723429
Visit us at: www.centrumpress.com

Non-formal Education

First Edition, 2009

PRINTED IN INDIA

Printed at Balaji Offset, Delhi

Contents

Preface

Non-formal education is instruction that is not obligatory and structured and is learned outside the context of a formal school. The term is often used in reference to adult education. Non-formal Education (NFE) organised educational activity outside the formal system of education. It is simple and flexible and can be delivered at any place convenient to the learners. It is generally designed to meet the basic learning needs of disadvantaged groups and can be availed of at any age. NFE is provided to those sections of the community who have no access to or are dropped out from formal education. Non-formal education became part of the international discourse on education policy in the late 1960s and early 1970s. It can be seen as related to the concepts of recurrent and lifelong learning. Tight (1996: 68) suggests that whereas the latter concepts have to do with the extension of education and learning throughout life, non-formal education is about 'acknowledging the importance of education, learning and training which takes place outside recognized educational institutions'. In many northern countries the notion of non-formal education is not common in internal policy debates - preferred alternatives being community education and community learning, informal education and social pedagogy. Adult and non-formal education are essential not only for eradication of illiteracy and universalisation of elementary education, but also for making life-long education a way of life and for bringing about the cultural revolution for the learning society. These alternatives are inter-related and interdependent and both should, therefore, go hand in hand for achieving the laudable objectives. Non-formal education has character of flexibility in respect of timings, vacations, curriculum and multiple point entry etc. and adjustment according to local specific need of the area and locality.

This book is designed to serve as an authentic reference tool on non-formal education. It is hoped, students and teachers besides the researchers and policy planners in the field will find this book much informative and useful. An attempt has been made to cover up most of the topics included in M.Ed. syllabus of the Indian universities.

—*Rajesh Verma*

UNIT-I

Principles of Non-formal Education

Non-formal Education—Concept, Definitions, Need, Aims and Objectives

A system of non-formal education is extremely important in the present context of India. Its incorporation in any country's educational system makes that system more useful. With the introduction of the new pattern in India, non-formal education becomes even more valuable to that country. In this pattern, a kind of selective admission after class X is in-built. Further, the addition of one more public examination upto the first degree course may mean more persons leaving the educational system and entering the world of work. For all such dropouts and others, a well organised system of non-formal education will be a boon. It might thus be urged that proper development and expansion of a non-formal system of education will provide for greater strength and stability to the new educational structure of 10+2+3. Accordingly, the Central and State governments are keen to give all possible encouragement and support to build up a strong and well-spread system of non-formal education.

A person's life has so far been divided, practically in all societies, in two stages: the student life and the working life. During the student life, he received knowledge and training and utilised the same afterwards in the world of work through self-employment or service. After he started working, he never thought of studying; and even if he felt its need, he could get no facility for it. In relatively simpler and static societies of the past, what he studied or learnt during his educational career was sufficient for his later life. But this is no more valid in modern days of explosion in knowledge, science and technology and of fast changes in practically every aspect of society. Education has now truly become a life-long process. If a person does not want to invite failure in the work he has chosen for his livelihood or does not otherwise wish to live as an obsolete human being, he has to acquire new knowledge and learn new methodologies relevant to him on a continuous basis. For doing this, he should make use of any form of education-formal, non-formal, or informal—whichever is more handy and pertinent to his needs.

There are a large number of young people who are already working in factories and other sectors of employment and are feeling handicapped in their career in the absence of a professional diploma. Similarly, there are students who have to leave their studies half-way for financial or other difficulties and who later wish to avail themselves of any opportunity for improving their employability or prospects for promotion by obtaining further education or training on part-time basis. For want of such facilities there are some students who have been taking examinations of the organisations like City and Guilds of London Institute, London, in various trades such as refrigeration, printing, electrical technician's course, telecommunication technician's course, etc. If proper facilities are made available in our own country for vocational and other diplomas through correspondence or otherwise, there is no reason why the students should look to a foreign organisation in future.

CABE and Non-formal Education

The Central Advisory Board of Education at its meeting held in November 1974 laid special emphasis on the development of programmes of non-formal education. As a general strategy, it urged that the exclusive emphasis on formal system of education should be given up and a large element of non-formal education should be introduced within the system. The scheme of multiple entry and other programmes of part-time education have to be adopted in a big way. At the secondary and university stages, part-time and correspondence education should be developed and all encouragement given for programmes of self-study. All state plans should, in future, include programmes of non-formal education as an integral part of educational provisions and a suitable machinery be setup in each state to formulate, devise and implement programmes of non-formal education, including functional curricula, integrated and inter-linked with the formal system.

With respect to universalisation of elementary education, the Board expressed conviction that the goal cannot be realised through an exclusive reliance on the formal system of education with its single point entry, sequential character and full-time institutional instruction with full-time professional teachers. The Board, therefore, recommended a large scale programme of parttime education for those children who cannot attend schools, for some reason or the other, on a whole time basis. The Board also urged that every state should prepare a concrete and realistic programme which should be made financially feasible through, *inter alia,* the introduction of non-formal elements within the existing system. In the field of higher education, the Board urged restraint in the establishment of new universities and colleges. In place of this emphasis should be on achieving expansion through existing institutions and through non-formal channels. In the field of vocationalisation of secondary education, the Board recommended that in designing the vocational courses, there should be considerable freedom, elasticity and experimentation; and wherever possible, non-formal educational methods, particularly correspondence and evening courses, should be used. Similarly, the Board welcomed and endorsed the proposals of the Union Ministry of Education for providing programmes of non-formal education to out-of-school youth in the age-group 15-25.

The Board also recommended that the programme of functional literacy; which represents the single largest on-going effort of intensive non-formal education linked to a developmental activity, should be strengthened and expanded.

Formal Education

We are all familiar with formal education. It constitutes the age-grade hierarchy of primary, secondary and higher education.

It is the traditional system in which the teacher and the taught face each other in a classroom situation on a regular and continuous basis, follow a fixed and pre-determined syllabus, secure promotion to the next class after passing the previous one, take a public examination at the end of the course and receive a certificate, diploma or degree. This system works in a rigid framework and one has to study under the constraints of these rigidities. But the system has continued to function for centuries and has had necessarily to be adopted as a basic system even by those countries where education has been introduced in an organised manner for the first time.

Non-formal Education

Over the years, a class of persons has grown in many countries who cannot make use of formal education. Their number is increasing every day. These persons include the school-dropouts (who could not complete even the minimum compulsory period of schooling for every citizen), the employed or working persons, those living far away from the centres of education or training, and the housewives, retired persons, and others many of whom are looking for information, knowledge or training without a diploma or degree.

Often, such people have experienced a "felt need" for further education, training or intellectual refreshment and are therefore already motivated.

A good portion of the need of such persons can be met through a non-formal system of education. That may also constitute a system most suitable to them. Such a system will include education through correspondence courses, radio or television, language laboratory, seminars, discussions or workshops, demonstration farms, sandwich courses, programmed lessons, paperbacks, popular literature (including that in science), modern public library system, open school and open university.

Informal Education

The individual does not live in a vacuum. He is constantly under the influence of his surroundings. In a way, he 'learns' all the time, from every event, from every experience, and from moment to moment. There is hardly a place or happening, *e.g.*, a market, a hospital, a railway station, a cinema house, a journey, an entertainment party or a court-case, from which something or other is not learnt. If one is observant, inquisitive and alert, one assimilates more and faster. Even those not so gifted receive something which affects their behavioural patterns in life. The education received in this indirect manner may be called informal education. Some people have called it incidental or accidental education.

Definitions

The expressions 'non-formal' and 'informal' education have in the past been used somewhat loosely and sometimes even with interchanged positions. Any education other than formal education has been called either non-formal or informal education. 'These two have been variously defined as the entire range of learning experiences outside the regular and graded system as an educational "unsystem", and as life-long learning.

Coombs defined *(Prospects,* UNESCO, Autumn 1973) formal education as one which is given through formal educational institutions: a school, a college or a university. He defined non-formal education as one which is imparted through organisations and institutions outside the formal education institutions. A sports association, for example, may educate promising children in various sports. Informal education, according to Coombs, is education which takes place all the time informally or incidentally.

In UNESCO parlance all education outside the formal system is out-of-school education. I would say that *Non-formal education* is education intentionally given outside the formal system, and informal education means education incidentally picked up in life situations like listening to a broadcast, seeing a puppet show, reading a newspaper, etc. It must be added that it is not possible to have water-tight divisions in this regard.

The suggested classifications are a matter of convenience and they are not mutually exclusive in toto. Non-formal education can be organised within the framework of a formal educational institution. Field trips, dramatics, club activities and other co-curricular programmes organised in a school can be classified as non-formal or informal in character. Similarly, there can be elements of formal education in a non-formal educational activity. The correspondence courses, for example, for the first degree given by a university do follow a prescribed syllabus, provide for a brief contact programme in which there is regular classroom teaching, and students of the correspondence course take the same public examination and in the same manner as other students of the corresponding formal course.

It should also be stated that the distinction between formal and non-formal education is one of degree and not of kind. The 'formal' system is characterised by rigidities of fixed hours during which a set of people assemble at a determined place and listen or otherwise participate in a teaching process. Usually the students who so assemble and the teachers who give the instruction have certain uniformities in terms of age and educational attainments. But if we remove the rigidities in regard to hours and place of study, type of students, methods of teaching and learning, content of courses, qualification requirements of students and teachers, and methods of evaluation, and still organise a systematic learning process with clear goals of learning, we will have a 'non-formal' educational system which will have different degrees of flexibility and hence different degrees of 'non-formality'. As regards informal education, it is clearly unstructurededucation imparted and imbibed through cultural and socio-religious functions as well as through political and scientific processes and social institutions. Though its impact has been great for generations, at least in the Indian way of life, its depth has never been scientifically assessed. Perhaps it cannot be so assessed.

Historical Perspective

Even in the earliest times it was seen that the natural learning which occurred in life was not adequate to meet the needs of life and the people-young and old-so they went in search of teachers. The 'gurukulas' in India, which have been in existence for the last several thousand years, provided non-formal education in the sense that there was no rigid curriculum and the instruction was individualised. With the increasingly complex organisation of society, specially after the industrial revolution in the West, the concept of providing education to children in organised classrooms resembling the factory model became increasingly popular and in due course an article of faith.

But with further development of the society, knowledge increased much in quality and variety and the means of acquiring that knowledge grew so diverse that the 'factory model' could hope to cover only a fraction of the needed knowledge and that too only for those who could attend the 'factories' during specified hours.

As the proportion of learning occurring within the school to the total Iearning needs diminished and as large learning resources became available elsewhere in society, education in schools and learning came to be distinguished from each other. Accordingly, efforts are being made in different countries to build up a non-formal system of education that will supplement the well-known formal system.

That such a system can meet a felt need of the society has already been pointed out. There are several other reasons why such a system is not only feasible but is also a practical possibility. The reasons for this include the following:

(i) The continuing acceleration of knowledge which cannot be imparted within a certain period of life.

(ii) The ever-expanding needs of society and of individuals more and more persons need to be taught and trained up to increasingly higher levels.

(iii) The ever-present shortage of financial resources, compelling the pooling together of all available resources.

(iv) The increasing need to use a large spectrum of persons to give specialised knowledge and skills in a given area, one or two teachers alone not being sufficient.

(v) The availability of audio-visual media and other aids which are developing.

(vi) The increasing knowledge about the process of learning.

All these reasons apply to the rich as well as the poor nations. For the underdeveloped countries attempting to make headway on several different fronts at the same time and facing grave financial constraints, non-formal education on a large scale is a good solution for maximising returns from the given resources. If education is to reach millions of children and adults, there is no other alternative and a more effective path. There is no doubt that millions have to be reached within a given time span, if genuine development and progress are to take place and the quality of life of the masses of people has to be improved.

To those who consider that education is still synonymous with the classroom, hourly bells and a set of fixed rules, non-formal education will doubtless seem a nightmare spelling chaos in an otherwise well-ordered system. In truth, the concept of non-formal education is founded on hard pragmatic reality: that no socio-economic development is possible unless. (a) every citizen reaches a minimum level of educational maturity, and (b) the educational system provides for continued learning and growth of individuals according to their own pace and need.

Limitations of Formal Education

There is ample evidence to prove that the formal system of education cannot meet all societal, collective and individual needs for instruction, knowledge, skills and behavioural change. Even if the traditional schools and universities are ideally developed and their curricula and teaching methods perfectly elaborated, it is not possible to fulfil all requirements in education through the formal system alone. There are many reasons for it. They include the following:

(i) There is a trend towards democratisation of education. It is neither feasible nor realistic to offer formal education facilities to all people who are in need of some education or training. The obviously restraining factors are the enormous increase in enrolment, rise in educational cost per pupil, limitations of governmental expenditure, and practical difficulties of distance, transport etc. The working class, therefore, thinks that the full-time formal system of education is against their interests and the poor people opine that continuance of the formal system alone shows denial of education to them.

(ii) The environmental differences and the variety of people to whom educational opportunities are to be offered require considerable flexibility in the organisation, content, duration, timing and place of education.

(iii) The rigid patterns of formal education are easily adaptable to the constant evolution of science, technology and society.

(iv) It is against the requirements of life-long education if people who leave the educational system once are compelled to give up for good the use of the educational services.

(v) Formal education, by its very nature, requires continuity, accepts with difficulty the educational values of practical or professional life and responds slowly to new demands and to partial or individual educational requests. This situation is against the realities of present day living.

The Positive Side

There is also a positive side of the case of non-formal education. This reinforces the need for giving a non-formal orientation to the future growth of education. The positive factors are several in number.

The present society has new potentialities for education. The various types of work (*e.g.* job of a telephone operator and use of gadgets and machines in cleaning, washing, agriculture, industry, etc.), the civic life (*e.g.* use of electricity leading to replacement of a fuse-wire or bulb), the pattern of modern civilization (*e.g.* style of dressing, use of furniture, mode of laying a table, methods of entertainment), and the communication media (*e.g.* the satellite) are all offering new possibilities of education. In other words, the educational value of non-educational media is increasing constantly. This explains why the trend towards non-formal education has its basis in the fact that everybody can learn in many more ways and in many more different places than ever before.

There are now more facilities, in addition to the teachers and the books of the past, at one's disposal for learning. These include, as stated earlier, mass media, programmed text-books, pocket or inexpensive literature, educational film shows, extension lectures, professional or technical persons etc. In fact, there is hardly any aspect of life where the effort to learn and develop the individual further is not possible. The human factor also plays an important role in the expansion of non-formal education. In India, for example, besides lakhs of teachers, there are lakhs of other professionals and intellectuals, lakhs of college and university students and voluntary participants in the National Service Scheme, the Yuvak Kendras etc. All of them can contribute their share in developing non-formal educational activities. Our present society is much better equipped to carry out such a programme than its predecessors at any earlier period in history.

Removal of Misunderstandings

It is, however, not correct to think that non-formal education is invariably a better substitute for formal education or that it is only good for people without any formal education, for unskilled or illiterate men and women, and for those in the lower social strata. It should not, in fact, look paradoxical to say that a certain amount of minimum education (literacy at least) through the formal system may be considered desirable before one can make use of the non-formal system on one's own.

It is also not right to think that non-formal educational approach should be adopted only if the conditions for formal education are not possible. The best educational strategy is to provide for a comprehensive educational structure in which both formal and non-formal systems are put to most effective use, depending upon the circumstances and the pupils and objectives to be served.

It is very erroneous to think that non-formal education can be organised without any know-how, knowledge and experience, or professional preparation and methodological training. In fact, non-formal education may be more difficult to organise than the formal or traditional school or college education. Non-formal education should not be taken to mean a softer kind of education. It may be equally demanding in terms of effort from the students as well as the teachers. Actually, it may call for greater planning and preparation and more and better supervision. While being innovative and flexible in regard to methods and content, it may have to be inflexible in regard to goal and standards.

It is similarly unfair to believe that non-formal education is a remedy for all deficiencies of formal education. On the contrary, non-formal education by itself alone cannot deliver the goods. While this is true, it should also be recognised that non-formal education is by no means a cheap or inferior kind of education.

Integration of Formal and Non-formal Education

It is important to realise that in modern times both formal and non-formal methods of education have their due places in any organised system of education. In order to develop such an integrated system, we should undertake, among others, the following measures:

(i) Make people understand and realise the potential and value of non-formal education.

(ii) Take out non-formal education from its marginal position and put it in the mainstream of educational theory, planning and practice.

(iii) Establish links between formal and non-formal education and permit switching over from one to the other. For example, it should be permissible for a school drop-out to make up the deficiency through an evening institute, correspondence course or private studies and then join a centre for higher education along with other students who continued to pursue the formal system without a break. This necessitates a change in the attitude of some of our university authorities particularly.

(iv) Make non-formal education an integral component of the educational system by adopting the principle that the important thing is what a person has learnt and not which channel he has followed in his studies. For example, a certificate, diploma or degree obtained through the owntime or correspondence system should be unhesitatingly accepted equivalent to the one obtained through the formal system.

(v) Develop non-formal educational facilities in such a manner as to offer to the young and the grown-ups various opportunities to move from one branch of education to another, to enter freely at various stages and to leave at different points, and to combine a diversity of work and education according to one's circumstances and need.

The success of such measures as above will depend upon the understanding and appreciation with which issues connected with non-formal education are attended to by our educators, planners, policy-makers, administrators and the general community.

The Indian Education Commission of 1966 had recommended the growth of a parallel system of non-formal education in the country. Mathematically, two parallel lines never meet. So the recommendation should be interpreted to mean that a non-formal system of education should he so developed that it is as comprehensive and efficient as the formal system and that every knowledge or skill, which is attainable through the formal system, should be available through the non-formal system as well.

For, unlike the non-meeting parallel lines of the Euclidean geometry, the two systems should appropriately have a number of points of intersection so that any seeker of knowledge or training is able to achieve his ends through either of the two systems or through a combination of both as it suits his circumstances and convenience.

Some Projects in Non-formal Education

We are not treading on barren soil. Some work in the field of non-formal education has already been done or is going on in various parts of India. A few examples known to me in this regard may be mentioned:

(i) Correspondence courses for the first university degree in many Indian universities and for the master's degree in some.

(ii) Correspondence courses for the school certificates in three boards of secondary education.

(iii) Correspondence courses for the teacher training degree in the five regional colleges of education and the Himachal Pradesh University.

(iv) Correspondence courses for the study of Hindi as a second language by Indians and foreigners through the Kendriya Hindi Nideshalaya, New Delhi.

(v) The mobile education *shibers* of Maharashtra (A forum for primary school teachers and community improvement).

(vi) The Delhi Public Library, Delhi.

(vii) The Kisan Saksharata Yojana (The national programme of functional literacy for farmers in the high-yielding variety areas) merged from 1979-80 in the Rural Functional Literacy Programme.

(viii) Extension programmes organised by the Indian Agricultural Universities, the Institutes of Rural Higher Education and other agencies.

(ix) The summer institutes through the U.G.C., NCERT, etc., and other programmes of in-service training.

(x) Educational Extension activities of several universities in India.

(xi) The national programme of workers education organised through the Union Ministry of Labour.

(xii) The Shramik Vidyapeeth (*i.e.* Polyvalent Centre) at Bombay and Delhi.

(xiii) The orientation programmes organised by National Institute of Educational Planning and Administration,

New Delhi, Staff College, Hyderabad, and National Institute of Health Administration and Education, New Delhi.

(xiv) The scheme of Delhi.

(xv) The national programme Plan.

(xvi) The Open School in New Delhi. Hyderabad.

(xvii) The proposed programme of education through the Indian satellite. INSAT-1B.

In many other countries similar projects of non-formal education appropriate to the prevailing circumstances in those countries have been taken up and are in progress. Two of the most notable examples in this regard may be mentioned: the School of the Air in Australia and the Open University of England. In the School of the Air, teaching is provided through a two-way receiver and the pupils and the teacher may be as far as one thousand kilometres from each other.

The Open University in London constitutes the latest and largest experiment in non-formal education. The admission requirements for its courses do not prescribe the possession of any formal schooling, and correspondence, T.V., extension and other possible methods of communication are all utilised for the teaching work.

Building a National Programme of Non-formal Education

Talking of the future, a comprehensive national programme of non-formal education should conceptually cover all kinds of individuals and groups in the country. More specifically, such groups ought to include the following:

(i) Children of age group 6-14 years who have never been to school.

(ii) Children of age group 6-11 years who dropped out of the formal system of schooling.

(iii) Children of age group 11-14 years who dropped out of the formal system of schooling.

(iv) Illiterate persons of age group 15-25 years.

(v) Semiliterate persons of age group 15-25 years.

(vi) Rural adults working in the high-yielding variety areas, doing dry farming, or interested in horticulture, animal husbandry, fishery, poultry, agro-industry, etc.

(vii) Illiterate or semiliterate population of the age 15+ and residing in urban areas.

(viii) Vocational workers needing the upgrading of their skills.

(ix) Working persons who want to upgrade their academic or professional status.

(x) Housewives, retired persons and others who seek knowledge, information or skills mostly for leisure-time activities and without a certificate, diploma or degree.

Building up an effective programme of non-formal education which would ultimately cover the entire population of India is a challenging task before the educators, administrators and policy makers. In terms of knowledge, values and know-how to be imparted, in terms of age-groups, in terms of syllabi and curricular requirements and the terms of the educational methodology and technology to be used, the variety, complexity and magnitude of the task is baffling. As indicated above, the programmes have to span target-groups from the most illiterate to the highly educated persons.

However big and baffling the task, a start has to be made. There appear to be a number of principles which should govern the building up of the programme. The target group should be clearly chosen with priorities of development in mind. In our case, the rural children of age group 6-14 years who dropped out of school pre-maturely or never went to school and the illiterate and semiliterate youth of the age-group 15-25 are the two priority groups.

A variety of well-programmed material must be built up for these groups taking into account their diverse cultural, economic, and educational levels and occupations. A broad principle should be that while the curriculum is set at national or state level, the syllabus, the method of teaching, and the details be left to the district or even block level with appropriate guidance and supervision. This requires that capability for designing the learning material for non-formal education and for training of teachers should be built in every block and district. A group of persons who understand the developmental and learning needs of children and of adults and know-how to effectively cater to those needs have to be assembled; and with the help of leading experts the latest scientific knowledge in different fields like agriculture, animal husbandry, health, nutrition, and family planning have to be brought into the programme.

Age-group 6-14: For successful organisation of a programme of non-formal education at the primary stage, we will have to bear some crucial considerations in mind. They should include the following:

(i) These programmes should have an element of motivation in order to attract the children to the centres of non-formal and part-time education. Story-telling, drama, *bhajans* or devotional songs, and dance may provide a base for attracting this group of children to the centres.

(ii) The programme may vary from place to place. The rigid approach of the prescribed curriculum and the prescribed text-books may not lead to success.

(iii) The programmes should be related to proficiency in jobs available in the locality. Here the effort should be to help the pupils to acquire skills in processes of production in the earlier stages and more sophisticated training in course of time.

(iv) The programmes should emerge through a solution of problems faced by the pupils while working on different jobs.

(v) The attempt should be to enable the children to join the mainstream of formal education at different points as early as possible and to that extent condensed and simplified courses will have to be planned and provided in the centres of non-formal and part-time education.

Conducting programmes of part-time and non-formal education will not be the same as teaching in the schools. It will call for ingenuity, patience, and organisational work on the part of the teachers. The average teacher or the educated youth of the locality called upon to manage a centre of non-formal education would require special orientation or training, help and encouragement. The teaching techniques utilised in these centres will have to provide for individualisation of instruction. The State Institutes of Education should play a leading role in this field.

They may organise regular meetings of representatives of the departments of agriculture, community development, health and nutrition, family planning, Nehru Yuvak Kendras, and adult education in order to discuss issues related to the preparation and supply of appropriate instructional material and the participation of experts in the organisation of demonstrations and discussion groups at the centres of non-formal education.

Age-group 15-35: This is a heterogeneous group. Members of this group play an important role in the society. They are often engaged in productive occupations or are economically viable. Most people get married in this age-group and have to take decisions about the size of their families. They also belong to an age-group at which they are often imbued with curiosity and a thirst for learning. Their educational needs are, however, multi-faced and numerous: they are not simple.

A project called Non-formal Education for the Age-group 15-25 was launched by the Central government from the beginning of the Fifth Plan. This was to be supplemented by a massive scheme entitled National Adult Education Programme during the Sixth Plan. It was formally launched on 2nd October 1978 on Gandhi's birthday. It visualised giving of adult education to 10 crore illiterates belonging to the age-group 15-35, within a period of five years. In 1947, literacy in India was 14 per cent. It rose gradually to 34.45 per cent (excluding the age-group 0-4) in 1971. But due to population increase the number of illiterates in the country above fourteen years of age also rose from 24.7 crores to 30.7 crores during the same period. According to the 1971 census, the total number of illiterate persons above fourteen years of age was 20.95 crores, of which 9.71 crores were in the age-group 15-35. This figure may at present he around 10 crores. It is this last group which was the target of the National Adult Education Programme.

According to the policy statement issued by the Government of India in respect of the above programme, adult education while emphasising acquisition of literacy skills will also be: (i) relevant to the environment and needs of the learner, (ii) flexible regarding duration, time, location, instructional arrangement etc., and (iii) diversified in regard to curriculum, teaching and learning materials and methods.

This will apparently make the whole programme largely non-formal in character. It may be mentioned in this connection that education and literacy, seen as essential for human resource development, must form part of development strategy. It is on the acceptance of this assumption that the National Adult Education Programme was stated to have been launched. It is a challenging programme full of difficulties in practical implementation. The financial allocation for this programme has, however, been reduced much in the revised Sixth Plan which is under implementation since 1981.

The life experience of the adults is much greater and their psychology, needs, and aspirations different from the children. These factors have to be duly taken note of in providing motivation, preparing instructional materials, and handling the teaching-learning situations. As an illustration, mention may be made of the programme-design evolved by World Education in one of their publications in which the following principles of instructional methodology suited to the illiterate adults have been mentioned:

(i) Illiterate adults are literate in visual sense: they can appreciate and understand visual presentation such as pictures and photograph.
(ii) The primer by its very definition of being a book discourages the beginning learner because the difficulties faced in getting through the first pages seen like formidable obstacles to reach the end.
(iii) A functional literacy programme should from the out-

set present material that is of immediate use to the learner.

(iv) The highly developed memories of illiterates can be used in the designing of a methodology.

(v) From the outset of the programme, emphasis should be on content rather than on the instruction of literacy skills.

(vi) A dialogical rather than a frontal teaching approach is better suited to the needs of adults.

(vii) Subject matter derived from the environment and experiences of participants is more likely to facilitate dialogue than a methodology and curriculum designed without relation to the participants. The content of the methodology should, therefore, be situation-bound.

Conclusion

Our circumstances demand that a large scale programme of non-formal education should be built into the growing system of Indian education. Both the formal and the non-formal be integrated into one comprehensive system. But the success of any programme of non-formal education either for children or adolescents or adults will depend upon the understanding and appreciation with which the connected issues are attended to by our policy-makers, planners, educators and administrators. And many of the solutions in this sector of education may call for an unorthodox approach and an unprecedented disposal.

Historical Development and Progress of Non-formal Education Programmes in India—Formal, Non-formal and Informal Education

Governmental Programs: India's open universities, adult education programs, and widespread distance education cater to the needs of a diverse population. The Department of Education, since 1980, has been sponsoring non-formal education (NFE) for children of ages 6 to 14, especially those marginalized from the formal system for various reasons, especially poverty. In 2001, some 740 voluntary agencies were implementing NFE programs in 25 states. Another 85 agencies sanctioned 9,485 NFE centres during 2000.

The National Open School (NOS) was established in November 1989 as an autonomous registered society to examine and certify students up through pre-degree courses. NOS provides the following programs: (a) foundation course, (b) secondary education course, (c) senior secondary education course, (d) open vocational education program, (e) life enrichment program, and (f) basic education for Universal Elementary Education (UEE). NOS provides individualized support through a network of study centres. Also called Accredited Institutions, the 972 study centres serve about 400,000 students all over the country. The aforementioned Indira Gandhi National Open University (IGNOU) also provides distance education.

Community-based Learning: Traditional societies have thrived on their non-formal systems of education. Joshi writes: "Ancient records of the Indian tradition testify to the search for the Rishis and sages for higher knowledge (para vidya), and their discoveries have been continuously transmitted to posterity and kept alive through its history, marked by periods of expansion, specialization, decline and renewal" (1998). Long before the bureaucratized western structures of schooling mushroomed in the "less developed" nations, India's non-formal education was enshrined in its familial and cultural units.

Students and educators in India thus usually share a common history and a legacy of collective wisdom. This learning process reinforces the curricular thrusts in structured settings. To isolate the two systems from each other is to fracture the whole learning process. There are fields—fine arts, medicine, astronomy, and numerous other skills—where knowledge has been transmitted from one generation to another within familial ties without any formal structures. One can argue that India's cultural continuity is indebted to this informal system of education.

Venkataiah calls this education beyond structured curricula "a collective alternative self-curriculum, for over the years it involves learning, in the neighbourhood and more intensely in the playground, a succession of codes and adjustments and conventional learned responses through which children complement their development with collective experience" (2000).

Concept Non-formal Education

Within policy debates a common differentiation has been made between different forms of provision. Informal, non-formal, and formal programmes have been viewed as very different. Here we explore this categorization and some of the forms of work that exist under the non-formal label in southern countries.

Non-formal education became part of the international discourse on education policy in the late 1960s and early 1970s. It can be seen as related to the concepts of recurrent and lifelong learning. Tight (1996: 68) suggests that whereas the latter concepts have to do with the extension of education and learning throughout life, non-formal education is about 'acknowledging the importance of education, learning and training which takes place outside recognized educational institutions'. Fordham (1993) suggests that in the 1970s, four characteristics came be associated with non-formal education:

- Relevance to the needs of disadvantaged groups.
- Concern with specific categories of person.
- A focus on clearly defined purposes.
- Flexibility in organization and methods.

In many northern countries the notion of non-formal education is not common in internal policy debates-preferred alternatives being community education and community learning, informal education and social pedagogy.

The Idea of Non-formal Education

As Fordham (1993) relates, in 1967 at an international conference in Williamsburg USA, ideas were set out for what was to become a widely read analysis of the growing 'world educational crisis' (Coombs 1968). There was concern about unsuitable curricula; a realization that educational growth and economic growth were not necessarily in step, and that jobs did not emerge directly as a result of educational inputs. Many countries were finding it difficult (politically or economically) to pay for the expansion of formal education.

The conclusion was that formal educational systems had adapted too slowly to the socio-economic changes around them and that they were held back not only by their own conservatism, but also by the inertia of societies themselves. If we also accept that educational policy making tends to follow rather than lead other social trends, then it followed that change would have to come not merely from within formal schooling, but from the wider society and from other sectors within it. It was from this point of departure that planners and economists in the World Bank began to make a distinction between informal, non-formal and formal education.

At around the same time there were moves in UNESCO toward lifelong education and notions of 'the learning society' which culminated in Learning to Be ('The Faure Report', UNESCO 1972). Lifelong learning was to be the 'master concept' that should shape educational systems (UNESCO 1972:182). What emerged was an influential tripartite categorization of learning systems. It's best known statement comes from the work of Combs with Prosser and Ahmed (1973):

Formal Education: The hierarchically structured, chronologically graded 'education system', running from primary school through the university and including, in addition to general academic studies, a variety of specialised programmes and institutions for full-time technical and professional training.

Informal Education: the truly lifelong process whereby every individual acquires attitudes, values, skills and knowledge from daily experience and the educative influences and resources in his or her environment-from family and neighbours, from work and play, from the market place, the library and the mass media.

Non-formal Education: Any organised educational activity outside the established formal system-whether operating separately or as an important feature of some broader activity-that is intended to serve identifiable learning clienteles and learning objectives.

The distinction made is largely administrative. Formal education is linked with schools and training institutions; non-formal with community groups and other organizations; and informal covers what is left, e.g. interactions with friends, family and work colleagues. The problem with this is that people often organize educational events as part of their everyday experience and so the lines blur rapidly. As Fordham (1993) comments, these definitions do not imply hard and fast categories. In particular, there may well be some overlap (and confusion) between the informal and the non-formal.

Just how helpful a focus on administrative setting or institutional sponsorship is a matter of some debate. Once we recognize that a considerable amount of education happens beyond the school wall it may be that a simple division between formal and informal education will suffice. It has certainly been the argument of Jeffs and Smith (1990) that the notion of non-formal education has limited use when thinking about process.

Just because something does not make sense in terms of process, does not mean an idea doesn't retain its currency. It has been a convenient way of talking about funding rather than the actual process. As Graham-Brown (1991: 64) says, dividing formal education from out of school education or so-called non-formal education is artificial in many ways. But in some countries, this division reflects the gulf between government provision through the school system, on the one hand, and the needs and interests of marginal populations who are most alienated from the system on the other.

The range of initiatives and programmes that have adopted the title 'non-formal' are many and various. They include literacy and basic education for adults and young people, political and trade union education, 'catching-up' programmes for school drop outs, pre-school education for young children, political and trade union education and various kinds of educational work linked with development initiatives including agricultural extension and training programmes and health education. They also shade over into various examples of both state and private vocational training programmes. The McGivney and Murray (1992) collection Adult Education in Development gives a good feel of the sorts of initiatives this might include. They look particularly at health education, literacy, rural development and the role of women in development. However, it can be confusing to use terms like adult education in the context of Southern education-given the age distribution of populations and the large numbers of young people involved in non-formal programmes.

What is also apparent from the literature is that it was politically useful to use a term like non-formal education. As Shukla (1985) has argued by the mid 1960s it was becoming clear that an education system based around schooling could not be sustained because of the sheer cost to already fragile economies.

A search for 'new' techniques was therefore on. Second, within the north it was becoming clear that the school was only one amongst many potential educative elements. Concepts such as 'the learning society' were gaining some currency. Third, there was the impact of movements such as that of deschooling.

These were essentially 'western' concerns. At the same time a number of socialist countries initiated large programmes for changing the consciousness, skills and organizations of their populations. They typically used many of the forms that we now label as non-formal education:

- Specially trained educators (maybe for 4 or 5 weeks) (not teachers) sent out to local villages etc. to set up and run programmes and recruit further helpers and group members.
- The use of mass media such as radio and television, things like newsheets and comics.
- Provision on a mass scale-a whole region or country is targeted.
- Sometimes formal, sometimes informal sanctions against those who did not participate.
- Many of these programmes apparently met with considerable success. In this respect Russia, Cuba, Tanzania, Somalia, Ethiopia and Nicaragua were often quoted as having organised successful mass campaigns-particularly in respect of literacy (Coles 1987: 38).

By the mid 1970s a number of non-socialist countries were beginning to turn to the idea of mass non-formal education. It was clear that there remained a large scale and apparently growing problem of illiteracy. It was also clear that economic and social development depended on bringing about changes in many people's thinking.

The development process is in fact an educational process, or rather it should unfailingly be viewed as such. We cannot therefore conceive of development in the absence of education any more than education in the absence of development. (Faundez 1988 quoted by McGivney & Murray 1991: 10)

How, for example, were people to learn to plant new crops or varieties or to farm in ways that might increase production?

There was a further shift amongst the donor agencies working in the South. Whereas there had been a great emphasis on the provision of plant, and particularly prestigious projects, there was a growing realization that development primarily depended on the people themselves and that much more stress should be placed on improving their quality of life.

This called for new approaches to formal education; it also gave considerable impetus to non-formal education, and especially to basic education for those who had been largely neglected-the urban and rural poor (Coles 1987: 37). The problem was that these sorts of programmes had not been tried in the market and political conditions associated with Southern capitalist societies.

Contrasts between 'Formal' and 'Non-formal' Programmes

Simkins (1976) analysed non-formal education programme in terms of purposes, timing, content delivery systems and control, and contrasted these with formal educational programmes.

The resulting ideal-types provide a useful framework-and bring out the extent to which non-formal education initiatives, while emphasizing flexibility, localness and responsiveness remain located within a curricula form of education (in contrast with those forms driven by conversation).

Ideal-type models of normal and non-formal education

	Formal	**Non-formal**
Purposes	Long-term & general Credential-based	Short-term & specific Non-credential-based
Timing	long cycle/preparatory/ full-time	short cycle/recurrent/ part-time
Content	standardized/input centred academic entry require- ments determine clientele	individualized/output centred practical clientele determine entry requirements
Delivery system	institution-based, isolated from environment rigidly structured, teacher- centred and resource intensive	environment-based, community related. flexible, learner- centred and resource saving
control	external/hierarchical	self-governing/democratic

'Top Down and Bottom Up'

One of the enduring themes in the literature of non-formal education, according to Fordham (1993), has been that the education provided should be in the interests of the learners and that the organization and curriculum planning should preferably be undertaken by the learners themselves: that it should be 'bottom up'. It is also often argued that this should empower learners to understand and if necessary change the social structure around them. Fordham (1993) continues: 'Examples where there is a genuine sense of ownership are not easy to find; and almost all have an element of community outreach as part of the general organization'.

On the other hand examples of top-down non-formal programmes are all too common. Almost all employer-led and State provided training falls into this category. This can be seen as paralleling the distinctions that Jeffs and Smith (1990, 1999) make between formal and informal education via curriculum. In this way formal education would broadly approximate to top-down curriculum formation (c); non-formal to bottom-up or negotiated curriculum formation (b); and informal education would arguably be a non-curriculum or conversational form (a).

Pointers to the Success of Non-formal Programmes

As Graham-Brown (1991: 74-77) has argued in respect of literacy programmes there are a number of dimensions that have proved to be crucial to effectiveness:

- Training and motivation of literacy workers.
- The quality and relevance of materials.
- The reinforcements of literacy.

It is clear from the studies of literacy campaigns that both the commitment and skills of literacy promoters are very important. Enthusiasm is not enough. It is not that straightforward to facilitate learner participation in dialogue and discussion. Certain skills are needed to put across ideas and so on. Many of the literacy workers are young (mostly between 18 and 25 in the successful Botswana campaign). This meant that they need not be automatically accepted or appreciated. In some campaigns there has been a considerable effort to try to recruit older workers and those who are known and held in good regard in a locality. In many campaigns workers are paid, and the job accords them some status (although not necessarily accreditation or certification). Where volunteers are recruited, for example in the Kenyan initiative, and who live in the local communities, the main incentive is often the hope that this might lead to a full time job.

There has also been an emphasis on developing appropriate materials. Most of the various national literacy campaigns have had some central unit which developed materials etc. for the workers etc. to use. To this must be added things like the production of regular radio programmes to support initiatives. However, this is both expensive and sophisticated and it is not proved that easy, for example, to update and change materials quite as has been needed.

Then as Graham-Brown (1991: 76) suggests, once people achieve basic literacy, whatever its precise form, the process creates further demands for post-literacy education, whether to 'catch up' on missed formal education, or to develop organizational or practical skills. At this point things can become quite expensive and complex. The demands are now more sophisticated.

To these specific questions must be added some further problems. To begin with, given that initiatives involve voluntary participation-how are people to be attracted on sufficient scale. This is much less of a problem in systems where there is large scale schooling some legal basis for attendance. The successful campaign in Botswana, for example, touched about 20 per cent of the population-it still left quite a few people illiterate.

In addition, unless the school system is discredited for some political reason, a lower valuation tends to be put on non-formal education, especially for young people. They do not hold the same status (they are local and not special) and often do not lead to accreditation.

In Conclusion

The notion of non-formal education has been a significant feature of policy debates around education in southern countries for three decades. It has drawn attention to the importance and potential of education, learning and training that takes place outside recognized educational institutions. There are questions about usefulness of the notion when looking at the process of education.

It has also gone in and out of fashion. Fordham (1993) comments that if we try to correlate the flourishing of non-formal education and political change then the 1970s can certainly be described as the decade of non-formal education (Rubenson 1982).

Similarly the 1980s saw the neglect of non-formal education and Fordham suggests that this was in tune with the politics of the decade, accompanied by greater inequalities both within and between countries. Given the extent to which notions of lifelong learning and associated ideas have gained ground in recent years it will be interesting to see how the language of policy debates will change over the next few years.

Basic Principles of Non-formal Education—Paulo Friere's Concepts: Conscientization—Culture of Silence—Culture of Poverty

A careful analysis of the teacher-student relationship at any level inside or outside the school, reveals its fundamentally narrative character This relationship involves a narrating Subject (the teacher) and patient, listening objects (the students). The contents, whether values or empirical dimensions of reality, tend in the process of being narrated to become lifeless and petrified. Education is suffering from narration sickness.

The teacher talks about reality as if it were motionless, static, compartmentalized, and predictable. Or else he expounds on a topic completely alien to the existential experience of the students. His task is to "fill" the students with the contents of his narration—contents which are detached from reality, disconnected from the totality that engendered them and could give them significance. Words are emptied of their concreteness and become a hollow, alienated, and alienating verbosity.

The outstanding characteristic of this narrative education, then, is the sonority of words, not their transforming power. "Four times four is sixteen; the capital of Para is Belem." The student records, memorizes, and repeats these phrases without perceiving what four times four really means, or realizing the true significance of "capital" in the affirmation "the capital of Para is Belem," that is, what Belem means for Para and what Para means for Brazil.

Narration (with the teacher as narrator) leads the students to memorize mechanically the narrated content. Worse yet, it turns them into "containers," into "receptacles" to be "filled" by the teacher. The more completely she fills the receptacles, the better a teacher she is. The more meekly the receptacles permit themselves to be filled, the better students they are.

Education thus becomes an act of depositing, in which the students are the depositories and the teacher is the depositor. Instead of communicating, the teacher issues communiques and makes deposits which the students patiently receive, memorize, and repeat. This is the "banking" concept of education, in which the scope of action allowed to the students extends only as far as receiving, filing, and storing the deposits. They do, it is true, have the opportunity to become collectors or cataloguers of the things they store. But in the last analysis, it is the people themselves who are filed away through the lack of creativity, transformation, and knowledge in this (at best) misguided system. For apart from inquiry apart from the praxis, individuals cannot be truly human. Knowledge emerges only through invention and re-invention, through the restless, impatient, continuing, hopeful inquiry, human beings pursue in the world, with the world, and with each other.

In the banking concept of education, knowledge is a gift bestowed by those who consider themselves knowledgeable upon those whom they consider to know nothing. Projecting an absolute ignorance onto others, a characteristic of the ideology of oppression, negates education and knowledge as processes of inquiry. The teacher presents himself to his students as their necessary opposite; by considering their ignorance absolute, he justifies his own existence. The students, alienated like the slave in the Hegelian dialectic, accept their ignorance as justifying the teacher's existence — but, unlike the slave, they never discover that they educate the teacher.

The raison d'etre of libertarian education, on the other hand, lies in its drive towards reconciliation. Education must begin with the solution of the teacher-student contradiction, by reconciling the poles of the contradiction so that both are simultaneously teachers and students.

This solution is not (nor can it be) found in the banking concept. On the contrary, banking education maintains and even stimulates the contradiction through the following attitudes and practices, which mirror oppressive society as a whole:

(a) the teacher teaches and the students are taught;
(b) the teacher knows everything and the students know nothing;
(c) the teacher thinks and the students are thought about;
(d) the teacher talks and the students listen—meekly;
(e) the teacher disciplines and the students are disciplined;

(f) the teacher chooses and enforces his choice, and the students comply;
(g) the teacher acts and the students have the illusion of acting through the action of the teacher;
(h) the teacher chooses the program content, and the students (who were not consulted) adapt to it;
(i) the teacher confuses the authority of knowledge with his or her own professional authority, which she and he sets in opposition to the freedom of the students;
(j) the teacher is the Subject of the learning process, while the pupils are mere objects.

It is not surprising that the banking concept of education regards men as adaptable, manageable beings. The more students work at storing the deposits entrusted to them, the less they develop the critical consciousness which would result from their intervention in the world as transformers of that world. The more completely they accept the passive role imposed on them, the more they tend simply to adapt to the world as it is and to the fragmented view of reality deposited in them.

The capability of banking education to minimize or annul the students' creative power and to stimulate their credulity serves the interests of the oppressors, who care neither to have the world revealed nor to see it transformed. The oppressors use their "humanitarianism" to preserve a profitable situation. Thus they react almost instinctively against any experiment in education which stimulates the critical faculties and is not content with a partial view of reality but always seeks out the ties which link one point to another and one problem to another.

Indeed, the interests of the oppressors lie in "changing the consciousness of the oppressed, not the situation which oppresses them"; for the more the oppressed can be led to adapt to that situation, the more easily they can be dominated. To achieve this end, the oppressors use the banking concept of education in conjunction with a paternalistic social action apparatus, within which the oppressed receive the euphemistic title of "welfare recipients." They are treated as individual cases, as marginal persons who deviate from the general configuration of a "good, organized, and just" society. The oppressed are regarded as the pathology of the healthy society, which must therefore adjust these "incompetent and lazy" folk to its own patterns by changing their mentality. These marginals need to be "integrated," "incorporated" into the healthy society that they have "forsaken."

The truth is, however, that the oppressed are not "marginals," are not people living "outside" society. They have always been "inside" — inside the structure which made them "beings for others." The solution is not to "integrate" them into the structure of oppression, but to transform that structure so that they can become "beings for themselves." Such transformation, of course, would undermine the oppressors' purposes; hence their utilization of the banking concept of education to avoid the threat of student conscientizacao.

The banking approach to adult education, for example, will never propose to students that they critically consider reality. It will deal instead with such vital questions as whether Roger gave green grass to the goat, and insist upon the importance of learning that on the contrary, Roger gave green grass to the rabbit. The "humanism" of the banking approach masks the effort to turn women and men into automatons — the very negation of their ontological vocation to be more fully human.

Those who use the banking approach, knowingly or unknowingly (for there are innumerable well-intentioned bank-clerk teachers who do not realize that they are serving only to dehumanize), fail to perceive that the deposits themselves contain contradictions about reality. But, sooner or later, these contradictions may lead formerly passive students to turn against their domestication and the attempt to domesticate reality.

They may discover through existential experience that their present way of life is irreconcilable with their vocation to become fully human. They may perceive through their relations with reality that reality is really a process, undergoing constant transformation. If men and women are searchers and their ontological vocation is humanization, sooner or later they may perceive the contradiction in which banking education seeks to maintain them, and then engage themselves in the struggle for their liberation.

But the humanist, revolutionary educator cannot wait for this possibility to materialize. From the outset, her efforts must coincide with those of the students to engage in critical thinking and the quest for mutual humanization. His efforts must be imbued with a profound trust in people and their creative power. To achieve this, they must be partners of the students in their relations with them.

The banking concept does not admit to such partnership— and necessarily so. To resolve the teacher-student contradiction, to exchange the role of depositor, prescriber, domesticator, for the role of student among students would be to undermine the power of oppression and serve the cause of liberation.

Implicit in the banking concept is the assumption of a dichotomy between human beings and the world: a person is merely in the world, not with the world or with others; the individual is spectator, not re-creator. In this view, the person is not a conscious being (corpo consciente); he or she is rather the possessor of a consciousness: an empty "mind" passively open to the reception of deposits of reality from the world outside. For example, my desk, my books, my coffee cup, all the objects before me — as bits of the world which surround me — would be "inside" me, exactly as I am inside my study right now. This view makes no distinction between being accessible to consciousness and entering consciousness. The distinction, however, is essential: the objects which surround me are simply accessible to my consciousness, not located within it. I am aware of them, but they are not inside me.

It follows logically from the banking notion of consciousness that the educator's role is to regulate the way the world "enters into" the students. The teacher's task is to organize a process which already occurs spontaneously to "fill" the students by making deposits of information which he or she considers to constitute true knowledge. And since people "receive" the world as passive entities, education should make them more passive still, and adapt them to the world. The educated individual is the adapted person, because she or he is a better "fit" for the world. Translated into practice, this concept is well suited to the purposes of the oppressors, whose tranquility rests on how well people fit the world the oppressors have created, and how little they question it.

The more completely the majority adapt to the purposes which the dominant minority prescribe for them (thereby depriving them of the right to their own purposes), the more easily the minority can continue to prescribe. The theory and practice of banking education serve this end quite efficiently. Verbalistic lessons, reading requirements, the methods for evaluating knowledge, the distance between the teacher and the taught, the criteria for promotion: everything in this ready-to-wear approach serves to obviate thinking.

The bank-clerk educator does not realize that there is no true security in his hypertrophied role, that one must seek to live with others in solidarity. One cannot impose oneself, nor even merely co-exist with one's students. Solidarity requires true communication, and the concept by which such an educator is guided fears and proscribes communication.

Yet only through communication can human life hold meaning. The teacher's thinking is authenticated only by the authenticity of the students' thinking. The teacher cannot think for her students, nor can she impose her thought on them. Authentic thinking, thinking that is concerned about reality, does not take place in ivory tower isolation, but only in communication. If it is true that thought has meaning only when generated by action upon the world, the subordination of students to teachers becomes impossible.

Because banking education begins with a false understanding of men and women as objects, it cannot promote the development of what Fromm calls "biophily," but instead produces its opposite: "necrophily."

While life is characterized by growth in a structured, functional manner, the necrophilous person loves all that does not grow, all that is mechanical. The necrophilous person is driven by the desire to transform the organic into the inorganic, to approach life mechanically, as if all living persons were things.... Memory, rather than experience; having, rather than being, is what counts. The necrophilous person can relate to an object — a flower or a person — only if he possesses it; hence a threat to his possession is a threat to himself; if he loses possession he loses contact with the world.... He loves control, and in the act of controlling he kills life.

Oppression — overwhelming control — is necrophilic; it is nourished by love of death, not life. The banking concept of education, which serves the interests of oppression, is also necrophilic. Based on a mechanistic, static, naturalistic, spatialized view of consciousness, it transforms students into receiving objects. It attempts to control thinking and action, leads women and men to adjust to the world, and inhibits their creative power.

When their efforts to act responsibly are frustrated, when they find themselves unable to use their faculties, people suffer. "This suffering due to impotence is rooted in the very fact that the human equilibrium has been disturbed" But the inability to act which causes people's anguish also causes them to reject their impotence, by attempting... to restore [their] capacity to act. But can [they], and how? One way is to submit to and identify with a person or group having power By this symbolic participation in another person's life, [men have] the illusion of acting, when in reality [they] only submit to and become a part of those who act.

Populist manifestations perhaps best exemplify this type of behaviour by the oppressed, who, by identifying with charismatic leaders, come to feel that they themselves are active and effective. The rebellion they express as they emerge in the historical process is motivated by that desire to act effectively. The dominant elites consider the remedy to be more domination and repression, carried out in the name of freedom, order, and social peace (that is, the peace of the elites). Thus they can condemn—logically from their point of view—"the violence of a strike by workers and [can] call upon the state in the same breath to use violence in putting down the strike."

Education as the exercise of domination stimulates the credulity of students, with the ideological intent (often not perceived by educators) of indoctrinating them to adapt to the world of oppression. This accusation is not made in the naive hope that the dominant elites will thereby simply abandon the practice. Its objective is to call the attention of true humanists to the fact that they cannot use banking educational methods in the pursuit of liberation, for they would only negate that very pursuit. Nor may a revolutionary society inherit these methods from an oppressor society. The revolutionary society which practices banking education is either misguided or mistrusting of people. In either event it is threatened by the specter of reaction.

Unfortunately, those who espouse the cause of liberation are themselves surrounded and influenced by the climate which generates the banking concept, and often do not perceive its true significance or its dehumanizing power. Paradoxically, then, they utilize this same instrument of alienation in what they consider an effort to liberate. Indeed, some "revolutionaries" brand as "innocents," "dreamers," or even "reactionaries" those who would challenge this educational practice. But one does not liberate people by alienating them. Authentic liberation — the process of humanization — is not another deposit to be made in men. Liberation is a praxis: the action and reflection of men and women upon their world in order to transform it. Those truly committed to the cause of liberation can accept neither the mechanistic concept of consciousness as an empty vessel to be filled, nor the use of banking methods of domination (propaganda, slogans — deposits) in the name of liberation.

Those truly committed to liberation must reject the banking concept in its entirety, adopting instead a concept of women and men as conscious beings, and consciousness as consciousness intent upon the world. They must abandon the educational goal of deposit-making and replace it with the posing of the problems of human beings in their relations with the world. "Problem-posing" education, responding to the essence of consciousness — intentionality — rejects communiques and embodies communication. It epitomizes the special characteristic of consciousness: being conscious of not only as intent on objects but as turned in upon itself in a Jasperian "split" — consciousness as consciousness of consciousness.

Liberating education consists in acts of cognition, not transferrals of information. It is a learning situation in which the cognizable object (far from being the end of the cognitive act) intermediates the cognitive actors — teacher on the one hand and students on the other. Accordingly the practice of problem-posing education entails at the outset that the teacher-student contradiction be resolved. Dialogical relations — indispensable to the capacity of cognitive actors to cooperate in perceiving the same cognizable object — are otherwise impossible.

Indeed, problem-posing education, which breaks with the vertical patterns characteristic of banking education, can fulfil its function as the practice of freedom only if it can overcome the above contradiction. Through dialogue, the teacher-of-the-students and the students-of-the-teacher cease to exist and a new term emerges: teacher-student with students-teachers. The teacher is no longer merely the-one-who-teaches, but one who is himself taught in dialogue with the students, who in turn while being taught also teach. They become jointly responsible for a process in which all grow. In this process, arguments based on "authority" are no longer valid; in order to function, authority must be on the side of freedom, not against it. Here, no one teaches another, nor is anyone self-taught. People teach each other, mediated by the world, by the cognizable objects which in banking education are "owned" by the teacher

The banking concept (with its tendency to dichotomize everything) distinguishes two stages in the action of the educator. During the first he cognizes a cognizable object while he prepares his lessons in his study or his laboratory; during the second, he expounds to his students about that object. The students are not called upon to know, but to memorize the contents narrated by the teacher. Nor do the students practice any act of cognition, since the object towards which that act should be directed is the property of the teacher rather than a medium evoking the critical reflection of both teacher and students. Hence in the name of the "preservation of culture and knowledge" we have a system which achieves neither true knowledge nor true culture.

The problem-posing method does not dichotomize the activity of the teacher-student: she is not "cognitive" at one point and "narrative" at another. She is always "cognitive," whether preparing a project or engaging in dialogue with the students. He does not regard cognizable objects as his private property but as the object of reflection by himself and the students. In this way the problem-posing educator constantly re-forms his reflections in the reflection of the students. The students — no longer docile listeners — are now critical co-investigators in dialogue with the teacher. The teacher presents the material to the students for their consideration, and re-considers her earlier considerations as the students express their own. The role of the problem-posing educator is to create, together with the students, the conditions under which knowledge at the level of the doxa is superseded by true knowledge, at the level of the logos.

Whereas banking education anesthetizes and inhibits creative power, problem-posing education involves a constant unveiling of reality. The former attempts to maintain the submersion of consciousness; the latter strives for the emergence of consciousness and critical intervention in reality.

Students, as they are increasingly posed with problems relating to themselves in the world and with the world, will feel increasingly challenged and obliged to respond to that challenge. Because they apprehend the challenge as interrelated to other problems within a total context, not as a theoretical question, the resulting comprehension tends to be increasingly critical and thus constantly less alienated. Their response to the challenge evokes new challenges, followed by new understandings; and gradually the students come to regard themselves as committed.

Education as the practice of freedom — as opposed to education as the practice of domination — denies that man is abstract, isolated, independent, and unattached to the world;

it also denies that the world exists as a reality apart from people. Authentic reflection considers neither abstract man nor the world without people, but pea-pie in their relations with the world. In these relations consciousness and world are simultaneous: consciousness neither precedes the world nor follows it.

La conscience et le monde sont dormes d'un meme coup: exterieur par essence a la conscience, le monde est, par essence relatif a elle.

In one of our culture circles in Chile, the group was discussing (based on a codification the anthropological concept of culture. In the midst of the discussion, a peasant who by banking standards was completely ignorant said: "Now I see that without man there is no world." When the educator responded: "Let's say, for the sake of argument, that all the men on earth were to die, but that the earth itself remained, together with trees, birds, animals, rivers, seas, the stars.... wouldn't all this be a world?" "Oh no," the peasant replied emphatically. "There would be no one to say: 'This is a world'."

The peasant wished to express the idea that there would be lacking the consciousness of the world which necessarily implies the world of consciousness. I cannot exist without a non-I. In turn, the not-I depends on that existence. The world which brings consciousness into existence becomes the world of that consciousness. Hence, the previously cited affirmation of Sartre: "La conscience et le mond sont dormes d'un meme coup."

As women and men, simultaneously reflecting on themselves and on the world, increase the scope of their perception, they begin to direct their observations towards previously inconspicuous phenomena:

In perception properly so-called, as an explicit awareness [Gewahren], I am turned towards the object, to the paper, for instance. I apprehend it as being this here and now. The apprehension is a singling out, every object having a background in experience. Around and about the paper lie books, pencils, ink-well, and so forth, and these in a certain sense are also "perceived", perceptually there, in the "field of intuition"; but whilst I was turned towards the paper there was no turning in their direction, nor any apprehending of them, not even in a secondary sense. They appeared and yet were not singled out, were not posited on their own account. Every perception of a thing has such a zone of background intuitions or background awareness, if "intuiting" already includes the state of being turned towards, and this also is a "conscious experience", or more briefly a "consciousness of" all indeed that in point of fact lies in the co-perceived objective background.

That which had existed objectively but had not been perceived in its deeper implications (if indeed it was perceived at all) begins to "stand out," assuming the character of a problem and therefore of challenge. Thus, men and women begin to single out elements from their "background awareness" and to reflect upon them. These elements are now objects of their consideration, and, as such, objects of their action and cognition.

In problem-posing education, people develop their power to perceive critically the way they exist in the world with which and in which they find themselves; they come to see the world not as a static reality but as a reality in process, in transformation. Although the dialectical relations of women and men with the world exist independently of how these relations are perceived (or whether or not they are perceived at all), it is also true that the form of action they adopt is to a large extent a function of how they perceive themselves in the world. Hence, the teacher-student and the students-teachers reflect simultaneously on themselves and the world without dichotomizing this reflection from action, and thus establish an authentic form of thought and action.

Once again, the two educational concepts and practices under analysis come into conflict. Banking education (for obvious reasons) attempts, by mythicizing reality, to conceal certain facts which explain the way human beings exist in the world; problem-posing education sets itself the task of demythologizing. Banking education resists dialogue; problem-posing education regards dialogue as indispensable to the act of cognition which unveils reality. Banking education treats students as objects of assistance; problem-posing education makes them critical thinkers. Banking education inhibits creativity and domesticates (although it cannot completely destroy) the intentionality of consciousness by isolating consciousness from the world, thereby denying people their ontological and historical vocation of becoming more fully human. Problem-posing education bases itself on creativity and stimulates true reflection and action upon reality, thereby responding to the vocation of persons as beings who are authentic only when engaged in inquiry and creative transformation. In sum: banking theory and practice, as immobilizing and fixating forces, fail to acknowledge men and women as historical beings; problem-posing theory and practice take the people's historicity as their starting point.

Problem-posing education affirms men and women as beings in the process of becoming — as unfinished, uncompleted beings in and with a likewise unfinished reality. Indeed, in contrast to other animals who are unfinished, but not historical, people know themselves to be unfinished; they are aware of their incompletion. In this incompletion and this awareness lie the very roots of education as an exclusively human manifestation. The unfinished character of human beings and the transformational character of reality necessitate that education be an ongoing activity.

Education is thus constantly remade in the praxis. In order to be, it must become. Its "duration" (in the Bergsonian meaning of the word) is found in the interplay of the opposites permanence and change. The banking method emphasizes permanence and becomes reactionary; problem-posing education — which accepts neither a "well-behaved" present nor a predetermined fixture— roots itself in the dynamic present and becomes revolutionary.

Problem-posing education is revolutionary futurity. Hence it is prophetic (and, as such, hopeful). Hence, it corresponds to the historical nature of humankind. Hence, it affirms women and men as beings who transcend themselves, who move forward and look ahead, for whom immobility represents a fatal threat, for whom looking at the past must only be a means of understanding more clearly what and who they are so that they can more wisely build the fixture. Hence, it identifies with the movement which engages people as beings aware of their incompletion — an historical movement which has its point of departure, its Subjects and its objective.

The point of departure of the movement lies in the people themselves. But since people do not exist apart from the world, apart from reality the movement must begin with the human-world relationship. Accordingly, the point of departure must always be with men and women in the "here and now," which constitutes the situation within which they are submerged, from which they emerge, and in which they intervene. Only by starting from this situation—which determines their perception of it—can they begin to move. To do this authentically they must perceive their state not as fated and unalterable, but merely as limiting—and therefore challenging.

Whereas the banking method directly or indirectly reinforces men's fatalistic perception of their situation, the problem-posing method presents this very situation to them as a problem. As the situation becomes the object of their cognition, the naive or magical perception which produced their fatalism gives way to perception which is able to perceive itself even as it perceives reality, and can thus be critically objective about that reality.

A deepened consciousness of their situation leads people to apprehend that situation as an historical reality susceptible of transformation. Resignation gives way to the drive for transformation and inquiry, over which men feel themselves to be in control, if people, as historical beings necessarily engaged with other people in a movement of inquiry, did not control that movement, it would be (and is) a violation of their humanity. Any situation in which some individuals prevent others from engaging in the process of inquiry is one of violence. The means used are not important; to alienate human beings from their own decision-making is to change them into objects.

This movement of inquiry must be directed towards humanization—the people's historical vocation. The pursuit of full humanity however, cannot be carried out in isolation or individualism, but only in fellowship and solidarity; therefore it cannot unfold in the antagonistic relations between oppressors and oppressed. No one can be authentically human while he prevents others from being so. Attempting to be more human, individualistically, leads to having more, egotistically a form of dehumanization. Not that it is not fundamental to have in order to be human. Precisely because it is necessary, some men's having must not be allowed to constitute an obstacle to others having, must not consolidate the power of the former to crush the latter.

Problem-posing education, as a humanist and liberating praxis, posits as fundamental that the people subjected to domination must fight for their emancipation. To that end, it enables teachers and students to become Subjects of the educational process by overcoming authoritarianism and an alienating intellectualism; it also enables people to overcome their false perception of reality. The world—no longer something to be described with deceptive words—becomes the object of that transforming action by men and women which results in their humanization.

Problem-posing education does not and cannot serve the interests of the oppressor. No oppressive order could permit the oppressed to begin to question: Why? While only a revolutionary society can carry out this education in systematic terms, the revolutionary leaders need not take full power before they can employ the method. In the revolutionary process, the leaders cannot utilize the banking method as an interim measure, justified on grounds of expediency with the intention of later behaving in a genuinely revolutionary fashion. They must be revolutionary—that is to say dialogical—from the outset.

Culture of Poverty

The culture of poverty concept is a social theory explaining the cycle of poverty. Based on the concept that the poor have a unique value system, the culture of poverty theory suggests the poor remain in poverty because of their adaptations to the burdens of poverty.

The term "subculture of poverty" (later shortened to "culture of poverty") made its first prominent appearance in the ethnography *Five Families: Mexican Case Studies in the Culture of Poverty* (1959) by anthropologist Oscar Lewis. Lewis struggled to render "the poor" as legitimate subjects whose lives were transformed by poverty. He argued that although the burdens of poverty were systemic and therefore imposed upon these members of society, they led to the formation of an autonomous subculture as children were socialized into behaviours and attitudes that perpetuated their inability to escape the underclass.

Lewis gave some seventy characteristics (1996 [1966], 1998) that indicated the presence of the culture of poverty, which he argued was not shared among all of the lower classes.

> The people in the culture of poverty have a strong feeling of marginality, of helplessness, of dependency, of not belonging. They are like aliens in their own country, convinced that the existing institutions do not serve their interests and needs. Along with this feeling of powerlessness is a widespread feeling of inferiority, of personal unworthiness. This is true of the slum dwellers of Mexico City, who do not constitute a distinct ethnic or racial group and do not suffer from racial discrimination. In the United States the culture of poverty of the Negroes has the additional disadvantage of racial discrimination. People with a culture of poverty have very little sense of history. They are a marginal people who know only their own troubles, their own local conditions, their own neighbourhood, their own way of life. Usually, they have neither the knowledge, the vision nor the ideology to see the similarities between their problems and those of others like themselves elsewhere in the world. In other words, they are not class conscious, although they are very sensitive indeed to status distinctions. When the poor become class conscious or members of trade union organizations, or when they adopt an internationalist outlook on the world they are, in my view, no longer part of the culture of poverty although they may still be desperately poor. (Lewis 1998)

Although Lewis was concerned with poverty in the developing world, the culture of poverty concept proved attractive to US public policy makers and politicians. It strongly informed documents such as the Moynihan Report (1965) and the War on Poverty more generally.

Since the 1960s critics of culture of poverty explanations for the persistence of the underclasses have attempted to show that real world data do not fit Lewis' model (Goode and Eames, 1996). Despite decades of this criticism by prominent sociologists, anthropologists and other academics who argue that descriptions of the poor as being culturally unique have little explanatory power, the culture of poverty concept persists in popular culture.

Relevance of Gandhian Philosophy to Non-formal Education

The real difficulty is that people have no idea of what education truly is. We assess the value of education in the same manner as we assess the value of land or of shares in the stock-exchange market. We want to provide only such education as would enable the student to earn more. We hardly give any thought to the improvement of the character of the educated. The girls, we say, do not have to earn; so why should they be educated? As long as such ideas persist there is no hope of our ever knowing the true value of education. (M. K. Gandhi True Education on the NCTE site)

In a piece published some years ago, Krishna Kumar, Professor of Education at Delhi University, wrote that 'no one rejected colonial education as sharply and as completely as Gandhi did, nor did anyone else put forward an alternative as radical as the one he proposed'. Gandhi's critique of Western, particularly English, education was part of his critique of Western civilization as a whole. There is a story that, on arriving in Britain after he had become famous, someone asked him the question: 'Mr. Gandhi, what do you think of civilization in England?' to which he replied 'I think that it would be something worth trying!'

On Education

Given Gandhi's values and his vision of what constituted a truly civilized and free India, it was not surprising that he developed firm views on education. Education not only moulds the new generation, but reflects a society's fundamental assumptions about itself and the individuals which compose it.

His experience in South Africa not only changed his outlook on politics but also helped him to see the role education played in that struggle. He was aware that he had been a beneficiary of Western education and for a number of years while he was in South Africa he still tried to persuade Indians to take advantage of it. However, it was not until the early years of this century, when he was in his middle thirties, that he became so opposed to English education that he could write about 'the rottenness of this education' and that 'to give millions a knowledge of English is to enslave them... that, by receiving English education, we have enslaved the nation'.

He was enraged that he had to speak of Home Rule or Independence in what was clearly a foreign tongue, that he could not practice in court in his mother tongue, that all official documents were in English as were all the best newspapers and that education was carried out in English for the chosen few. He did not blame the colonial powers for this. He saw that it was quite logical that they would want an elite of native Indians to become like their rulers in both manners and values. In this way, the Empire could be consolidated. Gandhi blamed his fellow Indians for accepting the situation. Later in his life he was to declare that 'real freedom will come only when we free ourselves of the domination of Western education, Western culture and Western way of living which have been ingrained in us... Emancipation from this culture would mean real freedom for us'.

As we have seen, Gandhi had not only rejected colonial education but also put forward a radical alternative. So what was this alternative? What was so radical about it?

First of all, I need to say a word about Gandhi's attitude to industrialization. He was, in fact, absolutely opposed to modern machinery. In his collected works, he refers to machinery as having impoverished India, that it was difficult to measure the harm that Manchester had done to them by producing machine-made cloth which, in turn, ruined the internal market for locally produced handwoven goods. Typically of Gandhi, however, he does not blame Manchester or the mill owners. 'How can Manchester be blamed?' he writes. 'We wore

Manchester cloth and this is why Manchester wove it'. However, he notes that where cloth mills were not introduced in India, in places such as Bengal, the original hand-weaving occupation was thriving. Where they did have mills e.g. in Bombay, he felt that the workers there had become slaves.

He was shocked by the conditions of the women working in the mills of Bombay and made the point that before they were introduced these women were not starving. He maintained that 'if the machinery craze grows in our country, it will become an unhappy land'. What he wanted was for Indians to boycott *all* machine-made goods not just cloth. He was quite clear when he asked the question 'What did India do before these articles were introduced?' and then answered his own question by stating 'Precisely the same should be done today. As long as we cannot make pins without machinery, so long will we do without them. The tinsel splendour of glassware we will have nothing to do with, and we will make wicks, as of old, with home-grown cotton and use hand-made earthen saucers or lamps. So doing, we shall save our eyes and money and support *swadeshi* and so shall we attain Home Rule'.

Within this context of the need for a machine-less society, Gandhi developed his ideas on education. The core of his proposal was the introduction of productive handicrafts in the school curriculum. The idea was not simply to introduce handicrafts as a compulsory school subject, but to make the learning of a craft the centrepiece of the entire teaching programme. It implied a radical restructuring of the sociology of school knowledge in India, where productive handicrafts had been associated with the lowest groups in the hierarchy of the caste system. Knowledge of the production processes involved in crafts, such as spinning, weaving, leather-work, pottery, metal-work, basket-making and bookbinding, had been the monopoly of specific caste groups in the lowest stratum of the traditional social hierarchy. Many of them belonged to the category of 'untouchables'. India's own tradition of education as well as the colonial education system had emphasized skills such as literacy and acquisition of knowledge of which the upper castes had a monopoly.

Gandhi's proposal intended to stand the education system on its head. The social philosophy and the curriculum of what he called 'basic education' thus favoured the child belonging to the lowest stratum of society in such a way it implied a programme of social transformation. It sought to alter the symbolic meaning of 'education' and to change the established structure of opportunities for education.

Why Gandhi proposed the introduction of productive handicrafts into the school system was not really as outrageous as may appear. What he really wanted was for the schools to be self-supporting, as far as possible. There were two reasons for this. Firstly, a poor society such as India simply could not afford to provide education for all children unless the schools could generate resources from within. Secondly, the more financially independent the schools were, the more politically independent they could be. What Gandhi wanted to avoid was dependence on the state which he felt would mean interference from the centre. Above all else, Gandhi valued self-sufficiency and autonomy. These were vital for his vision of an independent India made up of autonomous village communities to survive. It was the combination of *swaraj* and *swadeshi* related to the education system. A state system of education within an independent India would have been a complete contradiction as far as Gandhi was concerned.

He was also of the opinion that manual work should not be seen as something inferior to mental work. He felt that the work of the craftsman or labourer should be the ideal model for the 'good life'. Schools which were based around productive work where that work was for the benefit of all were, therefore, carrying out education of the whole person-mind, body and spirit.

The right to autonomy that Gandhi's educational plan assigns to the teacher in the context of the school's daily curriculum is consistent with the libertarian principles that he shared with Tolstoy. Gandhi wanted to free the Indian teacher from interference from outside, particularly government or state bureaucracy. Under colonial rule, the teacher had a prescribed job to do that was based on what the authorities wanted the children to learn. Textbooks were mandatory so that Gandhi found that 'the living word of the teacher has very little value. A teacher who teaches from textbooks does not impart originality to his pupils'. Gandhi's plan, on the other hand, implied the end of the teacher's subservience to the prescribed textbook and the curriculum. It presented a concept of learning that simply could not be fully implemented with the help of textbooks. Of equal, if not more importance, was the freedom it gave the teacher in matters of curriculum. It denied the state the power to decide what teachers taught and what they did in the classroom. It gave autonomy to the teacher but it was, above all, a libertarian approach to schooling that transferred power from the state to the village.

Gandhi's basic education was, therefore, an embodiment of his perception of an ideal society consisting of small, self-reliant communities with his ideal citizen being an industrious, self-respecting and generous individual living in a small co-operative community.

For informal educators, we can draw out a number of useful pointers. First, Gandhi's insistence on autonomy and self-regulation is reflected in the ethos of informal education. Gandhi's conception of basic education was concerned with learning that was generated within everyday life which is the basis on which informal educators work. It was also an education focused on the individual but reliant on cooperation between individuals. There is also a familiar picture of the relationships between educators and students/learners:

A teacher who establishes rapport with the taught, becomes one with them, learns more from them than he teaches them. He who learns nothing from his disciples is, in my opinion, worthless. Whenever I talk with someone I learn from him. I take from him more than I give him. In this way, a true teacher regards himself as a student of his students. If you will teach your pupils with this attitude, you will benefit much from them. (Talk to Khadi Vidyalaya Students, Sevagram, *Sevak*, 15 February 1942 *CW 75*) Lastly, it was an education that aimed at educating the whole person, rather than concentrating on one aspect. It was a highly moral activity.

Psychological Principles Underlying Non-formal Education

The following 14 psychological principles pertain to the learner and the learning process*. They focus on psychological factors that are primarily internal to and under the control of the learner rather than conditioned habits or physiological factors. However, the principles also attempt to acknowledge external environment or contextual factors that interact with these internal factors. The principles are intended to deal holistically with learners in the context of real-world learning situations. Thus, they are best understood as an organized set of principles; no principle should be viewed in isolation. The 14 principles are divided into those referring to cognitive and metacognitive, motivational and affective, developmental and social, and individual difference factors influencing learners and learning. Finally, the principles are intended to apply to all learners — from children, to teachers, to administrators, to parents, and to community members involved in our educational system.

1. Nature of the learning process.

   The learning of complex subject matter is most effective when it is an intentional process of constructing meaning from information and experience.

   There are different types of learning processes, for example, habit formation in motor learning; and learning that involves the generation of knowledge, or cognitive skills and learning strategies. Learning in schools emphasizes the use of intentional processes that students can use to construct meaning from information, experiences, and their own thoughts and beliefs. Successful learners are active, goal-directed, self-regulating, and assume personal responsibility for contributing to their own learning. The principles set forth in this document focus on this type of learning.

2. Goals of the learning process.

   The successful learner, over time and with support and instructional guidance, can create meaningful, coherent representations of knowledge.

The strategic nature of learning requires students to be goal directed. To construct useful representations of knowledge and to acquire the thinking and learning strategies necessary for continued learning success across the life span, students must generate and pursue personally relevant goals. Initially, students' short-term goals and learning may be sketchy in an area, but over time their understanding can be refined by filling gaps, resolving inconsistencies, and deepening their understanding of the subject matter so that they can reach longer-term goals. Educators can assist learners in creating meaningful learning goals that are consistent with both personal and educational aspirations and interests.

3. Construction of knowledge.

   The successful learner can link new information with existing knowledge in meaningful ways.

   Knowledge widens and deepens as students continue to build links between new information and experiences and their existing knowledge base. The nature of these links can take a variety of forms, such as adding to, modifying, or reorganizing existing knowledge or skills. How these links are made or develop may vary in different subject areas, and among students with varying talents, interests, and abilities. However, unless new knowledge becomes integrated with the learner's prior knowledge and understanding, this new knowledge remains isolated, cannot be used most effectively in new tasks, and does not transfer readily to new situations. Educators can assist learners in acquiring and integrating knowledge by a number of strategies that have been shown to be effective with learners of varying abilities, such as concept mapping and thematic organization or categorizing.

4. Strategic thinking.

   The successful learner can create and use a repertoire of thinking and reasoning strategies to achieve complex learning goals.

Successful learners use strategic thinking in their approach to learning, reasoning, problem solving, and concept learning. They understand and can use a variety of strategies to help them reach learning and performance goals, and to apply their knowledge in novel situations. They also continue to expand their repertoire of strategies by reflecting on the methods they use to see which work well for them, by receiving guided instruction and feedback, and by observing or interacting with appropriate models. Learning outcomes can be enhanced if educators assist learners in developing, applying, and assessing their strategic learning skills.

5. Thinking about thinking.

   Higher order strategies for selecting and monitoring mental operations facilitate creative and critical thinking.

   Successful learners can reflect on how they think and learn, set reasonable learning or performance goals, select potentially appropriate learning strategies or methods, and monitor their progress toward these goals. In addition, successful learners know what to do if a problem occurs or if they are not making sufficient or timely progress toward a goal. They can generate alternative methods to reach their goal (or reassess the appropriateness and utility of the goal). Instructional methods that focus on helping learners develop these higher order (metacognitive) strategies can enhance student learning and personal responsibility for learning.

6. Context of learning.

   Learning is influenced by environmental factors, including culture, technology, and instructional practices.

   Learning does not occur in a vacuum. Teachers play a major interactive role with both the learner and the learning environment. Cultural or group influences on students can impact many educationally relevant variables, such as motivation, orientation toward learning, and ways of thinking. Technologies and instructional practices must be appropriate for learners' level of prior knowledge, cognitive abilities, and their learning and thinking strategies. The classroom environment, particularly the degree to which it is nurturing or not, can also have significant impacts on student learning.

7. Motivational and emotional influences on learning.

   What and how much is learned is influenced by the learner's motivation. Motivation to learn, in turn, is influenced by the individual's emotional states, beliefs, interests and goals, and habits of thinking.

   The rich internal world of thoughts, beliefs, goals, and expectations for success or failure can enhance or interfere with the learner's quality of thinking and information processing. Students' beliefs about themselves as learners and the nature of learning have a marked influence on motivation. Motivational and emotional factors also influence both the quality of thinking and information processing as well as an individual's motivation to learn. Positive emotions, such as curiosity, generally enhance motivation and facilitate learning and performance. Mild anxiety can also enhance learning and performance by focusing the learner's attention on a particular task. However, intense negative emotions (e.g., anxiety, panic, rage, insecurity) and related thoughts (e.g., worrying about competence, ruminating about failure, fearing punishment, ridicule, or stigmatizing labels) generally detract from motivation, interfere with learning, and contribute to low performance.

8. Intrinsic motivation to learn.

   The learner's creativity, higher order thinking, and natural curiosity all contribute to motivation to learn. Intrinsic motivation is stimulated by tasks of optimal novelty and difficulty, relevant to personal interests, and providing for personal choice and control.

Curiosity, flexible and insightful thinking, and creativity are major indicators of the learners' intrinsic motivation to learn, which is in large part a function of meeting basic needs to be competent and to exercise personal control. Intrinsic motivation is facilitated on tasks that learners perceive as interesting and personally relevant and meaningful, appropriate in complexity and difficulty to the learners' abilities, and on which they believe they can succeed. Intrinsic motivation is also facilitated on tasks that are comparable to real-world situations and meet needs for choice and control. Educators can encourage and support learners' natural curiosity and motivation to learn by attending to individual differences in learners' perceptions of optimal novelty and difficulty, relevance, and personal choice and control.

9. Effects of motivation on effort.

Acquisition of complex knowledge and skills requires extended learner effort and guided practice. Without learners' motivation to learn, the willingness to exert this effort is unlikely without coercion.

Effort is another major indicator of motivation to learn. The acquisition of complex knowledge and skills demands the investment of considerable learner energy and strategic effort, along with persistence over time. Educators need to be concerned with facilitating motivation by strategies that enhance learner effort and commitment to learning and to achieving high standards of comprehension and understanding. Effective strategies include purposeful learning activities, guided by practices that enhance positive emotions and intrinsic motivation to learn, and methods that increase learners' perceptions that a task is interesting and personally relevant.

10. Developmental influences on learning.

As individuals develop, there are different opportunities and constraints for learning. Learning is most effective when differential development within and across physical, intellectual, emotional, and social domains is taken into account.

Individuals learn best when material is appropriate to their developmental level and is presented in an enjoyable and interesting way. Because individual development varies across intellectual, social, emotional, and physical domains, achievement in different instructional domains may also vary. Overemphasis on one type of developmental readiness—such as reading readiness, for example—may preclude learners from demonstrating that they are more capable in other areas of performance. The cognitive, emotional, and social development of individual learners and how they interpret life experiences are affected by prior schooling, home, culture, and community factors. Early and continuing parental involvement in schooling, and the quality of language interactions and two-way communications between adults and children can influence these developmental areas. Awareness and understanding of developmental differences among children with and without emotional, physical, or intellectual disabilities, can facilitate the creation of optimal learning contexts.

11. Social influences on learning

Learning is influenced by social interactions, interpersonal relations, and communication with others.

Learning can be enhanced when the learner has an opportunity to interact and to collaborate with others on instructional tasks. Learning settings that allow for social interactions, and that respect diversity, encourage flexible thinking and social competence. In interactive and collaborative instructional contexts, individuals have an opportunity for perspective taking and reflective thinking that may lead to higher levels of cognitive, social, and moral development, as well as self-esteem. Quality personal relationships that provide stability, trust, and caring can increase learners' sense of belonging, self-respect and self-acceptance, and provide a positive climate for learning. Family influences, positive interpersonal support and instruction in self-motivation strategies can offset factors that interfere with optimal learning such as negative beliefs about competence in a particular subject, high levels of test anxiety, negative sex role expectations, and undue pressure to perform well. Positive learning climates can also help to establish the context for healthier levels of thinking, feeling, and behaving. Such contexts help learners feel safe to share ideas, actively participate in the learning process, and create a learning community. Individual differences in learning.

Learners have different strategies, approaches, and capabilities for learning that are a function of prior experience and heredity.

Individuals are born with and develop their own capabilities and talents. In addition, through learning and social acculturation, they have acquired their own preferences for how they like to learn and the pace at which they learn. However, these preferences are not always useful in helping learners reach their learning goals. Educators need to help students examine their learning preferences and expand or modify them, if necessary. The interaction between learner differences and curricular and environmental conditions is another key factor affecting learning outcomes. Educators need to be sensitive to individual differences, in general. They also need to attend to learner perceptions of the degree to which these differences are accepted and adapted to by varying instructional methods and materials.

12. Learning and diversity.

Learning is most effective when differences in learners' linguistic, cultural, and social backgrounds are taken into account.

The same basic principles of learning, motivation, and effective instruction apply to all learners. However, language, ethnicity, race, beliefs, and socioeconomic status all can influence learning. Careful attention to these factors in the instructional setting enhances the possibilities for designing and implementing appropriate learning environments. When learners perceive that their individual differences in abilities, backgrounds, cultures, and experiences are valued, respected, and accommodated in learning tasks and contexts, levels of motivation and achievement are enhanced.

13. Standards and assessment.

Setting appropriately high and challenging standards and assessing the learner as well as learning progress — including diagnostic, process, and outcome assessment — are integral parts of the learning process.

Assessment provides important information to both the learner and teacher at all stages of the learning process. Effective learning takes place when learners feel challenged to work towards appropriately high goals; therefore, appraisal of the learner's cognitive strengths and weaknesses, as well as current knowledge and skills, is important for the selection of instructional materials of an optimal degree of difficulty. Ongoing assessment of the learner's understanding of the curricular material can provide valuable feedback to both learners and teachers about progress toward the learning goals. Standardized assessment of learner progress and outcomes assessment provides one type of information about achievement levels both within and across individuals that can inform various types of programmatic decisions. Performance assessments can provide other sources of information about the attainment of learning outcomes. Self-assessments of learning progress can also improve students self appraisal skills and enhance motivation and self-directed learning.

UNIT-II

Methodology: Teaching and Learning Materials

Theories of Adult Learning

Typical adult learning theories encompass the basic concepts of behavioural change and experience. From there, complexities begin to diverge specific theories and concepts in an eclectic borage of inferences. Up until the 1950's basic definitions of learning were built around the idea of change in behaviour (Merriam and Caffarella, 1999). After this point more complexities were introduced "such as whether one needs to perform in order for learning to have occurred or whether all human behaviour is learned " (Merriam and Caffarella, 1999).

Jean Piaget contends that there are "four invariant stages of cognitive development that are age related" (Merriam & Caffarella, 1999). According to the authors, Piaget contends that normal children will reach the final stage of development, which is the stage of formal operations, between the age of twelve and fifteen. As cited by Merriam and Caffarella (1999), Arlin (1975, 1984), established from the work of Gruber (1973) on the development of creative thought in adults, has attempted to identify a fifth stage of development, in addition to Piaget's formal operations. "She [Arlin] contends that formal thought actually consists of two distinct stages, not one, as Piaget proposed". Arlin (1975) proposes that Piaget's fourth stage, formal operations, be renamed the problem-solving stage. According to Merriam and Caffarella (1999), Arlin's hypothesized fifth stage was the problem-finding stage. This stage focuses on problem discovery. Though Arlin's proposed fifth stage produced more questions than answers, it opens the door to understanding the learning needs of adults; to be approached as thinkers.

According to a literature review by Ross (2002), humanism, personal responsibility orientation, behaviourism, neobehaviorism, critical perspectives, and constructivism are all important facets of, and perspectives on, adult learning theory. The most common treatments of the research of these areas of self-directed adult learning are learning projects, qualitative studies, and quantitative measures. Collins (1991) explores adult learning as the interactive relationship of theory and practice. In basic terms, the adult learner studies a particular theory and then puts it into practice when presented with the opportunity to do so. Thus, the understanding of an adult learning theory can prompt practice and practice can prompt adult learning theory revision.

Adult learning theories in and of themselves have very little consensus amongst them. There is great debate on an actual determined amount of theories that are even possible, as well as labelling those theories into groups like Hilgard and Bower's (1966) stimulus-response and cognitive theories as large categories of their eleven theories. Another groups dynamic labels theories as mechanistic and or organismic (Merriam and Caffarella, 1999). Overall it seems that the theory of adult learning is broken down into two elements; 1) a process that creates change within the individual, and 2) a process to infuse change into the organization.

Malcolm Knowles might well be considered the founding father of adult learning. He contrasted the "concept of andragogy, meaning "the art and science of helping adults learn,"...with pedagogy, the art and science of helping children learn" (Merriam & Caffarella, 1999). Knowles' original studies and writings arose from the assumption that there are significant, identifiable differences between adult learners and learners under the age of eighteen. Primarily, the differences, according to Knowles, relate to an adult learner being more self-directing, having a repertoire of experience, and being internally motivated to learn subject matter that can be applied immediately – learning that is especially "closely related to the developmental tasks of his or her social role".

Andragogy

Knowles (1968) popularized this European concept over thirty years ago. Andragogy, (andr-'man'), contrasted with pedagogy, means "the art and science of helping adults learn" (Knowles, 1980). Knowles labelled andragogy as an emerging technology which facilitates the development and implementation of learning activities for adults. This emerging technology is based on five andragogical assumptions of the adult learner:

1. Self-Concept: As a person matures, he or she moves from dependency to self-directness.
2. Experience: Adults draw upon their experiences to aid their learning.
3. Readiness: The learning readiness of adults is closely related to the assumption of new social roles.
4. Orientation: As a person learns new knowledge, he or she wants to apply it immediately in problem solving.
5. Motivation (Later added): As a person matures, he or she receives their motivation to learn from internal factors.

These five assumptions dovetail with the thoughts and theories of others. Merriam and Caffarella (1999) point to three keys to transformational learning: experience, critical reflection and development. The aspect of experience (the second assumption to andragogy) seems like an important consideration in creating an effective learning opportunity for adults. The learning opportunity needs to be relevant and applicable to a person's set of experiences. Argote, McEvily, and Reagans (2003) point to experience as an important factor in one's ability to create, retain and transfer knowledge.

Critical reflection is the second key to transformational learning and part of andragogy's self-directed learning.

Reflection/think time is yet another essential principle to creating an effective learning experience for adults. Garvin (1993) shares the importance of fostering an environment that is conducive to learning including time for reflection and analysis. Adult learners need time to contemplate the ramifications of the learning experience to their experience and responsibilities.

The third key to transformational learning is development (corresponding to the third assumption of andragogy). Merriam and Caffarella state that "the ability to think critically, which is mandatory to effecting a transformation, is itself developmental" (p. 330). If development is the outcome of transformational learning, then an effective adult learning opportunity needs to be created that will take personal development into consideration.

Andragogy assumes the following about the design of learning:

1. Adults have the need to know why they are learning something.
2. Adults learn through doing.
3. Adults are problem-solvers.
4. Adults learn best when the subject is of immediate use.

According to Knowles an example used to apply the principles to personal computer training:

1. Explain why certain skills are taught (functions, commands).
2. Task oriented instead of memorizing. Tasks should be common tasks.
3. Take diversity into play. Acknowledge different learning levels and experience.
4. Allow adults to learn on their own and from their mistakes.

Some would contend that Knowles only introduced a theory of teaching rather than a theory of adult learning. In commenting on this thought, Merriam and Caffarella (1999) referring to Hartree suggest, "that it is not clear whether Knowles had presented a theory of learning or a theory of teaching, whether adult learning was different from child learning, and whether there was a theory at all-perhaps these were just principles of good practice". It is further contended that Knowles did not establish a proven theory, rather he introduced a "set of well-grounded principles of good practice" (Brookfirle, 1986).

"Within companies, instructional methods are designed for improving adult learners' knowledge and skills. It is important to distinguish the unique attributes of adult learners so as to be better able to incorporate the principles of adult learning in the design of instruction" (Yi, 2005). Within this context, adult learning is aimed at not only improving individual knowledge and skill, but ultimately it is the goal to improve the organizational performance by transfer of learning directly to work applications. Yi suggest three methods to foster learning in adult organizations: Problem-Based Learning which seeks to increase problem-solving and critical thinking skills; Cooperative Learning, which builds communication and interpersonal skills; and Situated Learning, which targets specific technical skills that can be directly related to the field of work (Yi, 2005). Each of these methods support the assumptions about how adults learn; specifically they are more self-directed, have a need for direct application to their work, and are able to contribute more to collaborative learning through their experience.

Multiple Intelligences

Howard Gardner represents those theorists who have dismissed the idea of one type of intelligence as typically measured by today's psychometric instruments. He posited that there were seven (later eight) types of intelligences (Gardner, 1993):

1. Linguistic intelligence
2. Logical-mathematical intelligence
3. Spatial intelligence or the ability to form a mental model of the spatial world and to maneuver within it using this model.
4. Musical intelligence.

5. Bodily-kinesthetic intelligence, or the ability to solve problems using one's body as performed by athletes, dancers and other craftspeople.
6. Interpersonal intelligence or the ability to understand other people.
7. Intrapersonal intelligence or the ability to understand one's self.

Gardner (1993) maintains that the first two are the types of intelligence commonly measured by IQ tests, and which are commonly accepted as "intelligence."

Gardner later added an eighth intelligence to his taxonomy, Naturalist Intelligence, which he defined as "expertise in the recognition and classification of the numerous species — the flora and fauna — of his or her environment" (Gardner, 1999) Sternberg's Triarchic Theory can be viewed as an interpretation of intelligence as information processing. Li (1996) provides us with a useful summary of Sternberg's theory. He tells us that: "In Sternberg's general theory, there are three subtheories: the componential subtheory, the experiential subtheory and the contextual subtheory, each divided into subdomains of concern. The contextual subtheory deals with the context of intelligence. Intelligence in the real world requiring adaptation, selection, and/or shaping the environment. Measurement of contextual intelligence would relate to the issue of social perception, culture fairness, and cultural relativeness. The experiential subtheory deals with the issue of novelty and automatizing of processing. It is related to the notion of learning and the dynamic interplay between controlled and automated processing in the competition for cognitive resources. Finally, there is the componential subtheory, which is subdivided into (a) metacomponents, (b) performance components, and (c) knowledge acquisition components, which are directly related to learning".

Conditions/Environment

Some research suggests that situational circumstances constitute an environment that promotes or discourages learning. Those circumstances may be created by organizational structure, positive or negative environmental situations, or time constraints. Child and Heavens (2003) suggest, "The learning capabilities of organizational members are, at least in part, socially constructed by national, occupational, or other institutions". They further suggest that internal boundaries are established by specialities or departments within the framework of organizations that hinder cross-boundary learning.

In following the thread of environmental issues within organizations supporting or hindering learning, Starbuck and Hedberg (2003) suggest that positive outcomes are much more apt to result in a positive and successful learning experience. They contend, "Pleasant outcomes (successes) reinforce Stimulus-Response links whereas unpleasant outcomes (failures) break Stimulus-Response links. As a result, pleasant outcomes are much more effective at teaching new behaviours" (p. 331). This concept follows the transformational leadership theory providing positive opportunities for individuals to grow within the framework of organizational life. However, it may be contended that learning through failure (i.e. experiments which do not result in the anticipated outcomes) may provide a more thorough and circumspect understanding of the given topic or issue under examination, although this method will generally involve a longer learning curve. —The license to fail is often the surest key towards successful learning which an organization may provide.

Weber and Berthoin Antal (2003) suggest, "A key question is how long organizational learning processes take and whether the duration can be externally influenced" (p. 353). They further contend that learning processes that require practice are much slower than those that do not require practice. Time consideration is an important element in considering the process of learning within an organization that must meet specific deadlines or has a client base that needs to be managed continuously. The conditions may not be suitable for an elaborate training or educational program. Organizations must consider time pressure as a tool that can encourage learning and speed up processes. However, Weber and Berthoin (2003) contend, "Time pressure can both accelerate and slow down learning processes...is experienced as motivating or threatening...if the sense of threat becomes too excessive, however, learning can be slowed or made impossible altogether".

Experiential Learning

Experiential Learning Theory emphasizes the role that true experiences play in the learning process. It is this emphasis that distinguishes itself from other learning theories. Cognitive learning theories emphasize cognition over affect and behavioural learning theories deny any role for subjective experience in the learning process.

Scholars in the field of education have two contrasting views when it comes to the concept of experiential learning. The first view defines experiential learning as a sort of learning which enables students to apply newly acquired knowledge in a relevant setting. The relevant setting can be a sponsored institution of learning with trainers, instructors, teachers, or professors to guide the lesson. The other school of thought defines experiential learning as "education that occurs as a direct participation in the events of life" (Houle, 1980). Thus, learning is not achieved in a formal setting, but in the practice of reflection of daily experiences. Kolb furthers the second definition of experiential learning by developing a model which details learning process through experiences. Kolb and Fry's (1975) experiential learning model is a continuous spiral process which consists of four basic elements:

1. Concrete experience
2. Observation and reflection
3. Forming abstract concepts
4. Testing in new situations.

Immediate or concrete experiences are the basis for observation and reflections. These reflections are assimilated and distilled into abstract concepts from which new implications for action can be drawn (Kolb & Fry).

According to Kolb and Fry (1975), the adult learner can enter the process at any one of the elements. The adult learner moves to the next step once he or she processes their experience in the previous step.

Anxiety and the Adult Learner

In an interview with psychologist Edgar Schein, Coutu suggests that more often than not, organizations fail at transformational learning. They rarely fundamentally change the behaviours within the organization. Schein dismisses the notion that learning is fun, especially for adults. He equates adult learning within organizations with that of the brainwashing techniques he observed while studying prisoners of the Korean War (Coutu, 2002). Organizations must find a method to deal with the anxiety adults experience when they are forced to "unlearn" what they know and learn something new (Coutu, 2002). Schein discusses two kinds of anxiety: learning anxiety and survival anxiety. It is in this manner that he draws the parallel to brainwashing; that is "learning will only happen when survival anxiety is greater than learning anxiety" (Coutu, 2002). Each of these anxieties could be managed, for example learning can be constructed in a "safe" environment where the consequences of failure are minimal. Survival anxiety can obviously be increased by threatening job loss, a lack of security, or recognizing competitive elements of the market.

Jarvis's Learning Process and Adult Learning Theory

One of the most significant qualities unique to adult learning as compared to that of children, teens, and traditional college students is life experience. That experience offers adult learners a meaningful advantage in the learning process. The sum of those experiences provides many reference points for exploration, new application, and new learning.

Merriam & Cafarella (1999) review Jarvis's Learning Process in a wider discussion of adult learning. These authors quote Jarvis (1987a) who suggests, "All learning begins with experience." Real learning begins when a response is called for in relation to an experience. If an individual is unchanged by a situation, Jarvis questions whether real learning has taken place. He proposes that new experiences need to be experimented with, evaluated, reflected upon and reasoned about for the most effective change and therefore learning to take place. Jarvis continues, suggesting that these post experience behaviours culminate in the best and highest form of learning where change and increased experience have happened. Jarvis's model offers an excellent learning model that can assist both facilitators and learners in advancing education and learning situations.

A few questions come to mind in light of Jarvis's theory. Does Jarvis's model reflect a deeply postmodern worldview where experience is either ultimate or paramount? How might this worldview expand or narrow learning theory? Does Jarvis's model seem to accept the maxim that 'experience is the best teacher'? We can of course qualify this statement by asking whether there is any learning which does not consist of experience in some form, whether in the classroom, on the playground or on the battlefield.

Is it possible that some hurtful and negative life experiences could be avoided if a person learned from another person who has already encountered and experienced a significantly negative life situation? Learning from an older or more experienced mentor provides an incredibly valuable learning forum and support network. Listening, and learning from a mentor's successes, failures, or mistakes can help expand one's knowledge base and shorten learning cycles experience alone would require. It seems that living largely out of one's personal experiences also short-circuits meaningful, relational connections that expand one's horizons and better equip one to succeed in this world and avoid so many of its pitfalls. Yet, it may be reasonably argued, that personal experience provides the most integral and visceral form of learning (and I state this as no objective fact, but rather personal opinion, contrary to how articles are generally written in "Wikeality").

Case Studies & Workplace Examples

The adult learning experience presented itself in all of its glory and contradictions through a curriculum review taking place in a school setting. The objective was to examine the current school curriculum and evaluate it for strengths and weaknesses. The purpose for this review was to both align the curriculum with current practice and augment the curriculum to enhance student learning. Interestingly, the teachers involved in this process seemed to exhibit all the qualities of adult learners mentioned previously: learning through projects, applying self-direction to the process, challenging the process for purpose, and some approached the process with much anxiety. Engaging in the process illustrated that adult learning is individual and there were as many approaches to adult learning as there were people involved in the process.

At GM, there are several examples of learning opportunities in manufacturing operations that fulfil the key criteria of adult learning. That is, they provide adults with the need to know why they are learning something, usually via a review of competitive analysis and the importance of the topic to our improved competitive position. Secondly, they are often done in a workshop-type format, where adults can learn through doing.

Next, the format typically will cover an application that will have immediate use and will require the students to bring their experiences to the class to assist and involve themselves with problem solving. Typical courses or learning opportunities cover safety issues, quality improvements, and productivity improvements as they apply to specific departments in the plant. In these workshop-style classes, actual problems are brought to the class for the students to learn and practice problem-solving skills. The outcomes and recommendations are then immediately applied in the regular operations.

At Medical Protective, adult learning has been promoted and encouraged among the entire community. Some learning is required for work-related functions, but other types of courses are intended to benefit professional development. Motivational factors, such as monetary incentives, courses being paid for, recognition, and the hope of advancement have encouraged all employees to participate in a learning course. By utilizing various information technologies, knowledge programs can be accessed online, downloaded to a PC, or printed off for manual review, depending on the need of the individual learner. Medical Protective employees are constantly adapting to the changing

IT environment in the market around them, and are using these systems to become more efficient, knowledgeable workers.

Speck (1996) notes that the following important points of adult learning theory should be considered when professional development activities are designed for educators:

- "Adults will commit to learning when the goals and objectives are considered realistic and important to them. Application in the 'real world' is important and relevant to the adult learner's personal and professional needs.
- Adults want to be the origin of their own learning and will resist learning activities they believe are an attack on their competence. Thus, professional development needs to give participants some control over the what, who, how, why, when, and where of their learning.
- Adult learners need to see that the professional development learning and their day-to-day activities are related and relevant.
- Adult learners need direct, concrete experiences in which they apply the learning in real work.
- Adult learning has ego involved. Professional development must be structured to provide support from peers and to reduce the fear of judgment during learning.
- Adults need to receive feedback on how they are doing and the results of their efforts. Opportunities must be built into professional development activities that allow the learner to practice the learning and receive structured, helpful feedback.
- Adults need to participate in small-group activities during the learning to move them beyond understanding to application, analysis, synthesis, and evaluation. Small-group activities provide an opportunity to share, reflect, and generalize their learning experiences.
- Adult learners come to learning with a wide range of previous experiences, knowledge, self-direction, interests, and competencies. This diversity must be

accommodated in the professional development planning.

- Transfer of learning for adults is not automatic and must be facilitated. Coaching and other kinds of follow-up support are needed to help adult learners transfer learning into daily practice so that it is sustained."

Motivation

Adults engage in continual education for various reasons. Our unique motivations help us stay focused and stick with a topic until we solve the current problem and gather enough information to complete our current task.

Cyril O. Houle conducted one of the most famous studies on what motivates learners. He identified three subgroups to categorize motivational styles.

(1) Goal-oriented learners use education to accomplish clear-cut objectives.

(2) Activity-oriented (social) learners take part mainly because of the social contact. Houle wrote, "Their selection of any activity was essentially based on the amount and kind of human relationships it would yield."

(3) Learning-oriented learners seek knowledge for its own sake. "For the most part, they are avid readers and have been since childhood.... and they choose jobs and make other decisions in life in terms of the potential for growth which they offer."

Allen Tough simplified Houle's motivational model by suggesting that adults learn because of (1) an increase in self-esteem, (2) a sense of pleasing and impressing others, and (3) certain pleasures or satisfactions. Recognizing our unique motivational styles can also help us identify the types of educational products and problems that will satisfy our needs. For instance, self-study programs are not going to motivate 'activity-oriented' learners unless the program contains some element of interaction. The more social the situation the better.

As certain things motivate, others discourage. Few things are more de-motivating than fear. Learning is, after all, a very emotional process. We must see, feel, and do. Fear, anxiety, and anger are emotional factors that negatively affect learning. On a physical level, stress can even cause cell assemblies to fire in unorganized patterns and ultimately inhibit transfer and retrieval. Our phase sequences can be in chaos.

Also, who likes learning something boring? If we don't care about a topic, we're less likely to stick with it and continue to learn. Even when we're interested in learning a topic, we're sometimes more motivated to play with the equipment or to daydream. We can get easily distracted from the task at hand and become more motivated to do something else perhaps not on task.

The big issues are relevancy and immediacy. Information has to be relevant to our current wants and needs, and it must feel useful to us. Most people don't have time to waste. We want to spend time learning what will make a difference now.

In one of the earliest studies of why adults volunteer for education activities, most said they do so to acquire the necessary knowledge and skills for vocational and professional advancement. While today another common reason may be to stay ahead of the influx of information in our jobs, career success motivates us to learn. No matter the motivator, if we can learn more of what we want and less of what we don't, learning becomes more appealing.

Literacy Curriculum

National Literacy Mission (NLM) has defined the desired level of competencies in the 3R's as follows:

Reading:

- Reading aloud, with normal accent, and at a speed of 30 words a minute, a simple passage on a topic of interest to the learner.
- Silent reading at 35 words a minute, of small paragraphs in simple language.
- Reading with understanding the road signs, posters, simple instructions, and newspapers/broadsheets designed for neoliterates.

- Ability to follow simple written passages relating to one's working and living environment.

Writing

- Copying, with understanding, at 7 words a minute.
- Taking dictation at 5 words a minute.
- Writing with proper spacing and alignment.
- Writing independently, short letters and applications, and filling in forms of day-to-day use to the learner.

Numeracy

- Reading and writing numerals 1-100.
- Doing simple calculations (without fraction) involving addition and subtraction upto 3 digits, and multiplication and division by 2 digits.
- Working knowledge of metric units weights, measures, currency, distance, area and unit of time.
- Broad idea of proportion and interest (not involving fractions) and their use in practical situations.

Language and Mathematics

Adult education in a multilingual country like India is the greatest challenge to the linguist. Faced with problems of instant communication to be linked up with the standardisation and modernisation of the languages, the linguist is called upon to develop a strategy of literacy which can steer through the maze of languages, dialects, styles, registors and such other varieties.

Most literacy workers have convinced themselves that the dialect has nothing to do with literacy. And yet when a farmer's literacy manual is written in 'Suddh Hindi' (Chaste Hindi) in Delhi and is not accessible to a farmer in Rajasthan or in parts of Bihar, they do not know what to do about it. It is not as if a linguist can solve all the problems of literacy. After all there is the Mahaboobnagar experiment in Andhra Pradesh (Deshmukh 1967) where one of India's well known linguists was associated in a programme for producing instructional material in the dialect. But the result was unsatisfactory. By the end of the course, the learners could read (and write)

Mahaboobnagar Telugu, but they could not read standard Telugu with facility. What, then, is the role of a linguist in an adult education programme ?

The Mahaboonagar programme clearly shows that unless adult literacy is functionally defined and all steps from the curriculum formation through apperception to self-actualisation are well integrated, adult education is bound to be incomplete. Unless reading the dialect is linked with the reading of the standard by a switch over mechanism, this problem cannot be satisfactorily solved. It is not enough to identify the needs and set the objectives, but it is necessary to structure experience through language in such a way that the competence in a language would be of a level which will not permit sliding back to illiteracy. Use of dialect in illiteracy is not an end in itself, but a means to attain necessary skills in the literary language in which sufficient reading material is available for him to maintain literacy.

Mahaboobnagar as well as similar experiences of the project run by the Council for Social Development, the Seva Mandir in Udaipur (Rajasthan), the Institute of Indian Education, Poona and Central Institute of Indian Languages, Mysore go to indicate that whether it is for motivation or for ensuring the functionality of the programme, material sensitive to local language use is more effective for bringing the learners quickly to the threshold of literacy. But this is not enough. Constant bridging at all levels of language is necessary to relate the local to the standard, which invariably is the high status language. The problem of literacy in case of language which have accepted another language as 'culture language' (Pattanayak 1977a) needs more serious attention. It is to be remembered that the purpose of literacy is not to develop the undeveloped languages and dialects, but develop the human potential through conscientisation. Therefore, a knowledge of language dynamics and language engineering becomes a must for a literacy worker in a developing country.

It is not as if the linguist can be eliminated if the problem of dialect is isolated. In a poona slum where the literacy worker asks the child tujhe vadil kay kartat and gets frustrated as the child does not understand, the problem is of a different order. Undaunted, the worker asks tujha bap ka karto and pat comes the reply daru pito ani aila marto 'drinks wine and beats mother'. This forcefully brings out the distance between the slum language and the standard spoken language, the problem of comprehension and the problem of status and attitude build into the language use. Linguists, who make it their business to study the structure of varieties of spoken and written languages in different domains, must be treated as indispensable allies of literacy workers to solve such problems.

In a meeting of the Scientific and Technical Terminology Commission, there was a discussion about the word for 'fishing rod'. Although many languages have the word 'bansi', the pundits rejected it in favour of a more Sanskritised word 'akheta danda'. Many people are in favour of such Sanskritisms without knowing their implication. The choice of a high culture word, whether Sanskritic or Perso-Arabic, determines the style of writing. Since this has serious consequences for literacy, it must be understood by the material producer. Take, for example, the Oriya word nasika and nake 'nose'. The choice of nasika will require kuncana kariba while nake modiba in the sense of disapproval. This not only is a problem in collocation, but the style of writing itself would be determined as a result of such choices. Hindi danta cikitsa and dat ka ilaj illustrate similar problems as the above.

Yet another dimension of the problem of language which has direct bearing on literacy is illustrated by the Tamil word which is written as patam, read as padam and spoken as pado or the Assamese word which is written as citi bach but read as siti bas. The language specific conventions of writing and reading need to be analysed and integrated in the literacy curriculum. The rules for moving either from the spoken to the written or from the written to the spoken have to be carefully worked out and graded before texts are prepared.

Telugu, where most textbooks and much of the printed material was written in the Granthika style presents another formidable challenge to those engaged in adult education. In spite of the decision to effect a phased change over to the SiÀa vyavaharika, the spoken standard style, the anomaly is bound to persist for some more time. The literacy workers even though working in a small homogeneous dialect area have to keep these broader aspects of language development in view. Otherwise devoid of the continuing flow of reading material which is likely to be available in the standard language for years to come, the neo-literates are bound to lapse into illiteracy.

Linguistic minorities pose a major problem to the literacy worker. In many cases people are to be made literate in two languages, the mother tongue and the dominant language. The linguists must stretch their ingenuity to develop the strategy of transfer, thus making it feasible to run simultaneous literacy in the home language and the dominant language wherever possible (Pattanayak 1977). Of course, those of the dominant language area may have to be made literate in either one o both the languages according to their choice. Facilities may be provided for this purpose. The West Bengal Committee for Eradication of illiteracy, for instance, has taken commendable steps in this regard. But very little research and experiment has gone in to making the other minorities literate.

Another peculiar problem is posed by linguistic minority communities who use a pidginised varieties of a language as contact language. The most important among these is the pidgin Naga, which is popularly known as Nagamese. This variety is not only a bridge among the mutually unintelligible Naga language speakers, but also a bridge between the various tribal language speakers and Assamese speakers. No literacy effort in this area can ignore the existence of this variety. The various tribal language speakers in the Koraput District of Orissa use Desia as a communication language in this manner. Similarly those in and around Ranchi in Bihar use Sadri or Sadni. Desia is a variety of Oriya and Sadri is a variety of Hindi. To what extent these intermediate languages can be exploited for furthering literacy has to be examined very carefully.

Problem of Santhali somewhat parallels the situation obtaining in the case of Konkani speakers. The Konkani speakers are spread in Goa, Maharashtra, Karnataka and Kerala. The Konkani language is written in four scripts, the Nagari,

Kannada, Malayalam and the Roman script. The Santhalis are mainly distributed in Orissa, Bengal and Bihar, though there are few thousands in Assam. The language consequently is written in five scripts, Nagari, Bengali, Oriya, Roman and the Ol scripts. The last is an indigenously developed script by one Raghunatha Murmu, himself a Santhali. Since the matter of script is an emotionally surcharged problem and the adoption of one or the other has many wider implications, literacy workers would do well to inform themselves about various aspects of this question with the help of linguists who have worked in these areas.

The above list is illustrative of challenges which literacy workers are likely to face. The various efforts at script and spelling reforms pose constantly renewed problems which need watching by trained linguists and their implications spelled out for the literacy workers. However, it is not only in the area of more language analysis that a linguist is relevant to a literacy programme. In the area of material production three major operations are envisaged in the years to come. Apart from writing materials which would presuppose language analysis, it is visulised that there will be need for translating and simplifying manuals and reading materials written by specialists.

Many international agencies are called upon to send specialists to prepare manuals are either designed for village level workers in health and education or for voluntary organizations engaged in extension work. As the knowledge of English of the workers themselves in minimal, the texts need to be simplified. Take for example an instruction from a manual (v.1 : 101) prepared by the Ministry of Health. "Schedule domiciliary visits to new acceptors of condoms at least one during the first two months and every six months after they have become regular users". This sentence has so many variables that for a person educated up to SSLC level it is difficult to comprehend it in one reading. Even after reading several times the chances of confusion cannot entirely be ruled out. Texts such as these need to be simplified. However the question is not as simple as it sounds at the first instance. How the simplification of an agreement between the governments of UK and Rhodesia assumed different nuances in the hands of government writers (Cripwell 1975 Aug.) goes to prove that a lot of expertise has to be brought to bear upon the problem. In Indian languages where prestige is often attached to the high style, texts have to be simplified to guide the inexperienced reader through graded steps into becoming an efficient reader. Here a parallel may be drawn with preparing textual material for purposes of second language learning. As in the case of learning a second language the learner is first introduced to the simple language used for native speaker he is guided to progress to greater complexities, in this case simplified language for neoliterate inexperienced reader slowly moves through simple language to greater complexities. Needless to say that the help of a linguist is essential in this operation.

Translations will have to be resoited to, as, for sometimes to come, the experts will write in English. Even if some good reading material is published in one Indian language it may have to be translated into other Indian languages. Translation is one of the most neglected fields in the country. Without going into the details of discussion regarding linguistics and translation (Pattanayak 1955; 57-63), it may suffice to point out that with language belonging to four language families and many languages of doubtful affiliation, almost all structural and semantic complexities of translation one is likely to find in the tour of the world can be illustrated by Indian languages. Fourteen languages as medium of higher education, administration and mass communication should indicate the extent of translation needed in the country. Apart from the problem of vocabulary, the presence or absence of verbs in equational sentences, passive and gender concord, the different modes of relativisation, the differing case relations are few of the important areas which pose obvious problems in translation. What is important to understand in this connection is that a research base has to be created in all these areas if functional adult education is to be achieved in a meaningful way.

The preparation of instructional material is not independent of the curriculum and philosophy underlying adult education in any country. Lyra Srinivasan (1977) speaks of four curriculum models. The four models, the Information model, the Problem solving model, the Projective model, and the Expressive, the Creative or the Self-actualising model, from a continuum on the basis of maximal and minimal role of a teacher. Each model will dictate its own material and teacher preparation. For example, when people speak in terms of textbooks and supplementary readers their thinking is essentially of the information model. The system in which the teacher engages himself in a one way communication of information where the textbook dominates the class, where education is not relevant to the important segments of living of the adult learner is incompatible with adult education. External incentives and pursuations may result in external allegiance to a programme but it cannot generate the necessary emotional and intellectual precondition for adult education.

The conventional thinking on the subject makes a distinction between adult literacy and adult education. Thus in a curriculum of 350 hours, 90-100 hours are given for literacy. This represents a gross distortion and misunderstanding of both literacy and education. First of all it must be understood that language is not taught in a vacuum. Unless the content of the language instructional material is closely knit with the needs and interests of the learners this itself may act as the greatest disincentive for them. Therefore, taking structures like lala tala la, lala la, tala la, selected on an ad hoc and random basis, and trying to generalise it for all groups of learners may not be the most efficient introduction of literacy.

Many perfer to use the primer prepared for native children for initial literacy. This thinking does not take into consideration the special psychological problem of an adult who either feels deprived, because of being bypassed by the school or has a low self-image, because of being a drop-out. He certainly resents when treated as a child. Secondly, a primer is a unit of formal schooling where it is structured differently with the curriculum. Thirdly, even the primers themselves are often not even properly designed for the children. For example, the first seventeen pages of the current Marathi primer contains mostly imperatives. Under these circumstances, no matter how convenient it is for the administrator from the point of sale of material, this is not the proper answer to adult education.

The knowledge sought to be imparted in an adult education situation must be need specific and the medium of communication location specific. This would indicate diversification of instructional material. But even accepting this diversity as basis, to what extent the initial material can be generialised needs to be studied more throughly and scientifically. So far only assertations of various literacy workers for and against such claims are available. For example, when one claims that the same literacy manual is being used for small and marginal farmers, industrial and mining workers, urban service workers, workers in different trades, tribals, scheduled caste groups and women it has to be examined a little more carefully and should not be taken at the face value.

Literacy to be functional, language must be well integrated with content. If the aim of adult education is to impart a level of competence to the learner so that he can sustain his interest of his own without lapsing into illiteracy, then it is not enough to give a mere recognition and manipulation of scripts, reading of controlled texts and writing letters to the grand child about one's health and the village fair. The adult learner must be made a competent reader with understanding of fairly complex structures so that he can read newspapers and make sense of various governmental forms and notifications. Very little research has gone into the officialise language of our country. The forms and notifications, even in English in many countries, are written in a language which need simplification in order to be accessible to the English knowing public (Wright 1975 : 213-220). Many of our forms and notifications, which are not originally drafted in Indian language, but are translations from English, are not even comprehended by highly educated native speakers. Therefore, it must be understood that both the content and language must be graded to carry the learner through successive skills while maintaining their relevance and creativity. This presupposes a team work in which a linguist is an indispensable component.

When we think of adult education, often, it is considered to be connected with writing and reading. Since every body speaks a language, spoken activity is completely ignored in the scheme of things. It must not be forgotten that India has a 2000 year old tradition of oral transmission of knowledge. In any case through dialogue it is not only possible to establish a personal bond between the teacher and the learners, but also lay the foundation of problem sharing and culture sharing. Very little research has been conducted about the structure of oral presentation in the formal class room, the radio and under more non-formal conditions. The research conducted by the Coimbatore Agriculture University (Sudarsanam 1975) tend to indicate that there is more similarity in the structure of the class room presentation and the presentation by the Radio. This may be because, the radio presentation is first written and then read. The linking of the oral structures to reading and writing must also engage the attention of linguists.

A question is often asked about testing those who pass through adult literacy programmes. In such situation the word 'assessment' should be used to include besides testing, such observation techniques as rating and interviews, class performance records, job records and evaluation of the total learning outcome to reflect developmental changes. This also requires formulation of the goals of literacy in a more meaningful manner. Functional literacy in terms of UNESCO norms was considered to be equivalent to education of the level of class V. But in the circumstances where the emphasis is on non-formality the specification of goals has to be spelled out in terms of skills, learner's confidence level creative interpretations of a stimulus, problem solving ability, etc. This is the only way to ensure fairness of assessment of both individuals and groups in a pluralistic society.

Terms such as motivations, animators, facilitators are being freely used in connection with adult education. Following the Indian tradition in this regard, some have even suggested a three-tier organisation where a motivator is the programme in-charge whereas the facilitator is the teacher. Those in-charge of adult education must ensure that the new lables are not used to either maintain status quo or smuggle in the formal class room authoritarianism. Malcolm Knowles developing the concept of Androgogy (Knowles 1971) describes it as the art and science of helping adults to learn. Androgogy has also been termed as 'A technology of involvement'. This involvement on the part of both orgnisers and learners is crucial to the success of an adult education programme. This is the biggest challenge before the educationists and linguists of this country today.

Mathematics

In adult and continuing education there seem to be two parallel and combined processes going on: *an institutionalizing process*, where schools or colleges for adults become subject to the sorts of regulation already experienced by schools for children and adolescents; and *a de-institutionalizing process* with a focus on adults' learning processes outside schools, some of which may be accredited as more or less equivalent to formal qualifications.

Adults are engaged in a range of social practices, such as working (or seeking work), parenting and caring for other dependents, budgeting and organising consumption, voting, etc. The term *lifelong* indicates that education takes place in all stages and spheres of life. By *mathematics* we mean multiple activities and knowledge, including academic mathematics, vocational mathematics, ethnomathematics, folk mathematics and adult numeracy. Regarding *education* we adopted the terminology of UNESCO (2000) as a point of departure: *Informal education* means the lifelong process whereby adults are learning mathematics in everyday life (e.g., work, family, leisure, society). *Formal education* refers to the adult educational system from adult basic education and vocational training through further and higher education. *Non-formal education* is defined as any educational activity organized outside the established formal system that is intended to serve identifiable learning objectives. Adult and lifelong mathematics education has multiple dimensions and the approaches represented in our discussions embraced, besides mathematics, a range of disciplines (psychology, sociology, politics, pedagogy, anthropology and androgogy), and a spectrum of concerns about inclusion – along lines of gender, class, ethnicity, age and language group.

Overviews of Recent Research and Practice in Adult Numeracy and Mathematics

After decades of neglect, adult numeracy and mathematics learning and teaching are coming to be recognised as worthy of serious research (Coben, 2003). Retical framework of Basil Bernstein which offers a coherent set of principles for linking the institutions of mathematics and lifelong education, and the emerging but contested construct of adult numeracy. At the macro or institutional level the positioning of mathematics and numeracy education and research in relation to each other and to discourses of lifelong learning. These are set within the arenas of knowledge production and distribution, influenced by policy formation at national and international levels. At the meso level, within the field of recontextualising where knowledge transmission takes place, curriculum formation and conditions of teachers' work. At the micro level, within the field of reproduction, where knowledge acquisition takes place, recontextualising texts and their possible impact on learners' identities.

Parents and Community as Intellectual Resources

The Cultural processes involving oral mathematics are produced and their curricular implications for the education of youths and adults in rural areas. This ethnographic study followed a group of 50 rural workers of the Brazilian Landless Movement, students in a teaching course belonging to this social movement, and illiterate youths and adults who participated in a workshop given by the course participants. *Marta Civil* (USA) presented two research projects on parents as adult learners of mathematics in a Latino/Hispanic working class community. The focus was on issues of content and learning environment: What mathematical content should we address when working with parents? What pedagogical approaches do they favour? The paper pays special attention to the voices of immigrant parents. The experiences of working with parents, guardians and community and interaction with them had shown that more than 90% of the parents of children facing difficulties in the learning of mathematics were found to have a phobia or repulsion towards mathematics.

Issues of Affect, Beliefs, Motivation, Resistance and Anxiety in Adult Learners

Continuing education is experienced by adults as a field of tension between needs and constraints. People's motivation and resistance to learning mathematics is interrelated phenomena. Mathematics and learning, based on the students' written reflections on the process of carrying out projects as part of a preparatory mathematics university course.

Pedagogic Resources and the Dialogic Approach

Cognitive trajectories in response to proportional situations in adult education", about learning of proportional situations in a school form adults. The perlocutionary speech acts can encourage learning, but can also create barriers when the speaker uses a position of power that breaks with egalitarian dialogue. It is important for everyone to be able to engage with quantitative materials, in particular tables, to enable them to extract information and make informed decisions.

Gender "Mainstreaming"

Opportunities and challenges in mainstreaming that has been widely adopted by the international community as a strategy for equality. Mainstreaming of research on mathematics education means that gender, ethnicity, social class and other difference defining categories are involved consciously and explicitly in every research agenda. In mathematics education, curriculum, context, instruction and values have a gender dimension that should be acknowledged in research. Literacy surveys present intriguing instances of gender blindness – the paper points out how gender is a possible confounding variable in a number of comparisons. The paper contends that gender mainstreaming must be expected to play a positive role in the search for better research in mathematics education and a more inclusive teaching of mathematics.

Issues for Pre-service Teachers and for Professional Development of Tutors

The development of a model of professional development for tutors of adult numeracy was needed. The model incorporates a view that professional development is not one of the activity, but something that allows for the development of a wide range of skills and knowledge, increasing complexity and specificity in the context of a tutor's own lifelong learning. The steps followed to design a remedial course in mathematics for adult participants within the bounds of a university study program offered to practicing teachers with no bachelor's degree. The contribution of this work is related to three main ideas: the social work it represents in a nation like Venezuela where there is a great number of non-graduate teachers; the opportunity to break paradigms and negative beliefs about the learning of mathematics; and the characteristics of the suggested evaluation instruments.

Roles for Functional Skills and Understanding and Commonsense

Education and Skills are to meet their requirements. The findings of some study confirm that for many, being "at a given level" is not meaningful for the individual, as notions of levels embody predetermined assumptions about progression and relative difficulty. The functional skills and understanding between four different analytical domains in adults lives (school, workplace, everyday life and democratic involvement) and considered functional skills from four different discursive perspectives (society/politicians, researchers, mathematics teachers, and the individual). This analysis emphasized that skills and understanding can be functional in one domain from one perspective and not functional in another domain or, from another perspective.

Sociological Characteristics of Learners—Classroom Interection—Communication

The classroom can be understood as the site of various forms of dialogical interaction. Taken together, engagement in such dialogues results in experiences for students that can impact positively or negatively on their personal and social identities. While the research literature acknowledges this in various ways, there is potential for a research programme more explicitly focused on how different learners respond differentially to classroom situations in terms of their developing identities in the broadest sense. Such a programme could complement life history-based approaches to understanding educational and career trajectories and evaluations of effective teaching based on narrow measures of performativity, by providing microlevel data in the context of a conceptual framework drawn from developmental and/or discursive psychology.

In this paper I explore the relationship between learning through classroom dialogu and identity development, as a move towards a re-evaluation of effective classroom teaching that associates deep learning with positive identity development, while acknowledging dialogism in all its dimensions. My aim is to encourage research that focuses on the role of classroom interaction, as it is variously defined, in identity development. Such research has the potential both to critique and to complement views of effective teaching as defined performatively, in terms of output measures such as test results. Several commentators have made the case for such a countermove (such as Blake et al 1998; Pollard 1999). The key question to be explored is, 'How can classroom learning, via the forms of dialogue possible in classrooms, impact on identity development?' This raises the second-order question: 'What forms of dialogue are possible within classrooms?'

In the concluding section, I shall speculate on a research agenda for coming to a very different understanding of effective classroom teaching to that envisaged in the current quest for evidence-based practice.

Teaching as Dialogue

Teaching involves communication; whether its purpose is to enable students to gain\ access to inalienable truths, or to promote intellectual or social exploration for its own sake. Nevertheless, within the literature and professional practice, there is considerable variation in the degree to which teaching is explicitly seen as dialogical. Much of the policy and professional literature stresses the need both for active student participation (often including collaborative work) and for clearly defined aims and objectives relating to curriculum and syllabus demands which do not appear open to interpretation. Perhaps it is inevitable that the conflicting demands of teaching as transmission and as empowerment should lead to some ambivalence in this respect.

It could be argued that, precisely because human beings are unpredictable, a degree o uniformity needs to be imposed on formal education. To follow this line implie acceptance that all forms of regulation -relating to teaching will inevitably valorize the attainment of pre-defined learning outcomes and the development of learner autonomy. Such regulation becomes counter-productive, however, where only one of these is effectively promoted, or where there is no evidence of potential symbiosis between the two. Certainly, the National Curriculum regulations for England and Wales (Qualifications and Curriculum Authority 2000), while promoting practical and collaborative work in a number of areas, tend not to express Levels of Attainment with reference to characteristics of effective dialogue.

Various models of teaching as dialogical process already exist in the literature, though such models seem only to have had a minor influence on (for example) National Curriculum guidelines in England. These models can all be seen as indebte to the developmental psychology of Lev Vygotsky (published in English in 1962, 1978), with many also influenced by the later Wittgenstein (1953), and perhaps the social constructionism of Berger and Luckmann (1966), among others. Vygotsky showed how learning was undertaken through largely linguistic interaction, with learner understanding depending on dialogue with a more learned other in a 'zone of proximal development' (Vygotsky 1978). Jerome Bruner specifically adapted this insight for teaching by developing the concept of scaffolding' (Bruner 1966), whereby teachers generate activities through which students can learn apparently unaided. Wittgenstein, in

Philosophical investigations, showed how concepts such as truth and meaning are contextualised within 'language games' (Wittgenstein 1953). An acceptance of this leads to an acknowledgement of the need for particular approaches to dialogue within the different areas of the curriculum (eg Driver 1994; Solomon 1998). Wittgenstein can be seen as a key influence on, for example, Pau Hirst and Richard Peters, in their development of the influential 'areas of experience' model of the curriculum (eg Hirst 1974), and later on the theories of situated learning particularly associated with Lave and Wenger (1991).

Berger and Luckmann (1966) showed how any contact with other perspectives enables individuals to understand the fluidity of structures and institutions, and thus gives them the potential to rework their own subjectivities in increasingly empowering ways. Berger and Luckmann's work can be used in support of arguments for group work and in defence of mixed ability or mixed gender groupings in classrooms.

In addition, a considerable body of literature concerning dialogue in teaching-and-learning draws on socially critical theories. A notable example is Robert Young who, in Critical theory and classroom talk (1992), specifically argues for a model o teaching he terms 'discursive', based on Habermas' Ideal Speech Situation. The adherence to a Marxist or post-Marxist tradition in such writing may, of itself, contribute to some polarisation of opinions regarding the role of dialogue in effective teaching in the educational community as a whole.

Clearly, any view of teaching as dialogue is liable to accentuate one of the above influences, sometimes at the expense of others: for example, proponents of the subject-centred curriculum may be more sympathetic to Wittgenstein; and those supportive of mixed ability teaching to Berger and Luckmann. An acceptance of the importance of dialogue in teaching by no means implies universal agreement on all issues of practice. However, a strong case remains for greater efforts at understanding effective teaching with respect to the effective conduct of dialogue. This invites a consideration of what can be held to constitute effectiveness in this regard.

Recent commentators have addressed this issue from various research o developmental perspectives. Neil Mercer (1995, 2000) has emerged as among the most influential developers of a social-constructivist research tradition focusing on the identification of 'learning talk'. Mercer himself has been greatly influenced by the earlier studies of, among others, Gordon Wells (1986), Douglas Barnes (Barnes 1976; Barnes et al 1969; Barnes & Todd 1995) and, in North America, James Dillon (1994). Such work tends to focus on process measures – for example, in identifying examples of 'exploratory talk' from transcripts – though some recent work claims to show concrete and sustainable improvements in reasoning as a result of training in such techniques (Gillies 2000; Mercer et al 1999).

Alec Webster, Michael Beveridge and Malcolm Reed (Webster et al 1996) are among the writers who stress the importance of classroom interactions for developing competence in aspects of the curriculum (in this case, literacy). Work by Robert Fisher (1995) and others (eg Lipman 1991) stresses the need for the development of certain kinds of thinking processes in children, via various forms of dialogic activity, as a precursor to improved performance across the curriculum. Thus, several recent commentators have promoted the role of classroom dialogue in enhancing the student learning experience, though none can make very explicit claims concerning the more general effect on learners – such as whether this dialogue can contribute to turning 'surface into 'deep' learners (Entwistle & Ramsden 1983).

Despite these efforts, contemporary commentators have not tended to radically oppose a policy adherence to fairly narrow outcome measures as indicators o success perhaps because they seem only able to identify process measures. As Blake et a (1998), among others, have pointed out, Jean-Francois Lyotard's notion of 'performativity' (Lyotard, 1986) has embedded itself as the dominant 'value' in an educational climate in which any consensus about more enduring values has been lost. Performativity drives the system.

Andrew Pollard (1999) has argued that movements in sociocultural theory offer the potential for developing a much-needed alternative to the performative paradigm. H stresses the usefulness of the cross-cultural case studies of children's upbringing undertaken by Richards and Light (1986), for example, and of Barton and Hamilton's work on 'local literacies' (Barton & Hamilton 1998). Pollard also quotes Jerome Bruner, who, in The culture of education (1996), argued: 'education must help those growing up in a culture to find an identity within that culture'.

Various researchers have pointed up the link between classroom language and identity development, but have either not pursued this in any depth with reference to particular cases, or have dealt with it on a general political level, focusing on group identities and social justice issues rather than personal positioning. For example, Gordon Wells discusses the impact of 'negative experiences' upon the learning orientations of particular individuals, but does not elaborate on this with reference to examples (in Lee & Smagorinsky 2000, p 56). Peter O'Connor exemplifies the latter tendency by stressing how 'standard accounts of literacy fail to see how literacy is integral to gender, cultural and language politics', but does not relate the genera insight to particular instances or identities (in Freebody & Welch 1993, p 199). Each of the writers cited in this section has made a significant contribution to the understanding of learning as a dialogical process.

None, however, have either attempted to map all the forms of classroom dialogue, or explored – wit much degree of specificity – how the learning and processes and outcomes they desire or identify relate to the emerging identities of young people. There is particularly a dearth of research illuminating this latter, broader concern via micro-level analysis of classroom interaction, taking full account of personal perspectives. Methodologically, perhaps the most sophisticated model yet made available is that posited by Putney, Green, Dixon, Duran and Yeager, who attempt to understand learning (rather than identity development more specifically) by 'bringing interactional ethnography together with sociocultural theory and critical discourse analysis' (in Lee & Smagorinsky 2000, p 121). Arguably, even this approach takes insufficient regard of actors' interpretations. Putney et al acknowledge the importance of 'close examination of the lived experiences of students' (2000, p 121). Lemke, writing about science and science education as communities of practice, goes a step beyond this in noting that 'social activities ... are definite only in retrospect' (Lemke 1990, p 4), while 'It is the sense we make of what we see, the meaning for us of what we see, that matters' (1990).

Learning as Identity Development

As the concern here is with teaching-and-learning as dialogic, there is a prima facie case for devoting particular consideration to the discursive psychologists whose work building on both social interactionism and more traditional development a psychology, is predicated on the assumption that human life is best understood as a kind of conversation: a series of social acts and actions that are essentially communicative (Edwards & Potter,1992; Harré, 1998; Harré & Gillett 1994). As there is now widespread acceptance that learning entails the social construction of meaning (variously interpreted), discursive psychology has the potential to provide conceptual frameworks for understanding development through sequences of dialogical interactions.

Such frameworks, of course, assume an understanding of learning as psychological change. A tentative start to such an approach was, in effect, made by Malcolm Ross and his colleagues at the University of Exeter during the late 1980s and early 1990s, in their application of Rom Harré's 'social reality matrix' (Harré, 1983) to the assessment of achievement in the creative arts (Ross 1993). More recently, a team based at the Universities of Bath and Swansea has suggested that Harré's work might be applied more broadly across the school curriculum (Stables et al 1999). In Personal being, Harré effectively construed learning as the undertaking of a series of 'Identity Projects' enacted through a 'social reality matrix' comprising cycles of activity involving Conventionalisation, Appropriation, Transformation and

Publication (Harre 1983). Such cycles might profitably be applied to lesson and course planning across a wide range (perhaps the complete range) of disciplines. The effective linking of learning to identity change by Harré and the other discursive psychologists invites, in its turn, closer attention to the ways in which classroom processes might contribute to identity change as configured by more traditional developmental psychology. We might, for example, draw on the work of James Marcia, who identifies four types of Identity Status (Marcia, 1994):

- Foreclosure – a narrow conventionality;
- Moratorium – an active exploration;
- Identity Achievement – a strong sense of relatively fixed identity; and
- Identity Diffusion – characterised by disaffection.

As Marcia clearly describes, two states can be seen as generally desirable, at least in educational terms (Moratorium and Identity Achievement), and two as less desirable. The question arises as to how classroom processes can contribute to the development of the former two, rather than the latter. In terms of an holistic understanding of identity change, there is currently a surprising dearth of literature on the role of classroom teaching, despite the wealth of work undertaken regarding wider influences on the development of personal identity – with schooling acknowledged as one such influence, but only in the broadest sense. Classroom organisation at the policy level (mixed-ability vs setting) has of course been considered. However, in terms of the specifics of classroom interaction, there is little that moves beyond Bernstein's influential work on framing and classification (1975), or the essentially socially critical assumption that smallgroup collaborative work is empowering (eg Young 1992). Perhaps the most extensive work available to date is that of Pollard and Filer (1996, 1999), who explore the development of an individual's self-identity as a learner with a series of longitudinal case studies. Pollard and Filer (1999) define four 'dimensions of strategic action' that parallel Marcia's more broadly defined states of ego identity. These are:

1. Conformity – cf Marcia's Foreclosure;
2. Re-definition – cf Marcia's Moratorium;

3. Non-conformity – cf Marcia's Identity Achievement, in that independence is marked out with confidence; and
4. Anti-conformity – cf Marcia's Identity Diffusion, though implying a more active form of disaffection in the classroom context.

Pollard and Filer's work shows how a variety of contextual factors, within and beyond the school, impact on students' classroom identities. These factors include relationships with teachers, but not specific teaching-and-learning events. In terms of scope, their focus on identity is somewhat narrower than that attempted in this paper.

Nevertheless, there is much in Pollard and Filer's work to indicate that effective teaching must be more than the decontextualised transfer of 'good practice'. Set against this, the UK's recent Teaching and learning initiative (Economic and Socia Research Council 1999) actively seeks an evidence base for effective practice, but its specifications pay little heed to the dialogic and psychologically saturated nature of teaching-and-learning, according to which it must be impossible to generate guidelines for good practice that take little account of the contextual. This notwithstanding, certain projects funded under the scheme have acknowledged the contextual, notably one by Bloomer and Hodkinson (2000), and the 'Home School' project (unpublished). Neither of these, however, attempts any microanalysis of classroom interaction.

Contexts of Dialogue for Effective Teaching

It has been argued that any sustainable definition of effective teaching should acknowledge outcome measures – in terms of learning results that cannot apparently be interpreted – and the development of creative individuals, capable of working flexibly alongside others. Unfortunately, most existing definitions strongly valorize one of these two criteria over the other. Most existing conceptions of Added Value in relation to schooling tend to focus principally on improvement in examination results, while critical theorists such as Young (above) take no account whatsoever of such measurable outcomes. In both cases, a limited view of teaching is presented.

One well-respected view of quality in teaching that does acknowledge both elements is that of Edwards and Mercer, who regard effective teaching as aiming for cognitive socialisation, undertaken via language (Edwards & Mercer 1987). This view acknowledges the work of the Vygotsky school, Wittgensteinian language games and the importance of seeing schoolwork in the context of broader interaction. The model has informed many pieces of later work, much of it by the two originators, yet has not effectively been superseded. Indeed, if anything, its emphasis on the distinctive nature of discourse in each curriculum area has become increasingly recognised during the last 15 years.

What has been added to the canon during this period is a much better\ comparative understanding, relating classroom discourse events in Britain to those in other parts of the world. Robin Alexander (2000), in the most comprehensive of such studies, shows how national and regional contexts impact on classroom dialogue, with a much greater emphasis in France than in England on 'les disciplines' at primary level, and a much greater preponderance of informal teacherpupil talk in England and the USA than in France, India or Russia.

As Westgate and Hughes (1997) acknowledge, there remain no firm criteriab for assessing quality in classroom (or other forms of teacher-learner) talk. However, Edwards and Mercer continue to provide a useful basis for the development of such criteria, despite the intercultural differences noted by Alexander and others. There is a significant gap in research knowledge, however, between the conceptualisation of teaching as (something like) cognitive socialisation through language, and understanding how patterns of classroom discourse build towards conceptual understanding and, by extension, psychological change.

Alexander (2000) offers tantalising leads here but does not pursue this line in any great depth. Edwards and Mercer's advocacy of the development of common knowledge within shared contextual assumptions is far from comprehensive in this respect. Bearing in mind that contextual assumptions can, at best, be only partly shared – so that the same classroom interchange can never mean quite the same for any two people or at any two different moments – it may be impossible to move to any greater level of specificity in terms of prescribing good practice in the sense of 'practice that can be copied'. However, it is at least possible to identify the various kinds of contexts in which classroom dialogue occurs, as a precursor to investigating what seem to be, have been, rich learning experiences in the classroom. This is addressed under the following four headings.

Context 1: Teacher-student/teacher-class Dialogue

Much of the earliest work on classroom interaction has a strong focus on the teacher-student/teacher-class condition. Edwards and Mercer (1987) present key findings from this set of studies. They particularly draw our attention to the effects o asymmetrical power relations on classroom discourse in schools, whereby most teacher-pupil interactions are controlled, typically following a pattern often defined as an Initiation-Response-Evaluation (IRE) or Initiation-Response-Feedback (IRF). This pattern tends to dominate teacher-student interaction even when teachers espous non-didactic models, and seems to be an inevitable result of the institutional constraints of schooling, which require teachers to control, as well as teach, large numbers of potentially disruptive pupils. More recent work confirms this general pattern, showing that classrooms are still dominated by teacher talk, which is itself dominated by teacher control of questioning (eg Bearne 1999) – though there is now strong evidence of intercultural variation than previously (Alexander 2000; Mercer 1995).

Such research has failed to convince British policy makers that whole-class teaching is of limited value, to the extent that it is given prominence (albeit in conjunction wit collaborative group work, and not merely as 'transmission') in the British government's National Literacy and Numeracy Strategies (Qualifications and Curriculum Authority, 1999). Perhaps such scepticism towards research is no without justification, as there may well be compensating factors that researchers have not considered. In this case, the evident success of whole-class teaching methods in other countries was not so assiduously studied for a considerable period by researchers in the West and Australasia, for example. Also, the various and skilful ways in which some teachers use even the limited IRE or IRF pattern is arguably still not fully recognised (Sahin et al 2002), while the UK's National Oracy Strategy paid scant attention to whole-class teaching (Norman 1992). Nevertheless, research does serve to develop a body of understanding that can inform, if never fully prescribe, future practice. In this case, the research has repeatedly revealed similar patterns of interaction, with various interpretations of what constitutes good practice espoused in relation to these: for example, good teachers build on 'Common Knowledge' between themselves and their students, and focus on principled rather than procedural knowledge (Edwards & Mercer 1987); good teachers tell stories and find alternative methods, thus reducing their reliance on questioning (Cortazzi 1993; Wood, in Norman 1992); and good teachers give clear instructions, set appropriate tasks, keep good classroom order and so on.

On the other hand, social and cultural differences determine that students will response differentially to the same teaching approaches (Bernstein 1975; Corson 1993); Maybin, in Norman 1992). This implies a relationship between teacherclass/teacher-student talk and student identity development, though few research studies have considered this explicitly. Nevertheless, there is at least plenty of material to draw upon to begin more sophisticated investigation into this first context for classroom dialogue.

Context 2: between-student Dialogue

A common response to the findings concerning the teacher-centredness of much classroom practice has been to promote increased collaborative work among students. While some of this work has been in part politically motivated, a strong corpus seeks to determine the cognitive (as opposed to the purely social) benefits of forms of collaborative pupil talk (for example, Barnes et al 1969; Barnes & Todd, 1995; Mercer et al 1999; Norman 1992). Despite occasional naivety both in the interpretation and the implementation of such work (Stables 1993, 1995) considerable progress has been made in this field;

recent studies systematically evaluated teaching approaches based, at least in part, on the results of earlier work, and claimed evidence for more than short-term effects (Gillies 2000; Mercer et al 1999).

While an openness has to be preserved about what constitutes effective learning in small-group contexts, where negotiation rather than completion of the task can become paramount (Yonge & Stables 1998) – and while considerable difficulties therefore remain with the formal assessment of collaborative work (Stables 1992) – we are now moving towards a much more explicit understanding of the kinds of discursive activity students engage in under this condition of dialogue.

However, beyond a vague exhortation towards 'balance' or 'mixed methods', research evidence remains limited on how whole-class and small-group teaching interact, or on how (to focus on the student) issues of personal identity are negotiated in the semi-public arena of the collaborative work group vis-à-vis the rather more public arena of the 'whole class'.

Context 3: Within-student Dialogue – Student and Text

In referring to 'within-student' dialogue, there is an acceptance of the validity of both Vygotsky's conception of 'inner speech' (Vygotsky 1962) and Bakhtin's work on the heterogeneity of voices (eg Todorov 1984). Even educators little versed in either set of theories may grant that it is hardly controversial to assert that learners are often required to 'engage' with a text, or with some other external stimulus physicall divorced from the teacher. This condition and the next relate to what Andrew Wilkinson (1986) referred to as A-A communication: i.e. the student talking to her/himself. Perhaps because such internal dialogue cannot be overheard, its value is often overlooked in discussions about classroom discourse (Stables 1995). Indirectly, such engagement is promoted through a variety of teaching strategies and measured, post hoc, through assessments of students' written and other more public communications. Directly, such assessments often rely on a largely intuitive feeling about classroom 'atmosphere'; about whether or not there is a 'good air of concentration'. We know little about the silent processes in which students engage in given contexts, nor about between-student differences in relation to this, though taxonomies of higher-order reading skills (for example) do exist that might prove helpful in providing some kind of starting point in the development of analytical frameworks here. There is also very little research on how the quality of this form of dialogue is promoted through the use of other forms.

Context 4: Within-student Dialogue – Reflection and Problem Solving

Similarly, while most teachers may wish their students to become reflective problem-solvers, little systematic work has been done on how to promote or evaluate this within the context of the lesson or wider teaching programme. The work of Robert Fisher (1995) and of other proponents of 'philosophy for children' (eg Lipman 1991), while generally respected, has had limited policy impact to date.

The work of Richard Andrews and his colleagues on the nature of argument (Andrews 1995) has similarly been little exploited so far, despite revealing significant gaps in awareness, even among able and advanced students. Teachers are often more aware that certain students are reflective and take initiative, without having much understanding of how or why. Similarly, readers of this paper who have engaged in teaching may be all too aware of the conscientious and successful student who plays no part at all in the spoken life of the classroom, yet whose levels of reflection and argumentation remain extremely high. Cultural differences seem to be significant here, too.

While the received wisdom of Western education is that verbal interchange promotes learning, there is plenty of evidence from around the world that this assumption is by no means universally shared. The reflective condition of inner dialogue also deserves, therefore, to be valued for its contribution to learning, and the oscillation of inner and outer speech can be promoted and utilised in a variety of ways that have not yet been clearly documented or evaluated. Identification of four discrete but potentially symbiotic general 'conditions' of classroom dialogue might form the first step in the formulation of guidelines for effective teaching that fully acknowledge its essentially dialogic nature. However, such an identification would still fall short of an account of effective teaching on two fronts: it would not define quality, and it would not consider peculiarities of classroom, personal and social contexts.

Teaching-and-learning as Dialogic Identity Development: Qualitative analysis requires two things above all: qualitative methods and a clear conceptual framework. It is beyond the scope of this paper to rehearse the argument for and against competing forms of qualitative research, except to stress that qualitative research can make use of quantitative data, just as positivist research can make use of, for example, in-depth interviews. The key point in this context is that numerical output does not directly measure quality of input (in this case, of teaching), since contextual factors beyond the classroom also influence tested performance. The issue is not whether this is so, but how. There is a strong case for looking to developmental and discursive psychology for the conceptual frame. Harré's Identity Projects serve as one example; Marcia's ego-identity types might serve as another. By working in depth with small numbers of students over significant periods of time, there is much that could be done to generate a rich qualitative data set around students' communicative and behavioural changes in terms of conceptions of personal and social identity, and the degree to which particular sets of classroom events seem to have influence these.

Particularities of Context

Consideration of situational context raises a different, though related, set of issues. These issues can be grouped as follows:

1. Issues of simple sequence: Given the heterogeneous nature of student readiness for the teaching event, how far is it possible to make universally valid statements about the most effective ways to start and end lessons? Similarly, are there forms of lesson transition that can be taken as universally preferable to others?

2. Issues of personal difference: How do different students behave under the different contexts for dialogue listed above? Judged by simple output measures, do some learn – effectively – the same things through smallgroup work that others learn through silent reading? Within a conceptualisation of learning as identity change, how do different students internalise given classroom events? Are students of different identity types differentially affected by immediate factors impacting on the classroom context (eg from the weather outside, to falling out with friends, or experiencing difficulties at home)?
3. Issues of teacher planning and preparation: To what extent can we generalise about 'best practice' in utilising combinations of different kinds of dialogic events? How can aims and objectives be conceptualized for forms of teaching that valorise, promote and make the fullest use of dialogue?

A body of research exists that explores how students make meaning dialogically Wegerif. Of the cited work, however, only that by Wegerif and colleagues is focused strongly on teacher planning and preparation for meaningful pupil interaction, and none explicitly addresses the issue of planning whole lessons, schemes of work or courses. Similarly, many models have been produced of cycles of learning, but literature on the application of this to classroom sequences, as opposed to classroom activities, is very limited.

If such an approach has any potential, it raises many questions for further research to explore. One key question concerns learning style and the Identity Project. In recent years Harré has called strongly for a science of positioning (Harré, 1998), in order to better understand how individuals construct their personal identities through social interaction. In the classroom, such work could have great benefits in helping us to understand the complex social psychology of the class.

Again, research exists here, but it has not been fully applied to pedagogy. In the 1980s, for example, Andrew Pollard found that the groups of pupils he came to refer to as 'Jokers' (Pollard

1985) were often the most successful in school, for the very reason that they took a more proactive role than other students in negotiating the progress of lessons; in effect, they took greater roles in the discourse of the classroom. There is surely scope for research into the conditions under which students are encouraged into, or discouraged from, becoming Jokers, or moving into other kinds of roles within the broader group dynamics of the class. Pollard's more recent work with Ann Filer concerns the forms of strategic action available to students as they develop their identities as learners with respect to a key concept of conformity.

There is the potential for work to build on this that is less closely wedded to the classroom or the school as the main driver of identity development, but continues to develop fine-grained analyses of classroom events as illustrative of, and instrumental in, the development of broader forms of personal and social identity. Indeed, Pollard and Filer's longitudinal study might provide-hypotheses that could guide the development of such work. For example, research informed by Marcia's ego-identity types might explore how different identity types– or strategic actors (in Pollard and Filer's terms) – respond to different sequences of dialogical activity intended for learning, and how different sequences of teaching and-learning events seem instrumental in effecting changes of identity status, more broadly defined.

Concluding Remarks

This paper has been speculative, but is intended to draw attention to the possibilities of developing a study of teaching as dialogical enterprise with the potential to contribute to positive identity development in a more refined sense than has hitherto been acknowledged. Such research would combine fine-grained microanalyses of classroom events and responses to them with a broader understanding of the development of personal trajectories.

For too long, it can be argued, debates about teachers' practice have failed to draw together insights from two concurrent streams of research: one that sees effective teaching as monological cultural transmission, and the other that views it as social empowerment. An important early step in such a process is the clear identification of the types of dialogical interaction that characterise the teaching-and-learning situation. The above identification of four contexts of classroom dialogue may prove of use in taking such a step.

Non-formal Education and Sociolization

In the multilingual, multi-ethnic countries like India, the need for sociolinguistics can hardly be underestimated. Language variations in social and regional axes, through mutual isolation and interaction constantly reshape individual and social identities, which in turn have their impact on the environment of planning. Moreover, language use in education, administration and mass communication can fundamentally alter the character of the polity and thus influence the orientation and affect the foundation of planning itself. Sociolinguistics and the role of linguists in developing countries has to be viewed in this perspective.

Two hundred years of imperialist rule resulted in the creation of an elitist society in India where less than 4 per cent of the population enjoy the rank, status and wealth bestowed by English education. The large majority of people were alienated from the ruling group by the use of a language in administration which was nor accessible to them. Since audience in India is divided by language use, the use of English as the major language of mass media alienated the large majority of people from those privileged rulers, whether they were aliens or their countrymen. Thus the foundation of a society governed by the elites for their benefit in the name of the masses was complete.

The thirty years after independence have seen a different kind of isolation and fragmentation. In spite of lip service to Indian languages, English education is still very much the preferred education. Wherever Indian languages have been adopted as languages of education and languages of administration, without proper linkages at different levels and stages, small islands have been created, separating dialects from languages and one languages from another. Even within a single language the use of middle class language as the standard has left many, whose languages are different, disadvantages. The mass media which swears by the spoken word, uses it for the entertainments of non-users of these languages. No serious effort is made to make the Indian languages vehicles of knowledge, to define the domains of various languages and dialects and to use these with a view to ensuring people-oriented multilingual planning.

Under such circumstances, the role of a practitioner of sociolinguistics can only be that of a catalyst and a rebel. It is strange but true that all new revolutions are quickly adopted by the people in positions of power and translated into new slogans. These slogans provide them the necessary cloack to go about their work in the age old manner for their own purpose. Thus, those who were in charge of education for the last two or three decades and are responsible for establishing and nurturing the formal educational structure leading to an elitist society, suddenly have become votaries of non-formal and mass education. Mass education demands instant communication of knowledge to the masses. The masses of people being identified in groups in terms of language use, a rational policy decision must be implemented linking the twin problems of instant communication and the process of standardization and modernization in the country. Whether it is learning to be, writing a pedagogy of the oppressed or establishing deschooling society, the planning orientation cries for a distinctive change and a linguist committed to his/her profession is called upon to provide the leadership.

At a time when learners coming from families where there was no formal education for generations is pointed out to be the reason for falling standards, when leaning to write a petition for supplying clean drinking water, improved seeds and fertilizers and a homestead for those who have none is considered indulging in antisocial if not antinational activities, their is no wonder that a sociolinguist has to fight his lone battle. He is to raise his voice against the forces both inside and outside who are bent upon sabotaging from within the proposals put forward by the leadership. The linguist must expose this combine and help the radicalisation of education. Father Ferer called true education as subversive. It is subversive of the vested interest, of the elitist structure and a restrictive society. True education must ensure total freedom and equality of opportunity to all sectors of people as regards the accessibility to knowledge is concerned. It must ensure putting that knowledge to use for improving the quality of individual as well as corporate life.

The linguists in the country, however, are neither prepared no preparing themselves for such a role. Inter-disciplinary subjects such as sociolinguistics, psycho-linguistics are not fields for incompetent linguists, sociologists and psychologists. In fact a lot of what goes under the name sociolinguistics is nothing but linguistics. If sociolinguistics is pursued merely as a fashion in the same manner as the generative transformational linguistics, then in spite of all the good will it is bound to fail to deliver the goods. I would, therefore, urge universities and institutions in the country to train their people well before making claims to achievements in the areas of applied linguistics in general and sociolinguistics in particular.

A good example of how our training lacks relevance to the Indian context may be seen from issues like the three-language formula, adult education and primary education. It is sad to see that even Ph.D.s in Indian languages and linguistics are not fully conversant with the import of the three-language formula. The three-language formula does not set up an upper limit to language learning. It is a consensus which highlights the need to blend the local, the national and the international and seeks to promote a culturally integrative policy. It is a lunching pad for the exploration to the micro, mezzo and macro dimensions of language use and cultural synthesis.

It needs a linguist to delineate the methods, materials and the media for teaching mother tongue, second language and the foreign language. But our children, who even today are asked to study mother tongue English and the mother tongue as a mirror image of second language English do not have even the vaguest idea of such distinctions. Fed with ancient and medieval literature taught in a perfunctory manner and starved of functional conceptual prose, the children in schools and colleges fail to manipulate their mother tongue for expressing themselves in any field of study. For language and linguistic scholars are aware of the ramifications of such a situation.

The deficiency at the higher stages is the cumulative effect of bad language teaching at earlier stages. It must be admitted that without proper understanding of the problems relating to language use neither the problems of primary education nor adult literacy can be solved. India has 400 million adult literates accounting for 50 per cent of the total world illiterate population. But this problem cannot be solved unless primary education is universalised and stagnation and wastage is plugged. With 70 per cent drop out, stagnation by the end of the 5th standard, the primary education is the greatest contributor to adult illiteracy.

If one critically examines the cause of drop out and stagnation, difference between the home language and school language and lack of an academic strategey to move from one to the other in a smooth way loom large as causes. Yet neither the planners, the teacher educators nor the teachers have thought it fit to tackle the problem. Some of them, in their bind allegiance to English and in the mistaken notion that a language is better taught if it is taught for a longer duration have even pleaded for primary education through English. These pseudo-educators forget that in the absence of trained teachers, improved techniques of teaching and scientifically graded textual materials, if a language is merely taught for a longer duration it will create more learning problems than solving them. In States like Karnataka and A.P. where there are approximately 2500 secondary schools and 40,000 primary schools each, introduction of English below the 5th standard (and say from the 3rd standard) will require training of almost one lakh teachers in each case for which there is neither expertise no resources in the country. Whether it is mother tongue, second language or foreign language instruction when the simple differences among teaching a language, teaching about a language and teaching through a language have not percolated even to the level of teacher educators, one can imagine the colossal challenges confronting a linguist. Thus, whether it is teaching language as a subject, teaching subjects through a language, designing a bilingual curriculum for, those whose home language is different from the school language or designing improved methods and materials for teachers and teacher educators, there is greatest need for trained linguists with Indian orientation and social commitment. Our universities and training institutions must go beyond teaching the meta-language of the disciplines concerned and inculcate a problem solving orientation in the students. A healthy partnership between universities and institutes engaged in research and textbook production, located in close proximity to Centres of Linguistic Research shall take the leadership in this direction, so that a community of scholarship by bringing together leading practitioners in the field of sociolinguistics can be created to meet the colossal challenges before us.

Teacher Characteristics

Teachers of non-formal education (NFE)are usually called ?facilitators? since their main role is to facilitate learning processes based on the learners? existing knowledge and skills. The tasks of NFE facilitators are wide and complex, but their social and economic status is notalways high or stable in many countries, compared with formal school teachers.

The reason for this could be because many governments consider that NFE should be economical to provide learners with minimum literacy and numeracy skills for survival, even sacrificing the quality of classroom facilities, teaching-learning materials and staff. NFE programmes are often considered alternative or supplementary activities for disadvantaged population groups such as out-of-school children, youth and illiterate adults who missed formal schooling.

Consequently, NFE programmes are often organized under time and budget-bound projects by government or NGOs, rather than in permanent learning institutions. These project personnel often work under a short-term contractor temporary employment. Accordingly,little investment has been made in most countries for long-term career development and training mechanisms for NFE personnel.

The work of NFE facilitators is not as easyas one might think. They have to designand conduct the activities to meet the needs of learners, since most learners come to learning centres to improve their skills or solve problems in their daily lives. If the learning programmes do not accommodate such immediate needs, learners, in particular adults, may lose their interest in continuing their learning.

Facilitators do not just transmit information, but also assist learners in identifying issues and finding solutions by themselves. In fact, someadult learners have more experience and wisdom about practical life andvocational skills in the local community.Facilitators need to help learners link literacy and numeracy skills with their knowledge from daily life and find solutions and directions. In view of this, facilitators are often recruited from the local community because they know better about community life. In some cases, understanding local languages is also an important factor in selecting the facilitator when the community uses a different language from the national language. However, facilitators recruited locally often have a low educational background and little training experience, so many of them face difficulties facilitating the learning process effectively..

According to the EFA Global MonitoringReport 2006, it is estimated that 100 million children are not in school and 771 million adults can not read and write. It is not realistic to assume that all of them will go to formal schools in the near future. Achieving the EFA goals of universal primary education and a 50% improvement in adult literacy by 2015 will not be possible without alternative learning mechanisms through NFE. Since out-of-school children and illiterate adults are disadvantaged socially and economically with little power or voice, EFA partners should further encourage governments to strengthen the programmes, particularly, the capacity building of facilitators.

At the same time, it is not easy to create new institutions that focus on NFE. Synergizing available educational resources in the country would be an effective and feasible strategy. This includes involvement of school teachers, retired teachers and university/college students so that NFE programmes can benefit from their expertise and experiences. Cooperation with existing research and training institutions,especially teacher training colleges, and linkages with NGOs should be explored and developed.

Non-formal Education Programmes of Neo-literates

The term 'Neo-literacy' has come to have different meanings in various educational systems. In some countries, the term is used loosely to include all forms of education that follow after the achievement of basic literacy. In some other countries, post literacy is defined more narrowly to simply consolidate basic literacy skills to a level equivalent to the completion of formal primary school. In this definition, neo-literacy is considered as a 'bridge' between primary schooling or its equivalent and further study.

The definition accepted by the National Literacy Mission lies somewhere in between these two extremes. As a part of continuing education, post-literacy programmes attempt to give interested learners an opportunity to harness and develop their learning potential after completion of a course in basic literacy. Learning skills acquired by neo-literates during the short span on the literacy campaigns are at best fragile. There is a genuine danger of neo-literates regressing into partial or total illiteracy unless special efforts are continued to consolidate, sustain and possibly enhance their literacy levels.

Thus, the aim of the Mission's post literacy programme is to consolidate the basic literacy skills of speaking, reading, writing, numeracy and problem-solving and at the same time, transform these learners into an educated 'whole person', who is a productive socio-economic asset to the community.

Types of Programmes—Methods of Teaching

The National Literacy Mission has designed a one-year post literacy programme, to be implemented in a mission mode. In fact, it has laid a great deal of emphasis on the planning and launching of post literacy programme simultaneously after conclusion of the total literacy campaigns phase. In keeping with its aims, the Mission has formulated and circulated broad guidelines for implementation of post literacy programmes. The three basic elements are:

- Identification of learning needs of neo-literates
- Provision of learning opportunities to meet the needs
- Creating a socio-economic, political and cultural ambience to sustain the learning environment

Post literacy learning strategies as developed by the National Literacy Mission envisage the provision of learning opportunities both in structured and unstructured situations. Structured situation refers to organised learning where primers or graded textual material as well as suitably designed supplementary reading books for neo-literates. Unstructured situations refer to widely differing literacy abilities necessitating the provision of a wide range of learning materials and tools. These range from wall newspapers to book corners or libraries. Various media like radio and television are also used along with local art forms, study tours and excursions. Two novel and successful methods of imparting information are 'village parliament' as experimented in Bilaspur district, or 'Gaon Kacheri' in Pune district.

The post literacy programme thus serves as an umbrella under which a host of development activities are taken up; skill development forms a major component of post literacy; enterprising district collectors have been able to dovetail skill development within innovative development schemes. It is during the post literacy phase that linkages with other departments-especially with health, rural development and environment are forged.

One of the most important tasks of the post literacy is the 'mopping up' operation or remediation. Those learners who dropped out of the total literacy campaigns phase or could not achieve the prescribed norms of literacy, are enabled to achieve the required levels. The first phase of the post literacy programme envisages 40 hours of guided learning, focusing not only on remediation, retention and consolidation of literacy skills of neo-literates but seeking to ingrain the reading habit in them-so that they are able to put their literacy skills to good use in their daily life.

Preparation of Materials—Need for Research and Evaluation

The next phase of the post literacy programme provides opportunities for unstructured learning through self-directed processes. The Jan Chetna Kendras are used as an 'open window' for dissemination of information regarding ongoing development schemes. Many districts have brought out simplified booklets on development schemes for neo-literates that have helped them to make informed choices. Districts are encouraged to create a pool of literature by holding a writers' workshop and the tapping the talent of local story-tellers.

The village library movement is yet another initiative to promote self-reliance in learning. In each village where the number of neo-literates is substantial, small pathagars with a reading room or a library in the existing shikshan kendra/ youth club should be established. Similarly at the block level, preferably in the library of the secondary or higher secondary schools, separate sections for neo-literates can be created. This support library at the block level is expected to nurture the library at the village level. It could also lend books and rotate them to different villages on a weekly, fortnightly and monthly basis. The creation of a library for each village unit of 100 learners is central to the organisation of all post literacy activities.

Thiruchirapally district of Tamil Nadu has the distinction of having virtually completed the post literacy programme on a totally ad hoc grant. The Thiruchirapally Mavatta Arivoli Iyakkam headed by the district collector ran according to schedule and has now made the transition to the continuing education phase. The Arivoli strongpoint was that it had a wide reach and adequate presence in the rural areas-a large number of village panchayat residents, most of them women, say that they owe their posts won in the 1996 panchayat elections, to their newly acquired literacy. The 2,400 village libraries, a feature of the post-literacy stage are well used. Often little more than a tin roof shed, where books are displayed like buntings on string tied to poles, the libraries are also doubling as the headquarters of women's self-help group of the area. An interesting practice initiated by the Arivoli is to have library organisers send direct reports on post cards, on the state of basic amenities in the village ranging from hand pumps and streetlights to drinking water. These missives reach the district collector and the practice has accorded the library organisers importance in the community.

Post literacy programmes are open to everybody who takes reading and learning as a way to enrich life. But they are specifically designed to cater to:

- Neo-literates in the 9-14 age group who have completed the basic literacy course under the total literacy campaigns
- Neo-literates in the 15-35 age group
- Semi-literates/dropouts from the basic literacy phase
- Dropouts from primary schools
- Pass-outs from NFE programmes

Each district is unique. The learners are not uniformly endowed. Their ingenuity for learning, receptivity and retentitivity are varied. Therefore the National Literacy Mission has permitted and encouraged great flexibility and innovation in designing and implementation of post literacy programmes. The concerned zila saksharta samiti is free to create a model that suits the needs of the district and its learners.

Faridkot district showed the way for others way back in 1995. Under its post literacy programme, it formed the Lok Chetna Kendras, close-knit clusters of neo-literates and literacy volunteers. Membership-based the scheme elicited a remarkable response. In just two years, nearly 4,000 Lok Chetna Kendras had been registered with well over two lakh members. Lok Chetna Sabhas were set up to coordinate the activities of the kendras in each village. The office bearers of these bodies were elected democratically from among the executive committee members of the Lok Chetna Kendras of that area. Each kendra runs a library for neo-literates. To arouse discussion and free expression of ideas on topical issues, each kendra meets once a fortnight. The topics range from social evils like intoxicants and vulgar songs to voter awareness, and health. The kendras are also taking an initiative in other fields by organising eye camps and animal husbandry camps.

At the launch of a post literacy programme, a quick survey is undertaken to comprehend the realistic state of learners. A system of external evaluation is adopted for the assessment of post literacy achievement, in keeping with the National Literacy Mission's thrust on transparency and objectivity.

Post literacy programmes have done well in ensuring a successful transition of neo-literates from guided learning to self-learning and finally to life-long learning. The Post literacy programmes implemented so far have covered considerable ground and the cumulative experience has yielded valuable insights for the planning of post literacy programmes and the shaping of continuing education strategies.

Non-formal Education for Dropouts and Non-strarters—Problems and Environment Oriented—Curriculum for Different Categories

Adult Education is human resources development. Human resources development is necessary so that people's affairs can be left in the people's hands. Take, for example, law. Because of the lack of awareness among the people about their rights, duties and opportunities, and because administration including administration of law is conducted in a language not accessible to the people, there was great dependence on law courts and lawyers. Ignorance of law resulted from ignorance of language and literacy. Litigation often resulted in the ruination of both the parties. The purpose of measures underlying the setting up of village panchayats was to reduce the dependence of people on the law courts. But, unfortunately, while this was generally accepted, no effort was made to reduce the production of lawyers. On the contrary, law schools went on multiplying and the production of a large body of lawyers built into the system the antithesis of delivering the legal care of people in their hands.

Prohibition can be taken as another example. While the social reformists give sermons about the harmfulness of drinking, the diehard economists point out the revenue accruing to the public exchequer from this source. Therefore, law against drinking continues to be passed while breweries continue to multiply. It may be that part of the money so accrued to the public exchequer is spent on providing succour to the families ruined by drinking. But this is like killing the neighbour's cow and, when he complains, presenting him with a pair of shoes made of the cowhide.

Economic resources planning divorced from human resources development results in a system which invests the affairs of people in the hands of managers, who are self-appointed through make-believe democratic procedures. The imperialists all over the world have prided themselves in developing the economic resources of underdeveloped countries.

Even after their departure, the beneficiaries swear in the name of economic development and work vigorously to maintain the system. Both in the capitalist and the communist countries, one finds systems where the affairs of the people are run by a managerial class. The people everywhere need to be educated about education in all countries, irrespective of achievements of formal educational institutions.

In India, today, the scientific manpower is the third in the world. But this cannot be termed as human resources development. As exploitation of raw material in one country for being processed in and marketed by another cannot be termed as the economic development of that country, similarly creation of cheap exportable educated labour at great cost to the country cannot be called human resources development to the country concerned. Both in technology and education one must develop system appropriate to one's need. One does not make or buy big caps, one gets caps that fit. Similarly a country does not ape big technology, it must have technology appropriate to its needs.

Education can be human resources development when it brings out the perfection inherent in a learner. The learner can thus contribute his mite to the society of which he is a member, while expecting the society to fulfil his needs. Societies built on capital intensive economy develop a pattern of life where profit is shared by a handful of individuals or by a set of managers appointed by the State. Where capital is scarce such an economy is bound to create greater inequalities. A country with surplus population must develop its manpower resources and creates a labour intensive economy. Only then, can it expect full employment and establishment of a society based on distributive justice.

The Institutional education in a country like India has resulted in providing education only for a low percentage of the population. It is responsible, on the one hand, for the widening gap between a few well trained and millions of illiterates and, on the other, a large primary school enrolment and an equally large dropout, stagnation and wastage. It is inflexible, textbook-bound, non-competitive and largely irrelevant to the needs and aspirations of the society. Merely multiplying such schools is neither likely to ensure universalisation of education nor obliteration of adult illiteracy.

Thus it will be seen that adult education has a role different from the time and textbook-bound certified education imparted in the school. It is to make the adult learner aware of the factors which limit his opportunities of free development, thus enabling him to manage his own affairs. The alphabetic literacy, which is being most talked about in developing countries of Asia and Africa is only one of the means, however important it may be, for attaining this end.

In a country like India, the declining adult education is intimately connected with the declining autonomy of individuals and groups to manage their affairs. It is, therefore, important that the factors inhibiting literacy are examined with care.

The factors inhibiting literacy can be seen from different angles. If one takes into consideration the geographical factor one finds that the physical geography is responsible for disparate groups living in isolated areas. This is particularly true of the tribal population. Geographical factors which isolate one group from another also inhibit dispersion of linguistic elements facilitating standardisation. Thus geographical factors which restrict the scale of communication become a major contributing factor for illiteracy.

The linguistic factor is partly a consequence of the natural regions and partly of stratified society. Multiple languages divided into regional and social dialects, written and spoken, and formal and colloquial styles are a major deterrent to literacy, particularly when a foreign tongue enjoys the highest status in the society. Multiplicity of scripts adds a further dimension to this problem. The divergence of the language of education from the language of administration, on the one hand, and the language of mass communication, on the other, inhibits literacy. Bi-and multi-lingualism pose serious challenges to the students of adult literacy. For the linguistic minorities there may at times be need for literacy. For the linguistic minorities there may at times be need for literacy in two languages.

The linguistic factor is intimately related to the cultural factor. The Indian languages belonging to four or more language families indicate the diverse ethnicity of the people speaking them. In fact maintainance of multilingulism in India to a large extent is due to the will to maintain distinct ethnic identity of groups. The history of the development of Indian languages show that when a language or a variety of language, which becomes prestigious because of its being the career of all knowledge, is confined to a minority upper strata, simplified spoken languages emerge. They act as sluices which carry the knowledge so confined to the people in India, where even in early times literacy was limited. There is a long tradition of oral transmission of knowledge; social life and leadership was not linked with the ability to read and write. By and large the society which was illiterate was educated as a result of the oral transmission of the accumulated wisdom and there were even uneducated among the scribes, those know how to read and write.

The economic and political factors which brought about a near complete break with the past tradition have played a major role in the accentuation of illiteracy. It has even resulted in the blockade of natural communication between the literate educated and the illiterate, thus converting the large mass of illiterates into uneducated. Economically, with the British take-over of the country, the village self-sufficiency based on pursuits of agriculture and handicrafts, became the first casualty. With the imperialist policy trying to exploit the natural resources of the country and using them to the best interest of the British, very little was available for distribution among the local populace. With the scarce resources and growing demand, only the sectors favoured by the rulers got the better of it and it resulted in the inequal distribution of resources. The society was divided between the privileged few and the underprivileged many. The upper class interest in the stratified Indian society and the interest of the economically privileged became one and both conspired to perpetuate an elitist rule. This led to the policy of illiteracy and ignorance even though there was external allegiance to education by all concerned.

The political factor also aided illiteracy. The centralised civil service was meant for the British. But what ever little was opened up for the Indians required rigorous and prolonged preparation and was only accessible to the privileged. With the advent of the British all Hindu, Muslim and Sikh educational institutions which provided grass root level literacy and education closed down but the secular education began mainly through the missionaries in an alien tongue which further inhibited literacy. As through the thousand year old literacy tradition was nullified by this process. The alignment of the church and the State at this stage resulted in (a) a small group of Christians separated from the majority of Indians divided by the worship of many gods; and (b) a small English knowing elite separated from the majority of Indian divided by the use of many tongues. This excessive learning on English naturally resulted in large scale illiteracy and limited education.

If adult education is to be attempted in a serious sense in the above background, then it will entail radical change of attitudes and existing educational programmes. Adult education can neither be effective through formal institutions nor would it succeed by institutionalising it. An adult literacy curriculum has to be built on the expressed needs of a community. The needs as felt by the Community and as observed by a trained social scientist together constitute the expressed need. To that extent adult education cannot be centrally directed and its curriculum cannot be uniform. However, the objectives need to be selled out and instead of trying to fit the objectives in a rigid time mould, time must be found for the attainment of the objectives. It is in this context that a core or minimum curriculum for adult education is suggested below. This may, however, be modified on the basis of experience of adult education workers.

A Core Minimum Curriculum

A core curriculum of Adult Education must have a component of spoken language. It is necessary for both problem sharing and culture sharing and forms a necessary condition for establishing rapport with the adult learners.

A. Dialogue with the target audience about their aspirations, attitudes, perceptions, priorities, problems and suggested solution.

Emphasis on causal relationship. For example, Fire, Flood, Exploitation, Molestation, etc., are not acts of God, but caused by natural phenomena.

I. Ability to comprehend spoken word:

Lectures/Talks

Discussions

Radio

Newspaper

II. Ability to make an oral presentation of grievances/ needs.

B. Ability to Interpret Illustrations : Picture of a known object-emphasis on writing/narrating. Picture of an unknown object-Emphasis on clarity of meaning/concept.

Superficiality of the play way-(i) A Picture 'the cat taking pictures' created great confusion in the learners. (ii) hut in TV (Orissa experiment, where none could identify the hut which was taken out from a TV frame).

C. Recognition of symbols :

In isolation

In combination-Words, phrases and sentences.

Conventional arrangement

Symbols-their superfluity and inadequacy of sound-symbol fit.

i. Dictionary order

ii. Pictorial presentation : 'A' for apple.

iii. Key word presentation——
(ma rama bara ramara rabara)

iv. Sentence as the starting point——
(lala tala la. lala la tala la)

D. Ability to sign one's name.

E. Ability to read:

Why Read ?

1. To acquaint oneself with tradition
2. To satisfy curiousity
3. To obtain information
4. To acquire knowledge
5. To broaden outlook
6. To get an understanding of the relationship between immediate society, the country, and the world.
7. To develop critical thinking
8. To solve individual, social and cultural problems (including helping children at home in their studies)
9. To secure moral and spiritual guidance
10. To advance one's profession.

Materials : Simplified simple/complex materials are to be given to the neoliterate in a graded sequence.

Material suited to each of the above needs is to be chosen. An illustrative list is as follows:

Matters relating to health, sanitation, civic problems (Rights and Duties), political pamphlets, local newspapers,

Governmental forms, notifications, road sign, simple job-specific material, puranas, fictional literature.

F. Ability to write: Application to various District/State Authorities, Banks and FIR to Police.

Filling in different categories of forms-Money Order, Railways Reservation, etc.

Writing letters to near and dear relatives and friends. Simple narration of events and experiences.

G. To sum: Numbers and Numerals: The four operations. (Relevant to one's job or interest).

Basic idea of decimal system.

Currency-Rupees and Paise.

Weights and Measures-Kilogram, Quintal and Ton.

Foot, Inch, Yard, Acre and Hectare.

Time-Hour, Minute and Second.

Days of the Week and months in a year.

Distance-Kilometer, Furlong and Mile.

Liquid-Liters.

UNIT-III

Non-formal Education Programmes

Existing Scenario of NFE

A large number of children in then age group 6-14 continue to remain outside the formal system due to socio-economic constraints. These include working children who assist in domestic, chores, like fetching fuel, fodder, water, attend to siblings, graze cattle, etc., children from scattered habitations with population below the permissible school norms drop outs and over-age children. Any strategy for UEE must, therefore, take into account alternative strategies to reach this important but marginalised group of children. The National Policy on Education (NPE), 1986 and the Programme of Action, 1992, call for a large systematic programme of Non-formal Education (NFE) as an integral component of the strategy to achieve universalisation of elementary education.

The term Non-formal Education (NFE) has been used in a specific context in India to denote education of out-of-school children. Although planned and concerted efforts in Non-formal Education is barely two and half decades old in India, it has, travelled a long way from the early beginnings in 1970s to a full-fledged scheme of the Government of India reaching out to nearly seven million children in the age group 6-14.

NFE was experimented bit the NCERT in early seventies and was later initiated as a centrally sponsored scheme in 1978. It was originally available in nine educationally backward states. viz. Andhra Pradesh, Assam, Bihar, Jammu and Kashmir, M.P., Orissa, Rajasthan, U.P., and West Bengal. Later it was extended to Arunachal Pradesh and the educationally backward pockets of the remaining States.

The NFE programme seeks to provide out-of-school children with opportunities for primary education which are decentralised, flexible and permit them to study at a convenient place, pace and time. The programme is operationalised by setting Lip NFE centres in rural areas and urban slum with average enrolment of 20 learners under the charge, of a local instructor with modest academic qualifications who is paid an honorarium of Rs. 200/- p.m. The village community is expected to provide for space and make other arrangement for running these centres. NFE centres are expected to run for 1 1/2 to 2 hours for 6 days a week. As a majority of the centres are being run at night, lighting arrangements are generally made by kerosene lanterns.

The NFE course is condensed into 4 semesters of 6 months each for which specially developed teaching-learning materials and stationery is provided to children free of cost. There is a provision for testing and certification of children of NFE centres to facilitate their entry into formal schools. Instructors are provided with training by District Resource Units (DRU) in District Institute of Education and Training (DIETs). For supervision, monitoring and evaluation of the NFE programme a supervisory structure has been put in place which includes a part time supervisor for every 1 0 NFE centre; a Project Officer for 100 NFE centres, district and state level functionaries.

States are being given 60% of central assistance for co-educational centres and 90% for girls centres. Voluntary Agencies are given 100% assistance. The scheme covers around 70 lakh children (majority of whom are girls) in 21 States/UTs in about 2.79 lakhs centres. While 1.18 lakh centres are exclusively for girls, 38,000 centres are run by over 500 voluntary agencies. There has been a steady increase in the number of girls centres and also in the participation of NGOs in NFE in last few years.

While the NFE programme saw a major expansion during the Seventh Plan, it has been extended and consolidated during the 8th Plan. At present, there are 2.79 lakh NFE centres covering about 70 lakh children in 21 States/UTs. Of these, 2,40,787 are being run by State Governments and 37,808 by 544 Voluntary Agencies. Five States viz, U.P., Bihar, Andhra Pradesh, Madhya Pradesh and Orissa account for 81% of NFE centres. The scale of NFE programme is moderate in Rajasthan, and Assam. Coverage is very limited in Jammu and Kashmir and North-Eastern States. Arunachal Pradesh has started the programme recently.

Proposals for Improvements in NFE in 8th Plan

While reiterating the guidelines regarding NFE in the National Policy on Education, 1986 and its Programme of Action (POA) the 8th Plan envisaged that NFE will be developed as a complementary system to the formal elementary education system. It stressed the importance of making necessary investments in qualitative improvement of NFE and reiterated that the advantages of NFE lay in its flexibility, and adaptability to the needs of an important minority of children. The following were envisaged as aims of NFE in the 8th Plan:

a) Improved selection of instructors and their pre-induction training as a pre-requisite for start of NFE centres.

b) Increase in remuneration of NFE instructors to Rs.200 per month with provision of annual increment of Rs.50/ -after completion of two years of satisfactory service.

2c) Opportunities for continuing education, including improvement of qualifications for NFE instructors.

d) Much greater investment of resources on production of good quality teaching learning materials for NFE programmes and provision of these materials free of cost to every learner.

e) Continuation of a project until all out of school children are covered in the area.

f) Admission of children to be made annually and from time to time within the capacity of about 25 children per NFE centres.

g) Strengthening of the administrative and technical resource support system.

h) Increase in number, of women instructors, supervisors and administrators.

i) Enlarging involvement of voluntary: agencies to run programmes in a creative, flexible and efficient manner and to improve the system of training.

In the 8th Plan it was recommended that the Central Government should continue to play a crucial role for provision of funds for NFE till this complementary system of elementary system gets firmly established. The share of Central assistance for mixed NFE projects should be enhanced to 75% and there need not be any rigid proportion between mixed and the girls centres. Financial assistance may be restricted to educationally backward States and educationally backward districts in non-educationally backward States. It was expected that overall requirement of fund for each NFE centres would increase from Rs.5500/- to about Rs.12,000/- annually and that the number of projects in VII Plan would be doubled in VIII Plan.

Revised NFE Scheme

The NFE Scheme was revised on the above lines in 1993. The salient features of the revised scheme are as follows:-

i) Increase in remuneration of NFE Instructors from Rs.105 to Rs.200 per month.

ii) Increase in share of assistance for mixed NFE Centres from 50% to 60%.

iii) Ratio of Girls Centres to total Centres was increased from 25% to 40%.

iv) Expenditure on a NFE Centre was increased from Rs.5,500/- to Rs.8,725/- per annum.

v) Investments on teaching learning materials, training and equipment were suitably enhanced.

vi) A provision of contingent expenditure of Rs.250/- per annum was introduced.

vii) To provide a degree motivation to NFE Instructor, a system of cash incentives linked to the number of learners qualifying to enter upper primary level was introduced.

In addition to the above, the revised scheme provides that efforts at community participation in planning, locating, running and overseeing NFE projects be initiated. To cater to local needs it permits flexibility in the number of Centres per project. To ensure regular availability of funds delegation of financial and administrative powers to Project Officers has been envisaged.

Non-formal Education Programmes for Different Age Groups 6-14, 15-24 and 24-25 Years

The problems of non-formal education and adult literacy have continued to receive high priority during the year. The Conference of Education Secretaries held in July, 1976 discussed at length the concept and programmes of non-formal education and suggested strategies for their future development. The CABE Committee on Non-formal Education and the Standing Committee of CABE, which also met in July, 1976, discussed further the issue raised in the Education Secretaries Conference and made important recommendations. Along with selective programmes of non-formal education, emphasis was given to mass programmes of adult literacy through a larger involvement of students under NSS, and of teachers.

The Directorate of Non-formal (Adult) Education.-To provide technical support for the programmes of adult education, particularly to the State Governments and voluntary organisations, the Directorate of Non-formal (Adult) Education was established in 1971 by taking out the Department of Adult Education from the NCERT. Since then the Directorate has grown considerably in size and coverage and has expanded its activities to cover many aspects of adult education/literacy which were hitherto unexplored. It is now functioning as a national resource centre in the field of non-formal education and is providing useful assistance in planning programmes, training, preparation of teaching/ teaming materials, and evaluation and monitoring. Among the activities of the Directorate the following deserve special mention :

(1) The Directorate helped the State Governments of Andhra Pradesh, Kerala and Tamilnadu in organising training courses for their non-formal education workers at different levels.

(2) It prepared curricular guidelines for non- formal education programmes. The emphasis in these guidelines is on developing. methodology of curriculum preparation and promoting efforts in, developing diversified and need-based curricula with an inter-disciplinary approach.

(3) It undertook a project to compile information in respect of various non-formal education activities organised by various Ministries/Departments of the Government of India under their programmes. This is being brought out in the form of a compendium that will help in co-ordinating the efforts in this field.

(4) It brought out 34 publications on various topics relating to non-formal education under its normal publications programme. These publications helped in disseminating useful information and providing academic help in implementing the programmes.

(5) It processed and supplied learning materials worth Rs. 4 lakh to various adult literacy programmes run by NSS, Nehru Yuvak Kendras and other organisations.

(6) It provided professional guidance in planning and implementing the urban adult education programmes run by Shramik Vidyapeeths and Workers Social Education Institutes.

(7) It continued and strengthened its documentation service under which bibliographies, abstracts, etc were issued. The service has been extended to cover over 300 information cells for non-formal education located with different agencies all over the country. In addition, the service has also been extended to about 80 other national and international agencies identified as resource centres for non-formal education programmes.

(8) It continued to function as an associate centre for the

UNESCO's Asian Programme of Educational Innovations and Development.

In recognition of its contribution in the field of adult literacy' the Directorate was awarded an Honourable Mention of the Nadezhda K. Krupskaya Prize for 1976 by UNESCO.

Non-formal Education Programme for Youth in 15-25 Age. group.- Youth in 15-25 age-group constitute the most vital segment of the country's human resources. Since a majority of them are still illiterate or semi-literate, a comprehensive scheme of providing them non-formal education facilities was launched in 1975-76. The scheme which was expanded in its coverage and scope during the year, aims at providing functional literacy and non-formal education in the following areas :

(i) Society and environment-position of the individuals, their civic orientation and their rights and duties;

(ii) Employment and vocational development;

(iii) Food production, distribution and nutrition;

(iv) Health, hygiene and family welfare planning; and

(v) Home and family life.

The programme is being implemented on a sharing basis by the Central and State Governments. The Central Government financed the programme in 25 districts in 1975-76 and extended it to 50 districts during 1976-77, each district having 100 centres with an approximate enrolment of 30 in each centre. The programmes of the States covered about 100 districts. About 3 lakh youth have benefited from the programme during the year.

To provide academic support, to non-formal education programmes in the fields of training, material production, evaluation, etc., it is proposed to set up State Resources Centres in each State.

Three such centres, in Tamilnadu, Maharashtra and Rajasthan have already come into being and the Government of India have extended financial assistance to them.

Farmers' Functional Literacy Project : This project is a part of the integrated programme of Farmers Training and

Functional Literacy being implemented jointly by the three Central Ministries, namely, the Ministry of Education & Social Welfare, the Ministry of Agriculture & Irrigation and the Ministry of Information. & Broadcasting. The Ministry of Education and Social Welfare is responsible for the functional literacy component of the programme. The scheme had so far been confined to districts covered under high-yielding variety crop areas and covered 123 districts till 1975-76. During 1976-77, its coverage was extended to additional 21 districts. In each district the project is operated through 60 centres and each centre has an enrolment of about 30. The project covered about 2.5 lakh farmers during the year.

The scheme having demonstrated the benefits of an integrated approach to rural development, was diversified in its scope to provide linkages with other developmental programmes. In 1975-76 it was extended to cover one district under SFDA (Small Farmers' Development Agency) and during 1976-77 it was extended to cover one district under the drought prone areas programme and five districts under the integrated tribal development projects.

In operation for about a decade now, it has a fairly wide coverage. To evaluate the scheme and to advise on taking up similar other schemes, particularly in the context of the Sixth Five-Year Plan, a highpower committee of evaluation, under the chairmanship of Shri J. C. Mathur ICS (retd.) has been set up. Non-formal Education for Urban Workers : Urban workers constitute an important segment of the population and their education is an important component of the overall efforts in adult education. Their educational programmes require to be linked

with their economic activities, on the one hand, and social and cultural responsibilities, on the other. Two types of programmes have been in operation for them. The polyvalent adult education programme, which is offered through the three shramik vidyapeeths at Bombay, Delhi and Ahmedabad, aims at providing basic knowledge and skills to urban workers related directly to their jobs. The educational programmes in these vidyapeeths are more functional and related directly to the participants' work. The other programme is offered through the workers social. education institutes at Indore and Nagpur. The emphasis in these programmes is more on arousing a sense of social and civic responsibility and on stimulating a desire for knowledge in the working class.

To suggest future directions for the development and expansion of the urban adult education programmes and to reorient them in the light of past experience, a committee was set up to review the programmes of workers social education institutes, vis-a-vis, the programmes of the shramik vidyapeeths. The Committee, after studying different programmes offered by the two types of institutions, recommended a reorientation of workers' social education institutes on the pattern and approach followed by the shramik vidyapeeths. It further suggested that the social education aspect, expected to be the sole content of the workers' social education institutes, should be built into the shramik vidyapeeths and a network of such vidyapeeths should be set up all over the country in various urban and industrial centres.

Production of Literature for Neo-literates-To encourage the production of reading material for neo-literates, the Government of India organise each year a prize competition of manuscripts for neo- literates. The 19th competition was launched in 1976-77 and its scope was enlarged because the Department of Family Planning had decided to collaborate in that project.

From 1976-77, 65 prizes will be awarded for outstanding manuscripts written on various topics in different Indian languages, 25 of them being earmarked for manuscripts written on family planning. Under the other part of the scheme, State Governments are provided grants-in-aid for producing and publishing better quality material for the neo-literates.

The Raja Rammohun Roy-Library Foundation, which was established to strengthen library movement in the rural areas, further expanded its activities and covered 5800 libraries in rural and semi-urban areas. The Foundation decided to set up a committee to evaluate its working and undertake a review of the present status of rural libraries.

Assistance to Voluntary Organisations Engaged in Adult Education Programmes: The voluntary organisations share a substantial part of the responsibility in the field of non-formal education and adult literacy. The Ministry of Education continued to extend financial and academic support to these agencies. Emphasis during the year was mostly on projects of an innovative nature and those which benefited the deprived sections of the society. Some of the voluntary agencies took up very significant projects which benefited particularly illiterate women, urban slum-dwellers and tribals. Over 50 voluntary agencies were assisted during the year and the total amount of assistance was nearly Rs. 20 lakh.

Cooperation with Unesco: Greater cooperation with Unesco has been achieved during the year. The Directorate of Non-formal (Adult) Education with the cooperation of Unesco undertook three experimental projects of preparing curricula under different socioeconomic settings. The emphasis was more on the development of methodology. The three projects involved preparation of curricula for rural women with the help of the Literacy House, Lucknow, for slum-dwellers with the help of Bengal Social Service League, Calcutta and for fishermen with the help of the Department of Adult Education, S. V. University, Tirupati. All the three projects were completed during the year and the report was submitted to Unesco.

The Government of India hosted the first phase of the Regional Mobile Field Operational Seminar organised by Unesco in November, 1976, with the active help of the Directorate of Non- formal Education in which 42 persons participated and also deputed its officers to participate in similar seminars organised in Iran and Afghanistan.

Exchange of Experience with Other Countries: Exchange of experience with other countries in the field of adult education was further strengthened during the year. A 5-member delegation of experts in adult education visited the Federal Republic of Germany in May, 1976 and studied the adult education programmes of that country for a period of two weeks. The Cultural Exchange Programme concluded by the Government of India with Hungary, USSR & Czechoslovakia inter alia, contained provisions for exchange of information, experience, personnel, etc. in the field of adult and non-formal education.

Programmes for Rural, Urban and Tribal Groups

Lok Jumbish Project

Lok Jumbish Project (LJP) in Rajasthan seeks to achieve Universalisation of Elementary Education through a community based and decentralised approach. The project which commenced in 1992 with support of SIDA, GOI & GOR in the proportion of 3:2:1 has taken up non-formal education as one of the strategies for achieving UEE in rural areas of the State. Currently the programme covers about 20,000 children through approximately 1000 NFE centres. A detailed evaluation of the programme conducted by Operations Research Group (ORG), New Delhi commends it as a feasible design for providing primary education to out-of-school children who are working or have crossed the school admission age. The ORG study recommends that the NFE model of UP deserves to be studied with care for improvement of the State NFE programme in Rajasthan and other parts of the country. The following features of the programme have been highlighted in this context:-

* Efficient and decentralised system of management.
* Effective community mobilisation.
* Adoption of successful strategies for motivation and training of instructors.
* Clear focus on girls' enrolment (girls constitute more than 2/3rd of children enrolled).
* Stress on equivalence with the formal system.

Some of the other steps taken by UP to improve efficiency of the NFE programme are as follows:

- Appointment of local instructor in consultation with the community.
- Substantial increase in honorarium of instructors and supervisors from Rs.200 to Rs.550 per month and from Rs,500 to Rs,1000 per annum respectively.

- The per centre expenditure has been enhanced to about Rs. 19,000/- per annum.
- It has been decided that number of women instructors should be increased to about 1/3rd and special reorientation courses are organised for women instructors.
- Opening of NFE centres on the basis of community-based school mapping and micro-planning exercise,
- Experienced and innovative voluntary agencies have been entrusted with important responsibilities in implementation of NFE.
- A system of intensive, recurrent and rigorous residential training of NFE functionaries has been designed and developed in partnership with NGOs.
- Modifications in curriculum and text-books to Incorporate MLLs and, contextually relevant materials.
- Flexible duration of study for different age groups within the eligible group 6-14 years.
- Development of a comprehensive MIS for NFE.
- System of monthly review of NFE programme at the cluster and block levels and quarterly review at State level.

Shiksha Karmi Project

The largest experiment in Non-formal and alternative education outside the Centrally Sponsored NFE scheme has been undertaken under the Shiksha Karmi Project (SKP) in Rajasthan which was launched in the year 1987 with the assistance of SIDA to revitalise and expand primary education in the remote, inaccessible and backward villages of Rajasthan. The Shiksha Karmi Project (SKID) has utilised the services of local youth who are specially selected and are trained rigorously and regularly, to revitalise primary schools in the most difficult areas of the State. Currently the project is being implemented in 1590 villages and covers approximately 1.32 lakh children in day schools, Prehar Pathshalas (Schools of covnenient timing) and Aangan Pathashalas (Courtyard Schools).

Prehar Pathshalas (PPs) in SKID provide Non-formal Education to out of school children in the age group 6-14 years who are unable to attend day school due to socioeconomic and cultural constraints. It is obligatory for every shiksha karmi to run a PP in his/her village outside school hours, in addition to running a day school during regular school hours. The number of PPs is 3534 indicating that there are 2 PPs in every SKP village. In few villages no PP has been running as all school age children have been enrolled in and attend primary schools during the day regularly. One of the significant features of PPs is that out of 32570 children enrolled, as many as two-thirds are girls.

The other noteworthy features of this scheme are:

- use of condensed version of school text-books;
- development of curriculum of each semester, on the basis of minimum levels of learning;
- availability of teachers guides to enable Shiksha Karmis to handle multi-grade classes;
- special inputs on running of PPs during initial and recurrent training of shiksha karmis;
- provision of 2,000 solar lanterns for righting in PPs;
- continuous efforts to encourage children of PPs to enrol in day schools.

In addition, SKP has experimented with the concept of Aangan pathshalas (APs) i.e. Courtyard schools for young girls who cannot travel long distances to attend either day schools or PPs. A local person, preferably a woman, is selected to run a Aangan Pathshala in her own home after necessary training and provision of other inputs. At present 58 APs have 2,415 students of which more than half are girls.

Progress of NFE during 8th Plan

The scheme of NFE was revised and continued in the 8th Plan with emphasis on consolidation of the existing programme and greater financial and administrative decentralisation of management. The significant achievements of the programme during the 8th Plan are, briefly, as under:

i) Number of NFE centres increased by 42,000 and enrolment capacity increased by 10.00 lakh learners;

ii) Number of centres exclusively for girls, increased by 39,000 which resulted in additional enrolment capacity of 9.75 lakh girls;

iii) There was greater participation of voluntary agencies in implementation of the programme. The number of voluntary agencies increased by 227 during this period. The number of centres run by VAs increased by about 15,000;

iv) The annual expenditure on implementation of the scheme increased by about three times.

v) In a few States, powers have been delegated to Panchayat Raj Institutions and/or Village Education Committees for planning, locating, running and overseeing NFE centres; selection of instructors, payment of honorarium to instructors; and supply of teaching-learning materials to NFE centres.

Some Significant Achievements

During the last 17 years the concept of NFE as an instrument for providing primary education to out of school children in educationally backward areas has been by and large accepted and validated, However, NFE is subject to criticism in certain quarters as a low cost inferior and ineffective alternative for full time school. A few critics have gone to the extent of saying that NFE seeks to legitimize child labour as it is based on the assumption that poor and deprived children must work and, therefore, cannot attend regular schools. Nevertheless it cannot be denied that despite numerous shortcomings, NFE has provided access to primary education for millions of children in remote and inaccessible rural areas and urban slums, specially girls, and disadvantaged sections of society.

In this context, NFE may be seen as an evolving model emerging from existing socioeconomic realities. Where it has been effectively and properly implemented, NFE has been useful as a stepping stone for formal schooling, in addition to improving the self esteem, confidence and social skills of children. A few voluntary organisations have been able to provide vocational inputs to NFE thereby improving the employment prospects of children. More importantly, NFE is recognised as an alternative by parents and the community. Currently, the NFE programme has the potential of enrolling nearly half the number of children enrolled in the formal school system. Together, the formal primary school and NFE can fulfil the demand for primary education for all children in the country in the age group 6-11.

Shortcomings

The NFE programme has not emerged as a credible alternative to the primary school system mainly because of insufficient funding, inappropriate organisational structures, inefficient operationalisation, inadequate involvement of the local community and unrealistic expectations of completion of primary schooling in two years by working children through part-time instruction imparted by under-equipped and low paid para teachers.

Development of appropriate curricula as well as suitable teaching learning materials for the NFE clientele and recurring training of instructors/supervisors have not received adequate attention. Earnest and effective implementation of NFE by States is also generally lacking.

The programme of NFE has had to operate in the most difficult conditions. Aimed at out-of-school children, the programme generally addresses first generation learners who comet from economic and socially backward sections of the society. These children have, by and large, no educational or literacy background within the family.

Furthermore, the programme is implemented largely in rural areas, often in remote regions especially in tribal areas. It has not always been possible to provide the essential facilities which are a pre-condition for the success of the programme. At the same time, it is difficult to retain functionaries within the programme for any extended period of time because of the paltry honorarium which has been a Subject of widespread concern and repeated criticism. Even the small sum of money often does not reach the Instructors on time leading to not only discontentment but also disruption of NFE centres. This leads to discontinuity and wastage.

Training of Instructors, Supervisors and Project Officers have been inadequate and sporadic. MLL based, local specific curriculum for NFE learners has not been developed in most of the States/UTs.

Recommendations of National and State level Workshops on NFE

A National Workshop was organised in NCERT in January, 1995 to review the scheme of Non-formal Education. This was followed by a series of State level workshops in major States implementing NFE so as to address specific issues for improving the implementation of scheme, The major recommendations of the National and State level workshops may be summarised as follows:-

- NFE be perceived as a long-term intervention for achieving Universalisation of Elementary Education.
- Efforts be made for better advocacy and awareness of NFE.
- Strengthening of administrative structure at the national level.
- Creation of autonomous bodies at state level for efficient delivery of NFE programmes.
- Substantial enhancement in remuneration of instructors and supervisors.
- Provision of a minimum of two instructors for NFE centres, one of whom should be a woman.
- Delegation of powers for appointment of instructor's to village panchayats and Village Education Committees.
- Replacement of block level project approach with the concept of small clusters consisting of a few villages for effective supervision and monitoring of programmes.
- Increase in duration of course from 2 to 5 years to ensure attainment of minimum levels of learning.

- Increase in duration of instruction in NFE: centres from 2 to 3 hours daily.
- Availability of incentives such as Mid-day Meals for NFE learners.
- Strengthening provision of pre-induction and inservice training of NFE instructor's, supervisors and project officers.
- Increasing funding of NFE centres to bring it at par with the formal schools.
- Enhancement in funds, for teaching learning materials, training and supervision,
- Streamling flow of funds to ensure regular payment of honorarium to supervisors and instructors and timely purchase and supply of teaching learning materials.
- Provision of necessary flexibility for incurring expenditure by States within the approved budget.
- Provision for increase in cost parameters of the scheme by 10% per year to neutralise escalation in prices.
- Strengthening of vocational inputs in NFE courses at upper primary level.

Strategies for the 9th Five Year Plan

Gaining from the experience of running the NFE programme in the country over the last almost two decades, some of the major strategies which need to be adopted for revitalisation and expansion of NFE in the 9th Plan have been enumerated as follows:

i) Perception of NFE as an inferior system of primary education would have to be redressed through stronger advocacy, better environment building, higher investments, rigorous implementation, coordination, monitoring and review of all parameters of the programme. The endeavour should be to provide primary education of satisfactory quality through schools as far as possible and through NFE wherever necessary.

ii) NFE should no longer be considered as a low-cost model for primary education. Its unit cost ought to be comparable with that of formal schooling. An effort should be made to provide for indicative costs rather than detailed and rigid cost break-up as at present.

iii) The scheme should provide enough flexibility in regard to duration, nature, content and management of NFE and while ensuring achievement of MLLs.

iv) Revamping of organisational structure of NFE at National, State, District and Project levels so as to provide for greater professionalism, autonomy and space. A group of experts may be associated with the NFE programme at the national level to aid advise and provide technical resource support to the Ministry, State Governments and NGOs. At the state level autonomous societies may be created to devote exclusive attention to all aspects of the programme.

v) Emphasis should be on consolidation of existing programme and limited expansion so as to improve efficiency and quality.

vi) Development of certain non-negotiable principles and postulates on the lines of Lok Jumbish Project which may form the basis of M.O. Us with states for delivery of NFE of satisfactory quality. There is need for norm-setting with regard to each and every aspect of the programme, equipment, material, training, evaluation, certification etc.

vii) Provision of adequate remuneration and career advancement opportunities for Instructors, Supervisors and other functionaries responsible for NFE.

viii) Introduction of pre-induction training programme for NFE functionaries and strengthening of in-service training through DIETs, with special emphasis on multigrade teaching skills and competency based learning.

ix) Development of learner and area specific NFE models for girls, working children, tribal children, first generation learners, minorities, slum areas and street children.

x) Exploring the possibility of providing relevant vocational inputs in NFE, particularly at upper primary levels, in collaboration with experienced NGOs.

xi) Forging of effective partnership with NGOs, Panchayat Raj institutions and the local community for decentralised planning and management of NFE.

xii) Working out modalities for involvement of industry and business for provision of opportunities for non-formal education at the work place.

xiii) Viewing NFE as an instrument of women's equality and providing for appointment of larger number of women functionaries at all levels.

xiv) Development of necessary linkages with the Open school system and continuing education programmes to upgrade the knowledge and skills of NFE Instructors.

xv) During the 9th Plan focus would be laid on the development of selflearning material. Workbook and work-sheet type of self-learning material would be encouraged. This would entail increase in investments for teaching-learning material at the NFE centre for Primary as well as upper primary level of learning.

Programmes in NFE during 9th Plan

The effort during 9th Five Year Plan would be to expand the existing programme of Non-formal Education cautiously and to focus on its consolidation and improvement by enhancing investments, increasing operational efficiency, revamping organisational structures and providing for decentralisation as well as greater community participation. It is envisaged that a larger responsibility would be entrusted to voluntary organisations for promotion of non-formal and alternative schooling.

Expansion: It is proposed to expand the NFE programme in educationally backward states and backward areas of other States by establishing 50,000 new NFE centres, bringing the total number, of centres at the end of 9th Plan to 3,30,000 centres. The expenditure on these centres, in accordance with the enhanced pattern of investment would be Rs.2520.08 crores.

Since NFE is primarily a scheme for disadvantaged groups, efforts would be made to identify areas with high incidence of dropouts for opening NFE centres. The focus during the 9th plan would be to cover out-of-school children of migratory labourers at work site, nomadic tribes, street children, children in urban slums, remote rural areas and difficult and inaccessible areas. For this purpose the areas in non-educationally backward States which are hitherto out side the purview of NFE programme are also proposed to be covered. Credible voluntary agencies Would be encouraged to take up the NFE programme in these target areas.

Consolidation: Based on various evaluation in the States, It is widely acknowledged that a large number of existing NFE centres are dysfunctional or are not functioning at the optimum level. During the 9th Plan it is proposed to take necessary steps to increase the proportion of functional centres substantially or close down dysfunctional centres. For this purpose States would be expected to review the location or closure of all existing NFE centres so as to consider their rig-location on the basis of micro-planning and school mapping exercises with participation of Panchayat Raj Institutions and Village Education Committees. The relocation of NFE centres should also take into account the generation of a positive demand for primary education among women and disavantaged sections of society in backward areas as an outcome of successful Total Literacy Campaigns (TLCs).

Increase in Expenditure on NFE Centres: On the basis of review of NFE programme during 8th Five Year Plan, the feed back received from State Governments and the comparative success of non-formal components of Lok Jumbish and Shiksha Karmi Projects, it is imperative that the investments on NFE centres are increased substantially in the 9th Plan. Keeping this in view, it is proposed that the cost of running a primary NFE centre in 9th Plan would be increased from Rs.8725 at the present to Rs.23,670 and the cost of an upper primary NFE centre from Rs.14,150 to Rs.34,670. There would be a provision for annual increase 10% increase in the cost per centre to take care of the cost escalation. Within this amount it is proposed to provide States with necessary flexibility for incurring expenditure on approved items. For this purpose, the items of expenditure could be categorised as 'essential' and 'desirable'; the former being obligatory for, all States and the latter being optional. States may also be given the option to incur lesser expenditure on certain items, while increasing the expenditure on other items which in their judgement and experience require greater investment in their specific context. Increased cost per centre would entail increase in the honorarium to instructors and supervisors as also greater investments in teaching learning material and continuous training of instructors. Efforts will be made to increase the daily duration of teaching to about 3 hours and the duration of the programme to a course of 3-4 years. A special problem which needs to be addressed during the 9th Plan is the high incidence of drop-outs from NFE centres. Efforts would be to make NFE centre more attractive through group singing, sports and games, excursion trips, etc. In addition, cooperation of guardians, local community members and other opinion leaders would be sought to arrest the problem of drop-outs.

Equivalence with Formal System: Efforts will be made to establish academic equivalence between the products of formal primary schools and NFE centres. Such comparability will ensure the possibility of lateral as well as vertical transfer of students particularly from non-formal to the formal system. Competencies under MLL would provide the criteria for achieving and establishing equivalence. Accordingly, during the 9th Plan various programme parameters of Non-formal Education like time and duration of study, nature and quality of learning materials, styles of teaching and learning, competency and training of teachers and evaluation procedures should be modified with a view to establish MLLs for the NFE system.

Testing and Certification: During the 9th Plan a system of testing and certification of NFE learners will be, introduced whereby equivalence in learning achievements of NFE learners and formal school students would be established. This system will provide the basis for lateral entry from NFE to the formal system as well as facilities for, the further education of persons passing out from NFE in approximately the same fashion as available to persons in the formal system. These efforts would strengthen the NFE system as not only a complementary system to formal schooling but also as a supplementary strategy for achieving Universalisation of Elementary Education.

A radical change will be needed in the nature of learning materials and style of learning. It would be important to practice a system of self-paced learning in the NFE programme. Towards this end, the textbooks and other teaching-learning materials Would need a radical change for different levels of NFE and alternative schooling. Integrated textbooks, workbooks having in them the competency based text, competency based and evaluation oriented exercises and unit tests and materials for self learning to ensure mastery should be designed and provided to NFE learners and instructors.

Certain parameters need to be strengthened to result in genuine equivalence in terms of pupil achievement between the formal and non-formal streams of primary education. These parameters are place of learning, time of learning, motivation of instructors, lateral transfers, textual material, self-learning materials, evaluation system, accreditation systems, systems for reinforcement and enrichment of brighter children and remediation of weak children.

Revamping of Organisational Structure for NFE

National Level: It is felt that the existing organisational structure for non-formal education programme at the national level in the Ministry of HRD and NCERT is inadequate and insufficient. With the acceptance of criticality of NFE as an essential strategy for achieving Universalisation of Elementary Education, it is necessary that the existing structures at national level are suitably strengthened. While NCERT and the NFE Division in the Department of Education may be suitably strengthened to deal with the requirement of a larger and more efficient NFE programme, it would appear to be necessary to associate a body of professionals with the programe at the national level to provide technical resource support and to aid, advise and guide the Ministry, NCERT and State Governments in the proper implementation of NFE programme. This body could beset up on the lines of ED. CIL's Technical Support Group for DPEP, or as a part of the proposed National Elementary Education Mission (NEEM) or as anindependent Non-formal Education Commission (NFEC). In the 9th Plan a provision of Rs. 12.00 crores is being provided for strengthening the national structure for NFE.

State Level: It has been generally observed that from an organisational point of view NFE has not got the attention it deserves at the State level. In some States the programme is dealt with by the Directorate of Primary Education whereas in others it is being handled by the Directorate of Adult Education. In both situations the NFE Programme tends to become marginalised and neglected due to the preoccupation of the Directors and senior functionaries with other responsibilities and tasks which have a higher priority in the Organisation.

On the other hand the experience of Mahila Samakhya, DPEP, UP, SKP and TLC suggests, that an autonomous Society at the State level staffed by specially selected experts and educationists and with sufficient flexibility in financial and academic matters is able to devote the kind of exclusive and dedicated attention that schemes like NFE require if they are to achieve an acceptable degree of credibility and success. In this context it is proposed, that in the 9th Plan educationally backward States which have a large NFE programme would be required to entrust the responsibility for supervision monitoring and implementation of the programme to a specially created autonomous society on the pattern of societies which manage the above mentioned educational projects.

The Director of the State level autonomous society should be selected on the pattern adopted by Mahila Samakhya Project from among IAS Officers or experts in the field of education for a minimum tenure of 3 years. Other staff would be drawn on deputation from different departments and agencies includings reputed NGOs on the basis of their expertise and commitment to the NFE programme. Simultaneously action would be taken to strengthen the implementation machinery at district and project levels. During 9th Plan it is proposed to provide Rs 322.57 crores for creation of autonomous societies for NFE at State level and for, augmentation of field level machinery.

Role of PRIs and VECs: A few States have taken the initiative in the 8th Plan to delegate responsibilities and functions regarding NFE to Panchayat Raj Institutions and/or VECs. This trend would be encouraged and supported during the 9th Plan. It would be expected that by and large decisions in regard to the following may be delegated to Panchayat Raj institutions and/or Village Education Committees:-

- Planning and location of NFE centres on the basis of micro-planning and school mapping exercise;
- Overseeing the day to day running of NFE centres; including determination of timing for centres during different seasons.
- Provision of arrangements for accommodation, seating, lighting, drinking water, etc.
- Selection of instructors in consultation with the community;
- Payment of honorarium to instructors;
- Supply of teaching learning materials to NFE centres.

Role of Voluntary Agencies

During 8th Plan as many as 227 new voluntary agencies have been associated with the NFE programme. The NFE centres run by voluntary agencies have also gone up steadily to 38,000. Voluntary agencies have developed innovative strategies for teaching children in difficult circumstances, developed learner specific and contextually useful learning materials, experimented with community supported NFE programmes and taken the initiative to supplement the academic component of the curriculum with vocational and skill inputs which are related to the local situation. Such efforts need to be encouraged and supported by the central govt. There is also scope for greater involvement of NGOs in non-formal education in states where their presence So far is negligible. During the 9th plan NGOs would be encouraged to act as facilitators and take under their umbrella smaller NGOs in their region for undertaking this programme. It is conceivable that some NGOs may take up area based integrated programme for achieving UEE during the 9th Five Year Plan with a strong component of NFE. A provision of Rs. 639.44 crores is proposed for support to NGOs for running NFE programmes during IXth Plan.

NFE in Urban Slums

One of the distressing realities of urban life today is the massive proliferation of slums in most metropolitan cities and large urban agglomerations. It is estimated that approximately half of the population of Delhi would be residing in slums by the end of this century. However, the problems of primary education in urban slums have not been addressed specifically by government so far.

Several Voluntary agencies have come up with successful innovation; and experiments in educating primary school children in slum areas through a mix of properly designed academic and vocational courses which also have health and nutrition components. During the 9th Plan it is proposed to devise a special scheme for supporting NGOs who are interested in taking tip non-formal education programmes at primary and upper primary level for children of urban slums and street children. A provision of Rs. 10 crores has been made for this purpose.

Coverage of NFE Learners under Mid-day Meal Scheme

The existing guidelines of NFE provide that all facilities and incentives given to girls, children of SC/ST and others in formal system are made available in the Non-formal system. However, the National Programme for Nutritional Support to Primary Education known as Mid-clay Meal Programme which was introduced in 1995-96 for students of primary classes has not yet been extended to NFE learners. It is proposed that during 9th Plan ambit of the Mid-day Meal Scheme should be extended to cover NFE learners.

State Resource Centres (SRC)-Link with NFE

It is understood that originally State Resource Centres were envisaged for providing technical resource support, to the Non-formal Education Programme. Over the years their focus has shifted almost entirely to supporting the adult literacy programme. The 9-14 age group is included in the target group of the Total Literacy Campaigns. There is a felt need to develop appropriate teaching learning material for this Cage group as distinct from the primers in use for adult learners. The TLC and NFE clientele can be broadly categorised as non-formal learners. In this context it would be useful for a few selected SRCs to provide technical and academic support to the NFE programme for school age children also, For this purpose it is proposed to fund the creation of NFE unit in these selected SRCs during the 9th Plan. A provision of Rs. 20.00 crores has been made to meet this objective.

MOUs with States Incorporating Non-negotiable Principles & Postulates for quality Improvement in NFE

In order to improve the overall efficiency and credibility of NFE programme, it is necessary to ensure that quality of the programme is not diluted. The UP has developed a set of non-negotiable principles and postulates to achieve this objective. It is proposed that Memorandum of Understanding (MOU) on these lines may be signed by the Central Government with State Governments for safeguarding the interests of the NFE clientele. Non-implementation and/or violation of the provision of MOUs should result in suspension of central funding for the programme until necessary remedial action is taken up by the defaulting States.

These postulates are as follows:-

i) NFE instructor should be selected in consultation with the village community, but his/her ability to run the centre should be the paramount consideration for selection.

ii) No centre should be started unless the instructor has received due training and effectiveness of the initial and subsequent training should be ensured.

iii) Village community should provide suitable space for running the centre.

iv) Centres should run during the day wherever possible. If necessary they may be run in the evening or night but satisfactory lighting arrangement must be ensured.

v) Curriculum, pupil evaluation and certification should ensure equivalence between NFE and the formal system.

vi) Textbooks, teaching/learning aids and essential equipments should be made available before a centre is started.

vii) Proper arrangement should be made for seating of children and provision of other amenities, particularly drinking water.

viii) Creation of an effective system of management and supervision with participation of PRIs and NGOs. It should be ensured that a centre is not closed down as long as there are children to benefit from it.

ix) NFE should be viewed as an instrument of women's equality and it should be ensured that women instructors and girl students improve their self-image and building confidence to play an active role in society.

x) Centres should be started in groups and on fixed dates only.

Based on the above postulates, it is proposed that during the 9th plan MOUs would be signed with the autonomous, bodies at the State level to ensure quality and efficiency in NFE.

Advocacy for NFE

The focus of the 9th Five Year Plan would be to create an environment for credible VAs and Panchayati Raj institutions to contribute significantly to universalise elementary education through people friendly and innovative techniques of implementation, resource support and training to teachers, local functionaries, Village Education Committee members etc. Efforts will be made to alter the public and administrative mind-set through repackaging of the programme, better advocacy and environment building on a sustained basis. A provision of Rs. 20 crores has been made for the 9th Plan Period.

Scheme of Experimental And Innovative Programmes for Education at the Elementary Stage

There is a need for considerable innovation and substantial experimentation with a variety of modalities so that relevant and effective models of alternative schooling are developed that help the learners to learn at their own pace. With this objective, the scheme of experimental and innovative projects in Elementary Education was launched in the 7th Plan.

The scheme has shown very encouraging results and needs to be strengthened and continued further during the 9th Plan 6.1 During the 9th Five Year Plan the endeavour would be to expand the scheme in more States and to focus on coverage of under-privileged sections of society, minorities and girls. One of the priorities would be to mainstream and replicate successful innovations carried out under this scheme so far. It is proposed to constitute a core group of representatives of reputed voluntary organisations to assist and advise the Ministry in this regard. A provision for Rs. 21.72 crores has been made in 9th Plan.

Linkages with Vocational Education at Upper Primary Level

During the 9th Plan strengthening of upper primary level NFE centres would be a major concern. Suitable vocations would be introduced at the upper primary level as per the specific needs of the area while at the same time emphasising achievement of academic competencies.

The area specific emphasis of this scheme would necessitate greater involvement of Voluntary Agencies and local PRIs which would be encouraged during the 9th Plan. A provision of Rs. 20 crores has been made in the 9th plan, Efforts should be made to equip the learner with alternative forms of education both general and vocational after the completion of the NFE course utilising the same MLL competencies as for the formal system with necessary adaptation. This could be implemented through emphasis on the vocational input of the upper primary NFE centres or through the open school system or any other alternative form of schooling. This should be also viewed in the perspective of continuing education centres of NLM.

Monitoring, Evaluation and Research

During the 9th Plan emphasis would be laid on monitoring, research and evaluation. Regular Supervision at all levels will be ensured through greater mobility, study visits, field interactions and better reporting and monitoring procedures. During the 9th Plan a Management Information System would be evolved to monitor the programme and give decision support data.

Programme evaluation (internal and external) on a concurrent basis will be attempted through suitably devised methods. Research institutions and independent organisations will be involved in evaluating this scheme. Professional affiliations and study visits in India and abroad would be assisted to enhance capacity. A provision of Rs. 1000 crores is proposed for research, evaluation, study visits and professional affiliation.

Functional Literacy—Scope and Definition—Different Approaches

The Indian Institute of Education (IIE), Pune, India, which is one of the ten member institutes of the APPEAL Research and Training Consortium (ARTC), has undertaken an investigation of projects in India that emphasize innovative approaches to non-formal education for sustainable development. These projects focus on disadvantaged members of rural society (women, tribal minorities, lower castes) and (in addition to local empowerment) address literacy and primary education, vocational education, health education, improvement of the environment, and the decentralization of financial and administrative powers to local levels.

The IIE has been engaged over the last quarter of a century in experimenting with innovative ideas for the spread of literacy and primary education through formal and non-formal modes and for the empowerment of rural women and other oppressed people. Its model of non-formal primary education (called PROPEL or Promotion of Primary and Elementary Education) has been used in other parts of the country. The model is considered an appropriate replicable alternative for bringing primary education within the reach of all children with due regard to community lifestyles and people's expectations.

Two other IIE projects, the Vigyan Ashram and the Centre for Education and Development of Rural Women, have been widely acclaimed and are also covered by this survey. Learning while working and the latter is an action research project for the education and development of rural women with a view to empowering them to become agents of rural reconstruction.

India is a vast country and there are many projects in rural areas oriented toward improving both formal and non-formal education. However, there are three in particular that deserve special attention because of their focus on previously unserved or underserved populations:

1. Lok Jumbish and its programmes for literacy, education and the empowerment of rural women in Rajasthan
2. The Integrated Abujhmarh Tribal Development Project undertaken by the Ramakrishna Mission for the development of tribal people in Madhya Pradesh
3. Agragamee and its rural education programmes for the tribal people of Orissa The survey of these six programmes was conducted by an IIE research team under the leadership of its Director General, Dr. S.K. Gandhe. Outside agencies provided assistance in the case of two of the projects (Abujhmarh and Agragamee) The research team obtained data from available documents and supplemented their interviews of students and staff with first-hand observation of project activities. Full details of these projects and their programmes, as well as information about a seventh project (Rashtriya Seva Samiti, Andhra Pradesh) not included here for reasons of space, are found in the full version of the study report submitted to APPEAL, UNESCO Bangkok.

The PROPEL Project (Promotion of Primary and Elementary Education)

IIE believes that education and development are closely interrelated and that the people at the grassroots level are the makers of development while government agencies are merely facilitators. The PROPEL project assumes that Education for All can best be organized through community mobilization. PROPEL has evolved through three phases with an emphasis on action research and the mobilization of rural communities for educational development. During Phase I of the project (1979-1985), nearly 4,500 children from 110 villages in different agro-climatic zones were reached under the non-formal education programme involving local leadership and communities. For this purpose 263 NFE centres were established.

Phase II (1985-1988) covered 669 children in 40 NFE centres at 35 newly selected villages in poor, drought-prone and hilly areas. Emphasis in this phase was on testing measures for community involvement by strengthening village education committees as local motivators and managers of primary education. In the third phase, there have been attempts to develop a replicable planning and development model to facilitate training programmes in community-level planning for education that can be set up by voluntary agencies and government officials. During this phase more than 5,500 out-of-school children were brought into the stream of primary education through 178 NFE centres and learning camps. Emphasis has been on reaching girls, the largest group excluded from schooling because of the household division of labour and deep-rooted social prejudices.

Currently, PROPEL serves a population of 120,000 living in approximately 18,000 households scattered over 4 blocks or sub-districts in Maharashtra State southeast of the city of Pune.

Basic Philosophy

PROPEL believes in teamwork, good governance, and responding to local needs. It has encouraged micro-planning, thus passing responsibility for the project operation to people at the grassroots level. It acts as a catalyst and attempts to support community ownership of the project. Collaboration and participation of the villagers are prerequisites for all activities.

From the very beginning local community members are made aware of education problems in their community and participate in surveys of specific educational needs and facilities available. After the surveys have been analyzed and the community decides to take action, a village education committee is activated to help project staff set up an NFE centre, organize classes, and mobilize the community to serve the educational cause. The village education committees (VECs) have been the chief vehicle ensuring community participation in the PROPEL project. Since 1992 these VECs have received legal sanction as well as political and administrative support. VECs are established by consensus at village council meetings and are expected to play a major role in convincing parents to place their out-of-school children in NFE centres.

Learning Materials—Objectives—Organisation and Structure

The NFE community centre and its curriculum are the heart of the project's programmes in non-formal education. The curriculum espoused by PROPEL attempts to cover the basic content of the first four grades of the formal primary school curriculum. In addition, the curriculum emphasizes skills needed for everyday life in the community rather than securing entrance to further education. Local relevance is imperative as far as curriculum content is concerned, as all non-formal learners are poor, and most are older than children who attend formal schools. Curriculum content is designed to further the following ideals:

1. All children should become cultured, educated and self-respecting citizens.
2. Children's scientific temper should be nurtured.
3. The habit of self-learning should be encouraged.
4. The poverty in which children live should be countered

by enabling them to organize their work systematically and learn new skills.

5. Children should become aware of the social conditions around them as well as the need for social change.

The PROPEL project's NFE curriculum proposed in the 1990s includes such subjects as language studies, athematics, general and developmental knowledge, science, aesthetics, social skills, and physical fitness and relaxation. In particular, it emphasizes opportunities for girls to express themselves freely in speech, drawing, singing, drama, and other activities that help them to become socially competent, culturally creative citizens.

Unlike the formal system of education, PROPEL emphasizes locally relevant learning materials. The staff have regularly consulted local communities as well as specialists (linguists and psychologists) regarding the content and language of primers and readers. Many NFE materials are designed for self-learning and peer tutoring. Consequently, the materials have proven quite useful and efficient in the hands of semiprofessional teachers. Materials belong to an NFE class, and are collectively shared by all students, which keeps the costs down. All materials are meant to improve literacy skills, as well as disseminate useful and practical information for everyday life.

Student Evaluation: One noteworthy innovation in the NFE programme is the absence of formal examinations. Evaluation of learning is based on the NFE teacher's daily diaries and students' continuous self-evaluation as well as testing of learning by peers during the students' group work activities. Self-testing is made possible by the preparation of graded evaluation materials, particularly in literacy (language) and arithmetic. Students are also encouraged to demonstrate their learning achievements daily to family members and periodically to the rest of the community. Particularly useful for public demonstrations of achievement are the community meetings during which the students can give speeches and thus show off what they have learned.

In addition, there are the biannual bal jatras (children's fairs). These events, which take place in a centrally located village, provide opportunities for singing, storytelling and games, and are thus settings for both recreation and informal evaluation of children's accomplishments. Students display their skills in the three Rs and are evaluated with simple test materials by teachers other than their own. The rationale for this innovation was the assumption that tests administered in the class would be neither useful nor relevant, because teachers might be tempted to pass all students to show good results, and the students might be constrained to copy one another's answers. This is what often happens in formal schooling due to the anxiety of both teachers and students.

However, to continue studies in the formal school, NFE students may take the formal Grade III or IV examinations. Several former non-formal education students have been admitted to formal schools. Achievement tests show that the competence of these students in many subjects is on par with, if not better than, the competence of formal education students.

Conclusion: The PROPEL project has achieved some goals that clearly indicate changes in the social life of the project area. Over 90 out of 137 project villages had reached the goal of universal primary education by the year 1995. This means that in these communities all children of school-going age are either learning in formal schools, attending NFE centres or in some rare cases studying on their own and receiving systematic coaching from volunteers, teachers or family members. A great majority of the children in the area attend formal schools. This shows that the project has been able to raise awareness of the importance of basic education. Simultaneously, formal schools in the area have become more relevant to students' needs, and thus also more attractive to them.

PROPEL has reached children, especially girls, who would otherwise never have had the chance to learn. Moreover, it has shown that more lively, participatory teaching and community awareness of the importance of education can stem the tide of dropouts and increase the quality of education, bringing universal elementary education a step closer.

What PROPEL has demonstrated so far is that in the matter of Education for All, breaking the barriers of educational orthodoxy is a tough task, but it can be tackled successfully if communities are mobilized and helped to determine their own educational and developmental destiny.

The Centre for Education and Development of Rural Women (CEDRW)

In 1993, IIE's priorities – action research, social and economic development, improvement of the status of women – led to the establishment of the Centre for Education and Development of Rural Women (CEDRW) in the village of Shivapur about 25 kilometres southeast of Pune in Maharashtra State. The centre not only focuses on education and empowerment of rural women and girls, but also attempts to make them both participants in development as well as subjects of development.

A significant feature of the projects undertaken here is that they adopt an ethnological research approach combining the ideas of Paulo Freire on education and Gandhian principles of education for the rural masses. Freire argued that oppressed people had to reflect on their existing social condition and subsequently take action to bring about required changes. The Gandhian principles urge modification of the Anglo-Saxon model of education to include more participation by learners themselves.

The CEDRW is at present engaged in the operation of various activities, such as women's savings and credit groups, vocational programmes for dropout girls and for women 15-45 years of age, camps promoting health, nutrition and personality development, and the training of local farmers and artisans through farmers clubs.

The Centre: The CEDRW, which became functional in 1994, occupies one hectare of land outside the village of Shivapur. The infrastructure is simple and designed to harmonize with the rural setting. It consists of a workshop, administrative office, lecture-cum-dining hall, agro-exhibition hall and a preschool or child recreation centre. Apart from this, hostel facilities for 40 trainees, two self-contained guestrooms for visiting faculty, quarters for two academic staff and a residence for support staff are available.

From the total land allotted, one third is for the building and the remainder is used for a tree plantation and as experimental plots for various kinds of horticulture, including the cultivation of flowers, vegetables and medicinal plants.

Objectives: The Centre has the following objectives:

1. To develop a new system of rural education that will empower women to become agents of rural transformation
2. To evolve integrated activities for
   - women's personal development
   - women's educational development
   - community development
   - overall socio-economic change in the villages for sustainable development

Assumptions

1. Education that goes beyond schooling has a major role to play in the process of development. This education, which is a lifelong process, is required to preserve human dignity and stimulate creativity among individuals.
2. The process of development must be given a holistic perspective and hence the community as a whole must be involved in this process.
3. Women's development cannot be considered in isolation from the development of men. Mode of participation

During informal meetings and discussions, community members initially identify the local problems faced by the community. The identified problems are prioritized according to the needs of the community. Subsequently, local representatives or animators are chosen from the community in order to establish linkages between the institute and the community. With the assistance of the animators and the community, and in consultation with the research team, an intervention or strategy is selected to tackle the problems. After implementation, the community itself evaluates the intervention on the basis of its success.

Projects Undertaken: The following are the major projects undertaken and conducted by the CEDRW. Vocational education programme The CEDRW, in response to the demand from many villagers, developed a vocational education programme for school dropout girls and women aged 15 to 45 years. The programme was introduced in 1997 and is presently being conducted at the Centre with assistance from the Department of Education of the Ministry of Human Resource Development, Government of India. The minimum qualification for the course is literacy and numeracy skills equivalent to Grade 3. At present, 34 students are attending the course, which lasts 6 months. The course focuses on developing skills related to sewing, tailoring, embroidery, hand and machine knitting, and the preparation of items such as bags, purses and coverlets. In addition, there are lectures and discussions on topics related to social legislation, women's rights, work ethics, budget and accounts maintenance, marketing skills (communication), personal health and hygiene, family education, environmental health and labour law.

Self-help (savings and credit) Groups: Another major achievement of the CEDRW is the formation of savings and credit groups for women, which have now spread to 17 villages. The success of these groups has led to the formation of a consortium, where two members, the chairman and treasurer of each group, meet occasionally to review the work and provide guidance to the others. It is interesting to note that the success of the women's groups has motivated the men to form their own.

Health Education Camps: These camps were arranged especially for women who experience health problems. Simultaneously, there were attempts to make the community aware of the requirements of basic personal as well as environmental health and hygiene. For this purpose, doctors at the Primary Health Centre as well as private physicians offered their assistance. Later on, the villagers themselves requested information related to vision and oral hygiene, areas that posed special problems in the village. Village women, who volunteered and worked in teams, were responsible for convening the health education camp for these topics.

Child Recreation Centre: In 1997 the CEDRW set up this centre to show that the parents and the community play a major role in the integrated development of children during the pre-school stage. In addition to preschool activities for young children (i.e., storytelling, games), the Centre also has a training programme for rural women to serve as preschool staff members. Parents are actively involved through regular parent meetings. Farmers club This club, established by villagers in Shivapur and nearby communities, arranges meetings with visiting experts in order to keep up with advances in agricultural technology, especially as related to the cultivation of rice, a major crop in the area.

Conclusion: The activities described above and their results show that the interventions made by the CEDRW have been successful in mobilizing the rural community, especially in regard to education and women's development. The series of camps that were conducted in response to the demand of the village women are sufficient proof of the growing awareness in the community. Furthermore, researchers observed that the women also participated actively at Centre meetings by expressing their views on certain issues raised. Other indicators of project success include the various articles prepared by the girl school dropouts during their vocational training programme and the men's emulation of the women's savings and credit groups.

On the whole, the developments occurring so far in Shivapur and other villages strengthen the need for adopting Freire's approach and Gandhian perspectives in rural development.

The Vigyan Ashram

The Vigyan Ashram near the village of Pabal in Maharashtra State has developed a system capable of educating and empowering school dropouts through training in basic science and technology at affordable cost and in an acceptable time frame. (The word vigyan means science and ashram denotes a place of simple living and high thinking.) The experimental project initiated by Dr. S.S. Kalbag in 1983, under the auspices of IIE, has developed a skills training programme that emphasizes learning while doing and serving the community. In 1985 this programme was approved by the Board of Secondary Education,

Maharashtra, as a rural technology course and is still implemented in schools as a part of the technical stream. The course adopted in the school caters to both formal as well as non-formal education students. A similar course is also conducted exclusively for non-formal learners on a full-time basis at the ashram.

Principles

1. The basic principle governing the Vigyan Ashram model is learning while doing. It is based on the assumption that working with your hands stimulates the intellect.
2. Technology is the application of science, and is the collaboration of head and hand.
3. Basic scientific procedures such as observation, measurement, recording, classification, documentation, and formulating and testing hypotheses are essential for everyone and can also be easily practised ineveryday life.
4. Education means training for real life.
5. All labour is worthy of dignity and there are no such things as white collar or blue collar jobs.
6. Any education system to become relevant and life-based must enable learners to offer services to their community.

General Objectives

1. To integrate education with development
2. To stimulate the intellect in order to enable learners to reach their highest potential
3. To provide a broad spectrum of technical education through access to many modern technologies

4. To develop new opportunities in the rural economy through local support

Specific Objectives

1. To provide skill training in the areas of agriculture, animal husbandry, food processing, food preservation, soil science, sewing and knitting, electrical assembly, and equipment maintenance
2. To develop the ability to take appropriate management decisions, to quantify and document, and to do simple accounting, quality measurement and quality analysis
3. To develop individual self-confidence and self-respect

Courses: The ashram offers a course titled Introduction to Basic Technology exclusively for non-formal education students. This course lasts one year. At present, schools in 15 villages also offer this course. In addition, there is the course in rural technology, which lasts almost a year (300 days) and is open to 20 students aged 17-25. This course consists of four themes, with related topics and skills, as indicated in the following

Theme Topic Resource Centre Skills Developed

- Living Home Food lab
- Prepare preservative food products (human and society) e.g., jam, pickles, biscuits
- sewing and knitting
- Health Rural lab
- provide first aid
- conduct pathological tests
- home remedies for common ailments
- oral rehydration therapy.

Living Agriculture 3 acre Plot

- plant and grow vegetables, crops (plants and animals)
- use of pesticides
- irrigation.

Animals Poultry Farm

- undertake poultry and cattle raising

Cattle

- artificial insemination (goats, cows)
- diagnosing pregnancy Non-living Engineering Workshop
- undertake measurement (material)
- soldering, welding
- use carpentry tools
- repair tractors
- construct buildings, equipment and geodesic domes Non-Living Energy and Water resource
- prepare energy devices-pressure (Non-material) environment unit stove, bio-gas stove.

Electrical Lab

- maintenance of engines (diesel)
- measure water table
- install water pipeline, hand pump etc.
- make electric circuits.

The students are divided into four groups, one for each of the course themes. They are rotated through all four themes for the duration of the course. Each student is required to undertake a project related to each of the themes. In addition, all students receive training in financial management skills such as estimating a budget, maintaining accounts, managing stock, and analyzing costs.

Major Achievements

1. A survey conducted in an area 25 kilometres around Pabal revealed that a large number of ex-ashramites have started small enterprises, workshops and poultry farms. These include welding works, fabricators, a photocopy shop, and women entrepreneurs who raise poultry. Other graduates have acquired sewing machines and become tailors.
2. Schools in the vicinity have benefited from offering the rural technology course. There have been increases in enrolment due to the entry of students from the

neighbouring villages. The students have performed better in technical subjects as well as the subjects in the formal curriculum. There has also been an increase in the percentage of students passing the high school standard examinations administered throughout the state. Finally, the contributions of students to their home communities have facilitated closer cooperation between these communities and the schools.

Conclusion: The Vigyan Ashram provides vocational and technical education to NFE learners directly at the grassroots level. It makes the course content more locally applicable by emphasizing the dignity of all labour and the necessary cooperation between the head and the hand. Nevertheless, in the future the Vigyan Ashram intends to move into the area of information communication technology by developing and applying computer software applicable for rural development programmes. Various kinds of software have already been used Theme Topic Resource Centre Skills Developed as feasible and efficient media of instruction. However, computers do not replace instructors, nor will they reduce the importance and necessity of practical work.

The Lok Jumbish Project: Education for Girls

If primary education is a matter of concern for the whole of India, it is a major worry for the state of Rajasthan, whose literacy rates are the lowest in the country. In 1991, the literacy rate for men was around 60 per cent but only 19 per cent for women. In other words, only one of five women in Rajasthan was able to read and write. In rural Rajasthan the situation is even worse, with only 11.6 per cent of the women being literate. In this context, a project like Lok Jumbish becomes essential. The Lok Jumbish Project aims at achieving the goal of Education for All through people's involvement and participation. (The name, lok jumbish, combines the Hindi word for people and the Urdu word for movement.) While many evaluations and reports have appeared dealing with Lok Jumbish and its success in the spread of primary education, here we focus on its work with respect to innovative programmes for the spread of education among girls.

Although the project's efforts in improving enrolment and retention through intervention in the formal education process have been widely recognized, the emphasis here is on the various non-formal methods of education that are used to target marginalized populations, especially girls.

Project Objectives: The Lok Jumbish Project (LJP), an offshoot of earlier efforts, began in 1992 with funding from SIDA and support from the state and federal governments. The philosophy of the project is based on the belief that the mere provision of physical inputs is not sufficient for ensuring universal access to primary education.

Instead, a strong partnership between parents, children and teachers is essential. The basic aim of this project is the universalization of primary education, with emphasis on both formal and non-formal education.

For all children up to 14 years of age. Non-formal education was indeed considered as a necessary tool for the spread of literacy to remote villages and socially conservative communities. The LJP has developed a three-fold approach:

1) improving the quality of education through training teachers and overhauling the curriculum,
2) changing attitudes and developing trust in education among communities that are resistant to education due to socio-cultural values, and
3) creating an environment for women to participate in the system, thereby increasing girls' access to education. The long-term objectives of the LJP are:
    - To provide access to primary education for all children below age 14
    - To ensure that all children complete primary schooling
    - To emphasize the quality of education
    - To bring girls to the same level as boys and make education an instrument of women's equality
    - To enable the poorest sections of society to participate equally in basic education

- To provide opportunities for lifelong education
- To effectively involve people in education management
- The LJP's primary strategy has been to mobilize and involve the local community in the demand for better delivery of education services. The idea behind this is that in the course of time it becomes the community's own agenda and therefore sustainable. The LJP achieved these objectives by environment building, school mapping and micro-planning, improving existing school facilities, producing and supplying textbooks and learning materials, training teachers, and promoting non-formal education and women's development. The village education committee (initially the village core team) in each community is ultimately the body responsible for the long-term education of its children.

Starting up in 1992, the LJP completed its first phase in 1995. The second phase began in 1995 and ended in 1998. Unfortunately, the third phase, which was planned to begin in 1998, is still not yet under way.

The total project expenditure over the five-year period amounted to Rs.1,524 million of which the SIDA contributed half, the Government of India one third and the State Government the rest. The project is implemented through blocks or sub-districts, each block divided into clusters of 25-35 villages and with an average population of 150,000. Altogether, 75 blocks were covered under the Lok Jumbish Project by October 1999 comprising more than 12,000 villages, 305 clusters and about 11 million people. By that time, 529 new primary schools and 540 Shiksha Karmi schools were opened, 268 primary schools were upgraded to upper primary schools and 5,010 NFE centres were opened to supplement the formal system.

At present, LJP is winding up its activities in some areas, which will be soon taken over by the Government. After the SIDA stopped funding, activities have almost come to a standstill. Another international funding agency has already agreed in principle to take its place.

Lok Jumbish Strategies for Educating Girls

The LJP has tried to influence formal schooling in the area it serves through teacher training and curriculum revision. Specifically, the aim has been to make both teachers and curricula much more gender sensitive than before, so that schooling becomes a more positive experience for girls. In addition, the LJP has introduced a number of innovative institutions related to non-formal education. In addition to village NFE centres, these include education camps and forums just for girls and workshops for adolescent girls and boys together.

In all these efforts, the principle of gender sensitivity is woven into the fabric of the Lok Jumbish educational approach. It serves the cause of education for girls indirectly by changing attitudes, challenging social stereotypes, and redefining girls' roles paving the way to the empowerment of women through education. Breathing life into schools: intervehtion in formal education.

Lok Jumbish took over malfunctioning government schools in backward areas for implementation of its agenda. The schools remained as they were in terms of structure and personnel. The intervention took the form of teacher training and introduction of a revised curriculum. The entire exercise was intended to improve the quality of education in government primary schools and make them attractive to village children and parents. At the same time, village committees and core groups worked to raise awareness of the importance of education amongst the villagers.

One important outcome of these efforts was an increase in participation, especially of girls in primary education. The average percentage of overall participation in primary education increased from 46.7 per cent in 1994 to a substantial 76.8 per cent in 1998. The girls' participation rate also jumped from 29.4 to 68.1 per cent. The following table provides a brief summary of the improved participation rate in primary education over the years. Other data show improved school retention rates among girls attending LJP schools, as well as higher test scores in Hindi language and mathematics.

In addition, it appeared that the single most important component was teacher training, which not only led to better teaching techniques, but also increased the motivation of teachers to perform well. Along with the new curriculum, this motivation contributed a great deal to improvement in quality.

Bringing Learning to the Village Courtyard: Sahaj Shiksha Centres

These NFE centres initially started in 6 blocks and eventually spread to around 33 blocks, with an increase in enrolment from 8,336 in 1993 to 45,839 by the end of 1997. By October 1999 there were 5,010 centres serving children who could not attend formal schools.

The dropout rate was negligible. It was heartening to find that 6,835 (out of the initial 8,336) moved on to formal schools after completing the Non-formal curriculum. The ratio of enrolment of boys to girls was 3:5, which indicated that the girls benefited more from this non-formal education opportunity than boys. In addition, an evaluation study found that the programme had been successful in attracting the target segment, namely girls belonging to scheduled tribes and castes.

The Sahaj Shiksha centres, unlike formal schools, were usually located within the boundaries of the hamlets and literally brought learning to the doorsteps of the girls. Most of these centres operated for two or two-and-a-half hours in the evening. Parents or grandparents were often present, which imparted seriousness to teaching-learning activities at the centres. Smaller children too young to go to school sat nearby with their sisters and became familiar with the process of learning.

The teachers were members of the local community who spoke the children's own dialect. They were recruited for the job by the village education committee or core team, who was also responsible for enrolling the children at the centres.

Short-term Interventions

In addition to the regular ongoing education programmes, the LJP also organized education camps of shorter duration. For example, the Balika Shiksan Sirvirs were camps held for adolescent girls who could afford neither formal nor non-formal education. The first camps were four months in duration but as they became more popular their length increased to six-and-a-half months. In addition to teaching the girls how to read and write, the camps provided opportunities for them to increase their self-confidence. One positive result was that 75 to 80 per cent of the girls from the camps went on to formal schooling.

In addition, the LJP held workshops attended by both adolescent girls and boys. The purpose of these residential workshops, which lasted five days, was to help girls overcome their shyness, develop selfconfidence, learn about their situation in society, question social stereotypes, and acquire information about the emotional and physical changes occurring during adolescence. Girls involved themselves in a number of activities, including traditional male ones like riding bicycles and playing cricket. They also participated in public excursions and mock elections. By the end of the workshops, most participants had developed the capacity to enter into dialogue with their peers (including boys) and had begun to acquire a new self-image.

Finally, the Lok Jumbish organized a variety of activities and institutions for specific purposes. These included arts forums for adolescent girls, camps for children with disabilities, empowerment forums for women teachers, hostels for girls, and the Women's Residential Institute for Training and Evaluation (set up in 1994), whose purpose was to train women in rural areas to be teachers.

Conclusion

In spreading literacy and primary education in a poor, undeveloped state like Rajasthan, Lok Jumbish's initiatives were successful basically because of its belief in participatory planning and implementation. Although the ultimate aim was to bring children into the mainstream education system, the focus has been on non-formal education in a variety of forms (centres, camps, etc.) according to the needs of each community. The most significant feature in this approach is the respect given to the needs of the community and an understanding of social, economic and cultural constraints.

The Lok Jumbish Project was able to transform village schools with its touch. Teachers from the primary school in Radhanagari, who were all praise for Lok Jumbish, were asked how they could believe that the LJP's intervention had changed education. Weren't they after all the same people as before? They replied unhesitatingly, "Within all human beings there exists goodness and the spirit of work and dedication, but it has to be woken up [jagrithi, which literally means awakening], and that is just what Lok Jumbish did". The transformation was evident in the manner in which they went about their daily routine work, in the enthusiasm with which they spoke of the movement and in the concern they showed about the school. It seemed like the movement was theirs. And that was what made the difference. The teaching-learning process also had changed with the new training. It had become child-centred and life-centred. The child had become an active participant in learning and the curriculum was made relevant to the immediate life experience.

Programme for Youth within the Formal Educational Setting and in out of School Setting, in Rural, Urban and Tribal Context—Occupation Orientation

The Bastar District is a remote plateau located in the extreme southeastern part of Madhya Pradesh State. The western part of the district, rugged and watered by numerous streams, is known as the Abujhmarh Hills. If any part of India is still terra incognita to nearly all travellers, it is Abujhmarh, which has the reputation of a land free from rules and regulations, inhabited by the Hill Marias as popularized in the anthropological literature. Abujhmarh, comprising 250 villages, is described as a tangled knot of hills, a back-of-beyond that remains cut off from the rest of the world for nearly half the year. Because of their extreme geographical isolation, the Hill Marias have a very primitive economy, their mainstay being the slash-and-burn cultivation practised on the steep hill slopes. Traditionally, they have bartered forest products (resin, cocoons) for trade goods like salt, chillies, tobacco and cloth. The barter system is still prevalent, and the tribal people are most unscrupulously and liberally exploited by traders.

The main problems of Abujhmarh, apart from extremely poor communication, are 1) the lack of medical facilities and a high mortality rate, especially among infants; 2) the lack of education facilities and extremely low literacy; 3) economic exploitation by various agencies; and 4) unwillingness on the part of government officials to work in the area.

In August 1985, the Ramakrishna Mission established a base camp or ashram at Narainpur, an administrative headquarters in Bastar District which is also the gateway to Abujhmarh. The objective of this centre was to direct activities aimed at eradicating illiteracy, ill health and economic deprivation amongst the Hill Marias of Abujhmarh, enabling them to eventually join the mainstream of the nation. With this objective in view, the Mission set up the Integrated Abujhmarh Tribal Development Project at Narainpur. The project serves an area of 3,905 square miles and a population of about 26,000. Despite adverse circumstances, the Mission has successfully started making major inroads against poverty, ignorance, sickness and economic exploitation. In addition to its own resources, the Mission relies on liberal grants-in-aid provided by both the state and federal governments.

A 60-acre plot of land provided by the state government is the setting for the Mission's model school, a 100-bed hostel for boys, a fully equipped modern 30-bed hospital, a vocational and agricultural training centre, an NFE centre, and a fair price shopping complex for local people.

Project Activities: The activities of the Mission, using innovative approaches, fall into the general areas of literacy and education, health, and economic development.

Literacy and education Missionaries of the Ramakrishna Ashram (both men and women), assisted by a devoted band of qualified and dedicated staff members, look after a number of education institutions that serve the needs of the tribes people. Foremost amongst these is a model residential school exclusively for tribal students, whose current enrolment is 341 boys and 161 girls. In addition, the Mission operates five residential co-educational schools currently serving 325 boys and 123 girls. Students at all six of these schools receive training in agriculture and horticulture using land that is part of the school premises.

The Mission also provides services for younger children. In collaboration with VISHWAS, a sister organization managed by devotees of the Ramakrishna Mission, the Narainpur centre administers 69 preschools located in the far-off villages of the Abujhmarh Hills. The purpose of these preschools is to prepare children 3 to 6 years of age to enter the regular school environment. Many of these preschools also have classes for girls and women between 11 and 65 years of age. Here they learn the three Rs and skills needed for everyday life.

It is an outstanding feature of the Mission schools that once students are admitted they continue to study uninterruptedly until the completion of their studies. This dedication, which includes taking on additional schoolwork during summer vacations, may account for their success in formal examinations at both primary and middle levels. In the last five years, the examination pass results have been almost 100 per cent, extremely positive for ethnic minority students. It was also heartening to note that out of 66 students who completed their studies in the Mission school, as many as 15 of them sought admission to engineering courses and 4 of them succeeded in securing admission to medical, veterinary, polytechnic and Ayurvedic courses respectively. About 20 entered graduate courses in arts, science and commerce, and 9 obtained regular employment.

Health and Nutrition

Activities in this area include maintenance of a 30-bed hospital and health centre, 5 clinics located throughout the district, a mobile dispensary, and a project in community health services for remote villages not reached by any of these. Economic improvement Project activities in this area include the operation of a tribal youth vocational training centre, an agricultural training and demonstration farm, and the Central Sector Scheme for Agricultural Extension. The purpose of the latter (begun in 1994) is to introduce the tribal people to modern, scientific methods of farming, thereby reducing their reliance on traditional shifting cultivation. In addition to the standard functions of extension services (demonstrating and supplying new inputs such as seeds, fertilizer, technology, etc.), the Project is involved in organizing village self-help groups, training farmers to use new technology, and promoting linkages between farmers and agricultural institutions in India (government agencies, universities, research centres).

Finally, in connection with agricultural development in the Abujhmarh Hills, there is the Rajiv Gandhi Watershed Project. The purpose of this project, which covers an area of 3,140 hectares, is to improve irrigation and reduce the effects of flooding. Since 1995, 54 tanks, 11 percolation tanks, 14 check dams and 6 stone weirs have been constructed. In addition, a number of trees were planted and fruit tree saplings distributed amongst 3,400 villagers.

Conclusion

The various activities undertaken by the Ramakrishna Mission Project have ushered in a new era in the life of the tribal communities. This success has occurred largely because of the holistic, integrated approach taken by the Mission, targeting the interrelated problems of illiteracy, poor health, economic exploitation, and ineffective agricultural practices. Looking at education, we find that the project adopts a similar integrated approach for the all-round development of learners. Children are admitted first to the preschools at a tender age and continue on to the primary and secondary boarding schools. They generally do not go home even during summer vacations. They learn how to lead well-disciplined and healthy lives under the guidance of a group of teachers who are dedicated and entirely devoted to their noble work. Education is totally free of charge. The quality of the graduates of the ashram schools is high and brings a good name to their efforts.

The project initiated by the Ramakrishna Mission at Narainpur is playing a vital role in achieving its objectives. But the Abujhmarh Hills is only a small corner of India and a single project does not touch even the fringe of the problem. Replication of this project in other similar parts of the country is a genuine and urgent need. Several ashramites observed that the State Government wanted the project to extend its activities to the entire district of Bastar. But it was not possible for them to take up the offer because their resources, especially in terms of devoted and selfless workers, were rather limited.

Keeping in view the approach adopted by the Integrated Abujhmarh Tribal Development Project, we can safely recommend that there is an immediate need for policy makers to bring under one umbrella the various activities affecting the welfare of tribal populations. The project is thus a worthwhile one to be adopted as a model. There is also a need to create a sense of confidence amongst tribal people before launching any programmes for their welfare. Anything imposed on them will certainly not be successful unless they themselves are convinced that the programmes will be of real benefit to them. The agencies functioning for their welfare must enjoy the full confidence of the target group. Moreover, the twin factors of dedication to work and devotion to duty are absolutely necessary.

The Agragamee Kishipur Project

In another corner of India, other ethnic minorities struggle with hunger, disease, landlessness, illiteracy and a situation characterized by a lack of basic services, leadership, and political will. The present-day district of Rayagada in the state of Orissa is inhabited by a mixed population of tribal groups (Kondhas, Parajas, Souras, etc.) and scheduled castes. In 1981, the NGO Agragamee undertook its first experiment in the block (sub-district) of Kashipur, fascinated by the overwhelming response and initiatives on the part of tribal people towards economic development opportunities. A group of tribal youths supported the project team and joined them during the second year of project activities. At present, the Agragamee Kashipur Project carries out a variety of education and economic development activities in si blocks of the district. Some of these have been replicated in other tribal districts of Orissa State.

General Objectives

1. To develop an alternative model of education for tribal areas to be replicated elsewhere
2. To make elementary education universal throughout inaccessible tribal areas
3. To encourage community participation in order to sustain programmes in the future
4. To link education with development
5. To increase literacy and classroom learning
6. To make education a medium for the empowerment of tribal students.

Specific Objectives

1. To use both traditional and mass media to generate awareness in the community
2. To ensure community involvement and participation in operating village schools by forming village education committees to assume responsibility
3. To develop and implement a child-centred curriculum
4. To help children develop a spirit of cooperation and mutual self-help
5. To strengthen classroom learning through practical experience
6. To introduce children to basic economic activities
7. To generate, with the people's cooperation, the initial capital for sustaining schools and NFE centres in the future.

Significant Activities: Agragamee intervention for tribal development combines educational inputs along with economic development activities for a holistic development of the community. In addition, the project has made systematic efforts to enable primary school age children to acquire literacy, numeracy and other basic skills. This is necessary because the majority of tribal children cannot benefit from the existing system of education provided by the Government due to a combination of reasons, including poverty, the need to work and the inadequacy of government schools.

In response the project has initiated a variety of programmes to meet the needs and priorities as identified by local tribal communities. These programmes include Non-formal Education for Elementary Children (70 NFE centres in two remote blocks), Innovative Education in Remote Tribal Areas (100 additional centres with curricula focusing on village economic development), district resource units for NFE teacher training and materials development, an education complex to improve the literacy rate amongst tribal girls, children's festivals, creative workshops for children, vocational training, science exhibitions, parent-teacher workshops, health checkup camps, and Bal Sansad, which is a programme to educate tribal children about the existing political system in India and their rights in regard to voting and other forms of participation.

Elements of Innovation: Ethnic minority communities have found it difficult to relate to the prevailing system of formal schooling. They require a different model of education that meets their own needs and priorities. The Agragamee Kashipur Project has attempted to provide such a model that includes a number of innovative features. First of all, members of the community are involved in selecting their own teachers for the NFE centre serving their children. This enables better rapport and communication between teachers and pupils, and bridges the language barrier. Parents and other village elders are encouraged to come to the classroom to share and learn. The village is also expected to provide a building where children can study.

Second, the curriculum is relevant to the local situation of the children. Teachers do refer to the formal school syllabus, in so far as it facilitates the learning process. But they also make use of additional material relating to the lives of the tribal people. Regular feedback from the teachers ensures that the material is being used and is acceptable to both the students and the community.

Third, teachers are encouraged to use the folk media of songs, dance and legends to enliven teaching and help the children learn faster. This method also helps to ensure the perseverance of tribal folk traditions, as well as helping the people identify more positively with the education model they are adopting. In addition, the teachers encourage children to participate more actively in the teaching-learning process by teaching each other, with older boys taking charge of small groups of younger children.

Finally, realizing that the process of education cannot be taken up in isolation, Agragamee's intervention combines economic activities with education and there are attempts to link education with the socioeconomic change and development activities in the villages. Children are encouraged to participate, even if as observers, in the planning processes, and issues related to development are incorporated into the NFE centre's curriculum. The teachers introduce topics concerning the children and their surroundings. They are not only teachers as such but have also received training to initiate participatory action for social change in the village.

Achievements: At present, Agragamee is managing 233 NFE centres in 7 tribal districts of Orissa. All of these institutions are operating with the active participation of the village communities. Currently, 7,584 children are enrolled, of whom 3,293 (about 45%) are girls. Village education committees have been formed and are responsible for the regular functioning of the centres. Of the 1,351 members of these committees, 559 are women. The educational process has helped to increase the self-confidence and capability of students to a great extent. In many of the villages where the NFE centres function, former students have taken over the teaching duties. In many instances, these people are doing much better than their counterparts who have undergone formal schooling. In some of the villages, youths who studied at the centres have now organized youth clubs.

Currently, there are 48 youth clubs and village development committees, 18 irrigation user societies, 15 education organizations at the panchayat level, 5 such organizations at the block level, and one at the state level. At each level of these forums, Agragamee tries to ensure people's cooperation. The youth clubs and village committees closely monitor the education programmes run by Agragamee in the villages.

They also take initiatives for increasing enrolment at the centres. At the panchayat level, members of the forum work together as a pressure group to ensure that the government schools in their own area are run more efficiently. They are also mobilizing parents to send their children to school. The state-level forum, the Adibasi Shakti Sangathan, tries to influence policy matters related to education in the tribal areas of Orissa.

Conclusion: The programmes of education for tribal areas developed by Agragamee have found wide acceptance amongst other voluntary organizations in the state. Four such organizations have received funds from the

Government to initiate education programmes based on this model. The Social Work and Research Centre (SWRC), a national-level voluntary organization, has also adopted this model, as have 125 NFE centres located in other underdeveloped areas of the country.

The success of Agragamee activities demonstrates that NFE programmes are more successful than the formal school system in making primary education universal in tribal areas. Therefore, it would seem that additional salary support and training for NFE instructors is highly desirable, especially in areas with low literacy.

Conclusions and Recommendations

These six examples of NFE programmes in India demonstrate the success of using innovative, unconventional methods to reach populations mostly excluded from formal schooling. This success rests largely on two factors. First, the programmes feature non-standardized, locally developed curricula that correspond to the priorities and life ways of both children and adult learners. Second, innovations in programme content and delivery occur directly in response to the needs of the local community. Instead of directives from government bureaucrats, demand as expressed by local community members largely determines the input of the NFE programmes.

The six projects and their activities clearly show the urgent need to contextualize and decentralize education, especially in the rural areas. In this connection, there should be rural development centres established at the grassroots level to facilitate decentralization and to make the education system more relevant for sustainable development. Similarly, more funding is needed for materials development at the local level, especially in regard to the preparation of appropriate science materials.

Finally, these projects illustrate the importance of reaching out to those who have previous been neglected or under-served. Whether they are ethnic minorities in remote parts of Orissa or Madhya Pradesh, or rural women and girls in conservative Rajasthan, the marginal sections of society deserve the same opportunities for education and social betterment that others in more favourable circumstances already receive.

Programme for Women—Objectives—Women's Potential Contribution in Hone Making, Child Care and Community Life

It is now globally acknowledged that investment in human resource development must accompany investment for economic development of any nation. Considering that human development proceeds along a continuum and that the process of development is essentially cumulative in nature, investment in programmes for the youngest age group of children in the 0 to 6 age range becomes a major priority as the very foundation for basic education and life long learning and development.

Research has also consistently indicated the first six years to be the critical years for the development in view of the rapid pace of development characteristic of this stage. Recent neurological research on the brain's development has further endorsed the significance of appropriately timed intervention for maximum impact, identifying the early years as a key stage for intervention. Interventions introduced subsequent to the early childhood stage are therefore not likely to reap expected benefits if the early childhood stage is left unattended/ inadequately attended.

It is in this context that Early Childhood Education (ECE) is considered a significant input to compensate for early environmental deprivations at the home front by providing an appropriately stimulating environment to the children. This is particularly relevant in the case of first generation learners. Multicentric research studies conducted by the NCERT and other institutions in the country have demonstrated a significantly positive impact of ECE experience on retention rates in primary grades. Quality ECE programmes have also positively influenced the learning and achievement of children at the primary level.

Realizing this crucial significance of ECE, the National Policy on Education (NPE-1986/1992) in an unprecedented way, recognized it not only as an essential human development programme but also as a support for universalisation of elementary education and a programme for women's development. While on the one hand it is expected to provide the necessary maturational and experiential readiness to the child for meeting the demands of the primary curriculum, it also indirectly impacts on enrolment and retention of girls in primary schools by providing substitute care facility for younger siblings. Envisaged as a holistic input fostering health, psychosocial and nutritional development, the policy emphasized the significance of making it play based while cautioning against the dangers of reducing it to the teaching of 3 Rs. The holistic and integrated concept of ECCE has now been further emphasized by terming ECCE universally as Early Childhood Development.

The Programme of Action drawn up for immediate implementation of the NPE, fixed specific targets in phased manner. It envisaged a coverage of 70 per cent children in the preschool age by the year 2000. A minimum of 2.5 lakh centres were to be established by 1990 to cover all tribal development blocks and blocks having Substantial Scheduled Caste population as well as urban slums. The POA fixed a target of 10 lakh centres by 1995 and 20 lakh centres by the year 2000. Though most of the coverage was to be through the ICDS, other models of pre-primary education centres and day care centres were also to be encouraged and supported. The POA also emphasized strengthening of all ECCE programmes in the direction of making them holistic and integrated in nature, improving their training component and evolving a Management Information System.

Integrated Child Development Services (ICDS)

ICDS is the largest ECCE programme at, present, in the country. It is an intersectoral programme which attempts to directly reach out to children from vulnerable and remote areas and give them a head start by providing an integrated programme of health, nutrition and early childhood education. Its package of services includes supplementary nutrition, Immunization, health check up, referral services, non-formal preschool education and. nutrition and health education for children below six years and to pregnant and nursing mothers. The nodal agency for coordination and monitoring of the scheme at the central level is the Department of Women and Child Development, Ministry of Human Resource Development and its counterpart departments at the state level. The scheme is centrally funded.

Although the scheme has now expanded and been made available to more deprived sectors, its pre-school education component continues to remain one of its weak components. The focus of the scheme has been more on health and nutritional aspects and only these aspects were reflected in early stages of the monitoring of the programme. In 1983, it was realised that preschool education needed further strengthening. As a first step in this direction, a monitoring and evaluation cell was set up in National Institute of Public Cooperation and Child Development (NIPCCD), to look into the ways and means of monitoring of preschool education and community participation in ICDS projects. The monitoring schedules have now been modified to include these aspects as well. Some effort has also been made to reinforce the preschool education component through revision of training syllabi and organisation of short-term refresher training in this area. Attempts to select and produce core material for distribution to anganwadis, and to the supervisory personnel to further strengthen their monitoring and guiding capabilities are being made as well.

Non-formal Education Though Balwadis and Creches

This scheme was started in 1975 to provide clay care services for children below 5 years. It caters mainly to children of casual, migrant, agricultural and construction labourers. The programme in the scheme is primarily custodial in nature. While some element of training is being given to the workers, the need to strengthen the early childhood stimulation component is still acute. The scheme is Sponsored by the Central Social Welfare Board.

Education Components

This scheme was introduced in the Sixth Plan as a distinct strategy to reduce the drop out rate and to improve the rate of retention of children in primary schools. Under this scheme, Central assistance is given to voluntary organisations for running pre-school education centres. A major lacuna of this scheme is total lack of health and nutrition component in its programme. There is also no provision for training of personnel although this aspect is now being attended to on a limited scale, by various quarters. The scheme was initially with the Department of Education, Ministry of Human Resource Development, but has recently been moved to the Department of Women and Child Development.

General Education

In addition to these schemes that reach out to the rural urban slum and tribal areas there are innumerable private, fee-charging nursery schools which cater to the needs of the parents living in urban and semi-urban areas. As; at present there is no system of licensing or recognition. No exact estimate can be made also regarding their numbers. Municipal Corporation of metropolitan cities like Delhi and Bangalore also run preschools attached to their primary schools. The Municipal Corporation of Delhi for example run more than 600 preschool sections covering approximately 20,000 children.

Vocational Training

The 8th Five Year Plan period from 1992-93 to date has seen an accelerated expansion of the ICDS scheme during the first three years of the 8th plan viz 1992-95, 911 new blocks were sanctioned bringing the total coverage of blocks under the scheme to 3072 as on March 31, 1995. The ICDS scheme has been universalized during 1995-96 through sanction of projects for all the 5320 community development blocks and 310 major urban slums thus increasing the total number of sanctioned anganwadis to about 7.98 lakh of which 4 lakhs are operational. At present, over 10.63 (DWCD June 1996) million children in the crucial age group of 3-6 years from the disadvantaged groups are availing this preschool education facility.

The training curriculum of different levels of ICDS functionaries has also been revised and updated during the 8th Plan period to provide required thrust to the preschool component. Efforts have been initiated to sensitise the key ICDS functionaries to the basic requirements to enable them to perform their roles effectively in the delivery of this component. Anganwadi training Centres have also been assigned the responsibility of developing at least 25 anganwadi centres so as to ensure the trainees get the required field experience. During the Plan period 2000 CDPO's offices in the country have been supplied with enriched early childhood education material developed in coordination with NCERT and SCERTs. Training input specifically in early childhood education has also been supplemented through the involvement of NCERT and SCERTs/State Resource Centres in 12 States of the country.

Convergence of inter-sectoral services in particular with the Department of Education has been pursued. Instructions have been issued to all the states for regular visits of primary school teachers to the anganwadi centres for enrichment of this component, for coordination of timings between anganwadi centres and primary schools with a view to relieve the girl child from the care of the younger siblings and for locating the anganwadi centres near the primary schools.

With the expansion and universalization of the ICDS scheme, the Early Childhood Education Scheme and Balwadi

Nutrition Programme are expected to be phased out by the end of the 8th Plan by merging their centres with the ICDS. Under the Scheme of Creches/Day Care Centres 12470 creches are catering at present to about 3 lakh children, In addition to this, the National Creche Fund has been set up in March-1994 which envisages that 25% of the creches assisted under the Fund would be Anganwadis-cum-Creche centres. Accordingly 642 creches and 150 Anganwadi-cum-creches covering about 20,000 children have been set up in the last two years under the National Creche Fund.

In terms of, ECE curriculum, a great deal of concern was generated for the 'mis-education' that is being imparted by the innumerable preschools and nursery schools in the private sector that have mushroomed all over, who are extending the primary curriculum down to the primary, level. This distortion is likely to be detrimental rather than facilitative to the development of the children. The impact of this is visible all over since it has percolated even to the level of the rural anganwadi where the worker is more often teaching the 3 R's than offering any development activities to the children Advocacy efforts were initiated particularly by NCERT and Indian Academy of Paediatrics to help correct the situation. Subsequently, the Yashpal Committe Recommendations titled "Learning Without Burden" also recommended that admission tests and interviews should be abolished at this stages and there should be no formal teaching of 3 Rs. Recommendations were accepted by the Central Advisory Board of Education for implementation, but the actual implementation is still not very evident.

Major Thrust Areas for Ninth Plan

While the 8th Plan period has witnessed a quantum leap in ECCE services primarily through universalization of ICDS, Early Childhood Education or non-formal preschool education as it is termed, continues to be only one of the 6 components of the ICDS scheme thus receiving only divided attention. Consequently it continues to remain its weakest component. It does not get due attention from the Education Sector either since, it is located in the Department of Women and Child Development. In the absence of any institutionalised mechanisms for convergence, particularly between these two sectors, ECCE continues to remain weak and of low priority.

The resources, material, financial and human available for ECCE are also not commensurate with the demands of a quality programme. Training provision for ECCE still need to tie further strengthened and professionalised for improved personnel preparation. Community mobilisation and support including involvement of NGOs and PRIs in more constructive mode is crucial to the success of the programmes and will need greater attention in the 9th Plan through large scale advocacy and extention activities. These areas of concern are detailed in the following sections alongwith the corresponding projections for 9th Plan outlay.

Education Work Though Women's Organisations—Role of Voluntary Agencies

It becomes imperative therefore in the 9th Plan that, in the context of the significance of ECCE for UEE, the Education Sector must come forward to give recognition to and assume responsibility for Early Childhood Education as an indispensable first step in the total educational continuum. This is particularly necessary in the context of the first generation learners who are expected to be inducted into the educational stream in large numbers.

This priority needs to be translated into specific action aimed at building resource capacity in ECE at all levels of the existing institutional structures in the education sector from state through district to sub district levels which can facilitate and be responsible for the qualitative improvement of the ECE programmes at the field level. Specifically this would involve:

(a) Creation of a Bureau/cell for ECE in the Deptt. of Education, M/HRD to initiate and monitor implementation of programme facilitate convergence and coordination between different related sectors and provide administrative support.

(b) Strengthening the national resource group for ECCE at the NCERT to carry out research, training, developmental and extention activities in ECCE. It would also serve a clearing house function for documentation, sharing and dissemination of information/experiences in a two way mode with the State and sub-state level institutions, NGOs etc. and undertake concurrent evaluation of ECCE programmes/ initiatives.

(c)-(i) creating ECE cells/expertise in all the 32 States/UTs in the DIETs, Block Resource Centres and school Cluster levels with a view to decentralize access to resource support. At present some capacity already exists in twelve states which was created under a UNICEF supported and NCERT guided Early Childhood Education Project. While these need further strengthening, ECE cells need to be established in the other states, by putting into position at least 3 faculty members in each SCERT and DIETs to serve as a resource unit for ECE programmes.

(c)-(ii) providing budgetary support for training of personnel and capacity building at all these levels in ECE.

(c)-(iii) making provision for organization of systematically planned, need based activities at these levels in the areas of training, material development, research, monitoring and evaluation. strengthening the ECE component of ICDS programme by providing an additional worker on a comparable honorarium as the AWW to take change of the ECE programme so as to relieve the AWW to take care of other responsibilities related to health, nutrition and early stimulation for the 0-3 age %group. This would ensure that ECE component in ICDS gets it due weightage. The additional worker known as the ECE Worker, could be given intensive job and refresher training in ECE through the DIETs/BRC/SRC structure. A sum of Rs.59436 lakhs has been proposed for Ninth Plan period.

Convergence and Coordination

Inter-sectoral convergence and coordination is crucial for the success of any ECCE/ECD programme and its linkage with primary education both since ECD is holistic in concept and since ECE is located in the Deptt. of Women and Child Development while being of significance for Deptt. of Education. It also becomes necessary to avoid duplication of services. Institutionalized procedures and mechanisms will need to be evolved and operationalized to ensure this at all levels in the form of interdepartmental coordination committees, interdepartmental resource teams at state/district/block levels, joint trainings, collaborative action plans etc.

Setting up of State level coordination committees by states to prepare state action plans is potentially a viable convergence strategy also which has been tried out by some states and can be encouraged in other states as well. To facilitate and periodically review the situation, a National Advisory group for ECCE can be constituted which can have representation from different regions and different sectors related to ECE. This group can in tulle with availability of sectoral resources meet twice a year, to take stock and make recommendations to the concerned departments. A sum of Rs.200 lakhs has been proposed for Ninth Plan period.

Provision of Minimum Basic Resources

Research has indicated that it is not any ECE programme but a programme of a certain minimum quality that can be expected to impact on and facilitate the realization of upper primary education goals. Research has also indicated that while a resource rich programme may not necessarily, be good quality, a basic minimum is absolutely essential in terms of financial, human and material resources for a good quality programme. It therefore becomes absolutely imperative that budgetary provisions be made to ensure conformity of the programme inputs with the Minimum Specifications for Preschools produced by NCERT selectively in a phased manner. The existing policy of large scale quantitative expansion at the cost of quality in view of limited resources, also needs review, in this context.

Efforts to mobilize local groups, craftsmen etc. for production of play materials for children should also be made and necessary support provided to them for this purpose both in terms of training and finance. A sum of Rs.200 lakhs has been proposed for Ninth Plan period.

Advocacy

To ensure developmentally appropriate play based programmes in ECCE for all children and elimination of pressures on children which exist presently due to the mis-education in the name of ECE, an appropriate climate needs to be developed and a strong parent lobby needs to be created. Focused efforts, will therefore need to be made to involve and educate the community/parents, and project to them the benefits of a play based ECE programme. Efforts to create correct community perceptions as Well as to develop in them, a sense of ownership particularly for the government sponsored: programmes will be necessary for making possible continuous support to the field functionaries in, terms of resources, supervision and monitoring. In view of this, large scale advocacy efforts aimed at environment building will be necessary, in a campaign mode using both folk and technologically modern media at all levels; These efforts will need to be directed not only at parents but also community leaders, school personnel, administrators, planners and policy makers. Appropriate budgetary allocations will be necessary to not only develop software but also in the case of audio: programmes and films for buying of broadcasting/telecasting time.

Orientation and, involvement of Panchayti Raj Institutions, VECs Mahila Mandals and convergence with TLC and Mahila Samakhya programmes can also be explored in this context.

Regulation and Monitoring of Quality

With the uncontrolled mushrooming of ECE: centres, particularly in the form of nursery schools in the private sector, and the working practices propagated by the especially interms of admission tests/interviews and formal content based on the 3 R's, there is need to institute legal provisions along with persuasive advocacy measures for regulation of quality in these programmes. Efforts should be made to enact appropriate laws in this context. The Departments of Education and Women and Child Development at the State level will need to initiate action in this regard.

Training

Personnel preparation in ECCE for all levels of functionaries will need to be given close attention with a focus on creating resource capacity for planning, implementation and monitoring of play based development oriented ECE programmes. There is a strong need therefore of reviewing the existing training programmes and facilities, both preservice and inservice and bringing in to them a degree of professionalism and rigour in terms of duration, content, methodology and approach. The NCTE specifications will have to be accordingly reviewed/framed and accreditation to these made compulsory for all preservice programmes. Selection of training institutes is crucial in this respect. Experienced institute like Home Science Colleges, Schools of Social Work University Departments can be identified for training purposes.

For inservice training also there is need for a coordinated strategy involving both governmental and non-govermental organizations at state and sub-state levels. Development of district, and block level resource tams and inclusion of ECE inputs at the cluster level resource Centre would facilitate decentralized and context-relevant inputs and strengthening of quality of ECCE programmes. There is also need to make training at all levels demonstration based with provision for hands on experience. The ECE cells in the SCERTs can be made responsible for coordinating and guiding this effort. Possibilities with the distance mode should also be explored particularly from the point of view of continuous training.

Strengthening of Ecce-primary Linkage

In the context of ECCE's crucial significance for UEE linkages between ECE and primary education initiated in the 8th Plan will need further strengthening in both operational and programmatic terms. Specifically, this will have to be realized through:

- * ensuring coordination of timings and location based on community appraisal and local micro-planning exercise
- * extension of the child centred and joyful learning methodology into the curriculum at primary stage in a systematic and scientific manner and capacity building for the same.
- * inclusion of a School Readiness package at the beginning of class 1 curriculum based on local needs to facilitate entry and adjustment of children who make a direct entry into primary school without any ECE experience
- * joint trainings of primary teachers and ECE workers/ personnel to facilitate better appreciation of the nuances of ECD-primary linkage and need for continuity.
- * experimentation on a pilot basis with innovative and alternative models like an Integrated ECCE centre or Bal Kendra comprising ECE and an ungraded unit of early primary level corresponding to grades 1 and 2.

Integrated ECCE centre or Bal Kendra, as conceptualized, can serve as feeder centres to primary schools in remote inaccessible areas e.g. among the Primitive Tribal Groups, with, multiple advantage of access, better pupil-teacher ratio, smoother bridging of home to standard language and space for pacing of learning of the minimum levels. 50C such centres may be established in the first phase in identified remote areas and their feasibility and impact in the context of U.P.E. goals malt be assessed prior to scaling up.

Expansion of creche and day care centres which is already envisaged from the National Creche fund with the Department of Women X2and Child Development could be in a limited way be further stepped up by establishing of additional creches attached to Anganwadis/Primary Schools to facilitate girls participation in primary schools. The AW facility is not adequate in this context since it caters to only 3 to 6 year olds and does not include the 0-3 group which is a greater liability for girls The programme in the creches/day care centres Should also be made more development oriented rather than being just custodial.

Micro and Need Specific Planning

With the growing realization that for any community based programme to be optimally utilised and to make an impact, it must be based on the local needs, and living patterns, for which decentralized, contextual, need specific planning is mandatory. A quality ECE programme also needs to ensure flexible response to local patterns of women's work, child care needs and local culture specific practices.

There is therefore need to orient/train community and programme personnel in participatory learning approaches to area mapping and micro planning identification of communities with low child related indicators. Involvement of and convergence with local women's groups, Mahila mandals, DWCRA groups, Indira Mahila Yojna should be Sought. Systematic capacity building action needs to be initiated by Director ICDS and Director of Education at the state level in collaboration with state level planning and management organisations for, this purpose.

Partnership with NGOs

Partnership with and participation of NGOs in than running of FCCE programmes and in providing resource support for qualitative strengthening of the programmes which was initiated in the Eighth Plan will need to be further, promoted. This should be done through

* encouraging adoption of projects and their independent execution within prescribed norms
* identification and capacity, building of proven individuals and organizations to participate by providing support and assisting in monitoring and evaluation
* providing a forum for networking of organizations and individuals at national, state and sub-state levels.

Research in ECCE

Action research in the area of ECCE needs to be also promoted to assess relative long term impact of ECE and Early Stimulation programmes on subsequent development and achievement of children vis-a-vis goals of UEE. Budget provision of substantial nature will need to be made for this purpose. The budget for ECCE for the 9th Five Year Plan period for Rs.108240.40 lakhs is proposed to be appropriately shared by the Central Government in the Department of Women and Child Development and Education in the Ministry of Human Resource Development and the State Governments and Union Territories.

Workers Education

The Central Board for Workers Education (CBWE), Nagpur, sponsored by the Ministry of Labour, Government of India was established in 1958 to implement Workers Education Scheme at National, Regional, unit and Village Levels.

- Tripartite in character, the Board consists of representatives from Central Organisations of Workers, Employers, Central/State Governments and Educational Institutions.
- Awareness is sought to be created among the working class about their rights and obligations for their effective participation in socio-economic development of the country.
- Different types of training programmes are organised by the Board for workers in organised, unorganized, rural and informal sectors as indicated in Table
- Board's programmes reflect the new orientation, direction and dimensions for meeting the wider educational needs of the worker, trade unions and managements, keeping in view the changed scenario.

Training Programmes of the Board

Training programmes of the Board for workers in organized sector are conducted at three levels.

- At the first level training is imparted to the candidates selected as Education Officers. After successful completion of the training, these Education Officers conduct various programmes from the centres of their posting.

- At the second level, workers from different establishments, sponsored by trade unions and released by employers are trained. These trained workers are called Worker-Teacher.
- At the third level, the worker-teacher conduct classes for the rank and file of workers in their establishments.

National Level Programmes

Programmes for representatives from Central Trade Union Organisations/Federations and Voluntary Organisations on different subjects are conducted by the IIWE in addition to giving pre-employment training to Education Officers and reorientation to Regional Directors and Education Officers of the Board as well. In view of the specialized training needs to tackle some of the specific issues by Trade Unions, three cells namely (i)

Industrial Health, Safety and Environment (ii) Education for Rural and Unorganised Sector Workers and (iii) Women and Child Labour have been established in the Institute.

Programmes at Regional Level

Organisation of Unorganised Labour and Training of Rural Educators

Initially the Board concentrated its activities in the organised sector. The Board shifted as emphasis to rural sector since 1977-78 on the recommendations of Workers Education Review Committee. Initially started with 7 pilot projects, the rural workers education programmes have now become a regular and continuing programme. The objectives of the programme are:

- To promote critical awareness of problems, privileges and obligations as workers and citizens;
- to enhance self confidence and build up scientific attitude;
- to educate them to develop their organizations through which they can fulfil socio economic functions and responsibilities in rural economy and strengthen democratic, secular and socialist fibre of rural society;

- to motivate for family welfare planning and to combat social evils. Rural Educators are imparted one month training at Regional Centres and the trained Rural Educators assist Education Officers in conducting of Rural Awareness Camps. These camps are attended by landless labour, tribal labour, rural artisans, forest workers and educated unemployed.

Tailor made programmes, 5-day camps, special programmes based on functional and educational needs of workers from Handloom, Powerloom, Khadi & Village Industries, Industrial Estates, Small Scale Units, Handicrafts, Sericulture; Coir Industry, Beedi Industry and workers of weaker sections such as women workers, handicapped workers, rickshaw drivers, constructions workers, civic and sanitation workers are also organised by the Board.

Literature and Audio Visual Aids

Simple literature in the form of Textual and Pictorial Booklets in Indian languages has been brought out. These are made available to workers at a subsidized price of Rs.3/- per booklet. Revision and reprint of the booklets is also undertaken. The Board also publishes Continuing Education Literature with a view to provide learning material to workers trained in various courses. During the Year 2001-2002, i.e. from April to October, 2001, the Board has brought out 7 Booklets.

The Board has also produced five multi-colour posters on "Workers Education and Awareness", "Rural Workers Education for Awareness", "Workers and Management – Two wings of Industry", "WE Stand against Terrorism" and "Remove clouds of Terrorism for Joyous Universe" in bilingual, one sticker on "Shram Eva Jayate" in Hindi and one "CBWE – A Profile". JOURNAL One combined issue of Quarterly Journal "Workers Education" i.e. June, 2001 and September, 2001 have been brought out during the period from April to October, 2001. Study material in the form of Seminar Papers, Case Studies, Talking points, etc. to supplement teaching at the Indian Institute of Workers Education and Regional Directorates have been prepared.

Cbwe New and Samachar

Monthly issues of "CBWE News" in English and "Samachar" in Hindi have been brought out from April, 2001 to October, 2001.

Grants in Aid

The Board provides grants-in-aid to registered Trade Unions and other Institutions for conducting their own Workers Education Programmes. The Board also sanctions grants-in-aid form National Level Courses to the Central Trade Union Organisations and National Federations. During the period April to October, 2001, the Board provided grantsin-aid amounting Rs. 2,75,536/- to 48 Unions/Institutions which conducted 106 programmes for 4,236 workers.

Use of Hindi

During the period April, 2001 to October, 2001, 15 employees of the Boardm were given incentives for doing the official work in Hindi. The Official Language Committee of the Board met twice and reviewed the progress made in the use of Hindi at Head Office, Indian Institute of Workers Education and Regional Directorates. During the year under report, two Rajbhasha Workshop was conducted at Head Quarters, Nagpur exclusively for Group 'C' employees of Head Office and other for Regional Directors of "C" Region in which 10 and 15 employees and Regional Directors respectively were imparted training for doing their official work in Hindi.

Observance/Celebration of Various Days

The Head Office, IIWE, Mumbai, all the Zonal and Regional offices of Central Board for Workers Education observed the following days to mark the occasion. Seminars, Symposia, special lecture, film shows, competitions were organised. Pledges wherever required were administered to the trainees and members of staff.

- Anti-Terrorism Day
- World Population Day
- Sadbhavana Day

- Hindi Diwas and Hindi Month
- Workers Education Day
- National Solidarity Day
- Anti-Corruption Day and Vigilance Awareness Week.

Impact

A feed back is obtained from the participants and management about the impact of various programmes conducted by the Board. The feed back has revealed that the participants have admitted and realized the importance of discipline, productivity, reducing the cost of production, improving quality to with stand global competition, feel enlightened on various problems of industry, changes in economic scenario etc.

The programmes have brought changes in their attitude and they have developed their identification with the interest of the organisation. Democratic process and practices in Trade unions have strengthened and the workers have approached managements for creation of common forum to discuss problems. The participants also gave up social evils like smoking, tobacco chewing, indebtedness and instead switched to savings.

In Rural camps the participants realized the importance of Rural Worker Organisation, small savings, health, hygiene and literacy etc. and undertook to carry on message of awareness to those who are not aware.

Upgradation of CBWE

Workers Education in view of the revolution in Information Technology in the emerging knowledge-based economy. He mentioned about the need for upgradation of CBWE into an institution of excellence.

In pursuance of this and also in recommendation of the Governing Body, Central Board for Workers Education, a Committee was constituted to study the upgradation/ restructuring of CBWE in May, 2001. The Committee has to study the status of labour education in the country and to suggest ways and means to enrich it; to redefine the concept of Workers' Education need to widen its scope, dimension and coverage and to assess needbased programmes so as to encompass capacity building of workers in all respects to meet the challenges of the country on account of globalization and intense competition from the MNCs by the workforce and industries. The Committee will submit the report very soon.

Programme for Workers in Industry—Objectives—Historical Perspectives—Distinguished from Vocational Education—Need

Workers on the organized sector have very few incentives and many heavy disincentives for seeking help with literacy difficulties. Literacy evaluation of a worker is seldom linked with evaluation of work efficiency nor the worker's role in cooperative development. Patronage and subsidy to the workers' education including literacy is not seen by the worker as organically linked with the work ethics of the firm or with its role as a responsible citizen.

On the contrary, voluntary revelation of their difficulty in reading, writing or spelling, is likely no only to lead a loss of face with the fellow workers, but to greater exploitation and threat of loss of work. Therefore, workers education must cater to the personal circumstances of workers and must be closely associated with their education and training for work.

Adults with literacy difficulties are in the main doing manual or unskilled work. They being below their potential, the normal system does not cater to their needs. The management which at times provides for vocational training or retaining is interested in the worker completing a set course. It is, therefore, essential that all vocational and industrial training institutions have a literacy wing and literacy become a compulsory component of further education and training. The dichotomy between education and training marginalizes the disadvantaged. Unless employers, trade unions, educationists and trainers recognise that literacy is a prerequisite of vocational education and training, the artificial dichotomy will continue and the working adults will not fulfill their potential as workers and be effective in their jobs.

Concept of Worker's Education—Techniques and Methods—Types of Programmes

It is important to emphasize the integration of different programme structures of workers education with recurrent systems of education. It is not an easy task. The child labour in skilled areas as carpet weaving, the women labour employed for tea or coffee picking or making incense sticks, the adult illiterate labour in an unskilled job or as a trade union worker have different needs. In all urban centres workers are drawn from different linguistic, ethnic and religious backgrounds and often do not even see their role as member of a responsible work force. Their education seldom give them introduction to the development perspective of the country or cooperative development strategies in management and citizenry.

There are educational theories which treat the child as a social and the learner's mind as an empty bucket to be filled with the wisdom of the teacher. As Prime Minister Rajiv Gandhi rightly points out, "we cannot bring in the institutionalized learning at the cost of destroying the intelligence and the wisdom that are already in our people. We must preserve them and together with them bringing institutionalized learning, bring in literacy which will help our people from being gullible, being exploited. It liberates them from servitude". This is a challenge to all those who produce material for literacy and education for workers, children as well as adults.

Education for Improving Skills and Competencies—Problems in Organizing Worker's Education Programme—Need for Support and Co-operation from Employers

India's massive adult education programme has many spectacular achievements to its credit. But its Achilles heel is the fact that it is run without reference to the language of the learners. That literacy is primarily a language problem, that language is the medium of education and training has been forgotten by the adult educators. Since everybody speaks a language, it is taken for granted that everyone is competent to speak about it.

One of the major tasks before us is the evaluation of all books used by Sramik Vidyapeeths round the country. Evaluation is a job for specialists. Institutions such as Central Institute of Indian Languages, which is the greatest repository of research and application in the fields of languages, linguistics and evaluation should be formally associated to avoid the tardiness in implementation. How can the Prime Minister's directive to forge many linkages be implemented if we don not shed the old habit of working in isolation?

The Institute of Applied Language Sciences has just completed evaluation of books prepared by the NCERT in 11 Indian languages funded by the UNICEF. About 35 specialists worked for about a year which has resulted in the production of a Handbook useful for material producers, teachers, teacher trainers and evaluators. Similar books will be ready for each of the languages. Such work should be the model for subsequent work.

UNIT-IV

Management of Non-formal Education Programmes

Basic Processes of Administration

A community-based learning centre (CBLC) is a place in the community where people come together to obtain knowledge, acquire skills and values that are relevant to their daily lives. These CBLCs may be set up by the government, development agencies, NGOs or by the local communities themselves. They are managed by facilitators with the support of a management committee set up by the community.

All CBLCs have a management committee consisting of local representatives (opinion leaders, women's groups, youth groups, religious leaders), local government authorities and parent organisations. This committee is responsible for the planning and implementation of CBLC activities, thus ensuring community ownership and sustainability. In addition to literacy activities, other training programmes are offered based on the expressed needs of the people.

A community-based learning centre (CBLC) is a centre where people learn a number of things based on their choices and needs. This centre is established by the community through its own initiative, with or without external assistance. It belongs to and is managed by the community that requested it. As a community owned centre it is open to all. The activities of the centre. In this role, it enjoys the continued support of the facilitator. It is accountable to the CGA and it includes both men and women. It fulfils several functions. In each management committee the following posts and sub-committees may exist:

I. *Chairperson:* S/he is elected from among the members of the community to lead the management committee.

II. *Secretary:* S/he is responsible for keeping record of the different meetings and actions of the management committee.

III. *Socio-cultural and Education Sub-committee:* It assists facilitators in maintaining a good learning environment and in the distribution of supplies, learning/teaching materials and furniture. This committee also supports the facilitators in the organisation of socio-cultural activities in the centre.

IV. *Financial Sub-committee:* It is responsible for the financial management of the centre. One member of the committee is nominated as the treasurer. It is also responsible for the mobilisation of both internal and external resources.

V. *Sub-committee for Organisation and Mobilisation:* It is responsible for the organisation and mobilisation of community resources, sensitisation of different emerging issues and social marketing. A participatory and coordinated process is necessary in the planning and implementation of activities of the centre with a real commitment of the different members of the community. Proper implementation of the plan requires regular supervision and monitoring by the facilitators.

In the village of Tambakunda the facilitator had not prepared nor sent out the mandatory quarterly progress report for the programme monitoring which was required for the release of funds. Moreover, the members of the management committee had complained about this lack of action, which had caused a delay in many of the planned activities. After repeated requests by his superiors, he sent a report of the second quarter which lacked information and was judged unacceptable. As a result, the funds were not released.

It is important that you regularly report both to the community and to your supervisors according to the agreed plan. The report must be detailed, reliable and verifiable and the deadlines for sending the report must be strictly respected.

For the community, the report may be in the form of a simple information meeting, but for documentation purposes and informing supervisors and implementing agencies, a written report must be prepared.

One of the most difficult jobs of a facilitator is to make learning relevant. When the learners are adults the job is even more challenging because adults learn best when learning is self-directed. The role of the adult literacy facilitator in non-formal education is not to teach but to facilitate, which means helping the adult learn.

At least four reasons justify setting up literacy and non-formal education programmes:

Firstly, basic education is considered a human right because a minimum of knowledge is necessary to live in a continually changing society.

Secondly, by targeting the most deprived communities, basic education is considered one of the best means of contributing to the improvement of the living conditions of its recipients by helping them to better organise daily activities, improve personal skills and abilities and develop income-generating activities.

Thirdly, the education of girls has a particularly significant impact on economic and social development. Research has shown that education for girls greatly contributes to higher family income levels, the reduction of maternal and infant mortality rates, improved nutrition and general health as well as longer life expectancy.

Fourthly, literacy contributes to the emancipation of the most deprived, an essential condition for building a civil society that all people feel part of, for contributing to better governance and for reinforcing democratic institutions.

Supervision

Adult literacy and non-formal basic education have several definitions based on social, cultural, economic and environmental contexts. Offered outside of the formal school system to adults and adolescents usually over 15 (although sometimes younger), adult literacy and non-formal basic education programmes aim to provide:

- A complementary or alternative primary education.
- A complementary or alternative secondary education.
- The acquisition of new and updated knowledge and skills.

Adult literacy and non-formal education programmes often target:

- Young women and adult women.
- Poor and other disadvantaged groups.
- Out of school youths and adolescents.
- Individuals who have not received a primary education.
- Individuals who had received an initial education but were forced to stop their studies.
- Individuals who have neither the knowledge nor the skills to adapt to economic changes.
- Marginalised groups, especially girls and women.

The contents of adult literacy and non-formal basic education usually include reading, writing and arithmetic. They can also cover other knowledge areas such as:

- Health (particularly on HIV/AIDS).
- The environment
- Information and communication technologies (ICT)
- Civil and human rights
- Income generating activities and credit schemes
- Etc.

Finally, they can include life skills such as:

- The ability to solve problems
- The ability to act responsibly and safely

- The ability to preserve the environment
- The ability to interact harmoniously with others
- The ability to generate an income
- Etc.

Adult learners are motivated to learn what they need to learn. They want to know how literacy will help them. Adults have established values, beliefs and opinions. They expect others to respect their differing ideas regarding beliefs, religions, value systems and lifestyles.

All adults have different styles and paces of learning. Although an adult's reaction and speed of learning may be slow, her/his learning capacity should not be underestimated.

The adult teaching method is different from the teaching methods for children. Indeed, adults do not have the same memorisation capacity (they are no longer used to learning things by heart), they do not accept preconceived ideas and need to be convinced (their minds are less easily influenced and they have many biases). In addition, learning questions pre-established certitudes, which can sometimes be regarded negatively. On the other hand, adults are experienced, which can be useful to the learning process, and they have a more developed critical mind. They need to understand the reasons for the training to be motivated: the actions taken must be justified.

Theories of Organisation and Management

Contemporary theories of management tend to account for and help interpret the rapidly changing nature of today's organizational environments. As before in management history, these theories are prevalent in other sciences as well.

Contingency Theory

Basically, contingency theory asserts that when managers make a decision, they must take into account all aspects of the current situation and act on those aspects that are key to the situation at hand. Basically, it's the approach that "it depends." For example, the continuing effort to identify the best leadership or management style might now conclude that the best style depends on the situation. If one is leading troops in the Persian Gulf, an autocratic style is probably best (of course, many might argue here, too). If one is leading a hospital or university, a more participative and facilitative leadership style is probably best.

Systems Theory

Systems theory has had a significant effect on management science and understanding organizations. First, let's look at "what is a system?" A system is a collection of part unified to accomplish an overall goal. If one part of the system is removed, the nature of the system is changed as well. For example, a pile of sand is not a system. If one removes a sand particle, you've still got a pile of sand. However, a functioning car is a system. Remove the carburetor and you've no longer got a working car. A system can be looked at as having inputs, processes, outputs and outcomes. Systems share feedback among each of these four aspects of the systems.

Let's look at an organization. Inputs would include resources such as raw materials, money, technologies and people. These inputs go through a process where they're planned, organized, motivated and controlled, ultimately to meet the organization's goals. Outputs would be products or services to a market. Outcomes would be, e.g., enhanced quality of life or productivity for customers/clients, productivity. Feedback would be information from human resources carrying out the process, customers/clients using the products, etc. Feedback also comes from the larger environment of the organization, e.g., influences from government, society, economics, and technologies. This overall system framework applies to any system, including subsystems (departments, programs, etc.) in the overall organization.

Systems theory may seem quite basic. Yet, decades of management training and practices in the workplace have not followed this theory. Only recently, with tremendous changes facing organizations and how they operate, have educators and managers come to face this new way of looking at things. This interpretation has brought about a significant change (or paradigm shift) in the way management studies and approaches organizations.

The effect of systems theory in management is that writers, educators, consultants, etc. are helping managers to look at the organization from a broader perspective. Systems theory has brought a new perspective for managers to interpret patterns and events in the workplace. They recognize the various parts of the organization, and, in particular, the interrelations of the parts, e.g., the coordination of central administration with its programs, engineering with manufacturing, supervisors with workers, etc. This is a major development. In the past, managers typically took one part and focused on that. Then they moved all attention to another part. The problem was that an organization could, e.g., have a wonderful central administration and wonderful set of teachers, but the departments didn't synchronize at all.

Chaos Theory

As chaotic and random as world events seem today, they seem as chaotic in organizations, too. Yet for decades, managers have acted on the basis that organizational events can always be controlled. A new theory (or some say "science"), chaos theory, recognizes that events indeed are rarely controlled. Many chaos theorists (as do systems theorists) refer to biological systems when explaining their theory. They suggest that systems naturally go to more complexity, and as they do so, these systems become more volatile (or susceptible to cataclysmic events) and must expend more energy to maintain that complexity. As they expend more energy, they seek more structure to maintain stability. This trend continues until the system splits, combines with another complex system or falls apart entirely. Sound familiar? This trend is what many see as the trend in life, in organizations and the world in general.

Management in India

For some period, much white collar work from the Western world has been exported to the Republic of India. This work has generally been in the field of information technology (IT).

Since IT is an essential component to any business these days, it is quite important that US managers have knowledge of how their managerial theories can be implemented in a country like India. In a study by Richman and Copen (1972), it was demonstrated that managerial practices developed in the United States and other industrialized countries were easily transferable to managers in India. The similarity is attributed to a number of variables including: the increased managerial education in India, the higher status being attributed to managers, the similarity between technology and management of technology, as well as India's trend toward the decentralization of authority. The only major difference comes about in the emphasis on certain managerial facets.

Earlier, the individualism-collectivism scale was discussed with regards to the United States and China. Somewhere in the middle of the bipolar extremes of the US and China lies India. While Indian society does reflect certain characteristics of collectivism as do many Asian cultures, the basic cultural orientation of India is rooted in the ideas of Buddhism, Yogic psychology, and self-discipline. Although Indian managers and workers will exhibit collectivist traits in family and other social interactions, in business management practices they tend to mix these collectivist traits with Western management philosophy.

For example, managers in India maintain close personal relationships with their peers and subordinates, which reflects their collectivistic attribute. However, in their business activities, Western management methods such as agendas and constant feedback are used. Leadership and communication also rank quite high in the evaluation of management in India, as they do in the United States. Modern Indian management practices have evolved from the British system prior to India's independence, and India has adopted similar practices in the management agency system since independence in 1947. However, Indian management practices have developed a distinct style, which is different from the British system (Neelankavil 125). For example, Indian firms are still run very paternalistically with the personal relationships playing a key role in the management of the organization. Besides minor differences in style, most characteristics regarding the evaluation of managerial performance tend to be similar between the United States and India. This suggests that India may be a lot closer to the US on the aforementioned individualism-collectivism scale. All in all, culture plays an important role in global business, and to achieve success in cross-cultural management, US managers should understand both themselves and others. This includes knowledge of one's self and the culture of those whom he or she is managing or working with. The competitive advantage for the firm comes about from the proper alignment between the external environment and the firm's internal strategies, structure, and management practices.

The Government seeks to follow an integrated approach to literacy. "This means, the Total literacy Campaign and the Post Literacy Programme will operate under one literacy Project. This approach would enable the enormous illiteracy problem to be tackled in a holistic manner. By treating the imparting of functional literacy as a continuum rather than as a one of benefit for the illiterate person, progress of literacy efforts would be made goaldirected.

Literacy campaigns would continue to run in those areas where there are large pools of residual illiteracy. At the same time, for those who have crossed the basic learning phase, programmes of consolidation, remediation, vocational skills, integration with life skills (emphasis added) and such other aspects would be considered the basic unit".

The characterization of life skills is not available; but speaking to MHRD officials; it appears that they follow the standard international definitions in relation to NFE.

Some NGO NFE providers ordered the life skills differently for the Indian context in a 2001 UNESCO-supported study conducted by an Indian NGO, REMEDIA Trust, on life skills education within the NFE sector; with a view to address issues related to drug abuse and HIV/AIDS prevention.

According to the NGOs participating in the study, 'self awareness is the first necessary life skill. By using the Socratic

Method, the students can be helped to debate the issue of an individual's place in a family, a social group, a community, and a country. The young people can be made aware of their rights and duties and their responsibilities to themselves and society. The need to preserve their physical and mental health has to be realized. The twin essence of self awareness is the life skill of empathy. Awareness of self should be counterbalanced by awareness of others, their different thinking, feelings, desires and wishes. This requires some imagination and fellow feeling. It is part of a process of socialization and self control. Indian culture emphasizes empathy with human beings, animals and the nature around us. This skill has to be cultivated carefully, especially among street and slum children as they often exhibit an aggressive stance in self protection.

Critical thinking and creative thinking is the next pair of life skills. Training in thinking is very rare in formal as well as non-formal classrooms in India; and today as the media sends out a constant stream of messages, it is important to begin critical listening and asking the right questions. Training young people to ask for cause-effect relationship and then for rational thinking is essential, if they are going to withstand pressure.

Decision making and problem solving comes somewhat easier to children who are on the streets rather than to children who are protected by the family. Since, in India, the group rather the individual are given importance, these skills may be fostered by debates where individual differences can emerge and can be defended by logical arguments.

Coping with emotions and stress first requires admitting emotions and stress. In the Indian society, emotions and stress are regarded as shameful and stoicism is encouraged. Therefore, the discipline of standing aloof from one's emotions, recognising them and coping with them is an exercise that has to be carefully taught so that the extreme positions of either denying emotions or totally giving in to emotions are avoided. Effective communication and interpersonal relations skills are important to young people in order to maintain both their independence and their friendships. In India, friendship between young people of the same sex has been more highly regarded than elsewhere. Even in India, family bonds, though strong, need careful nurture. Drugs do not tempt whose family bonds are strong. Families offer the young protection from drugs and stress. Two major life skills necessary are spatial orientation and orientation in time.

The nonverbal spatial skill is needed to practice arts and crafts, which are part of the Indian way of life. Most vocational programmes depend on spatial skills. Orientation to time helps the young to plan for their future. It has been discovered that the disadvantaged do not have this orientation, so they tend to live in the present and do not save or invest money they earn for their morrow. If the young who come to the NFE centres begin to understand the time-line and the cause and effect relationship, they will begin to appreciate how their effort of today will bear fruit tomorrow. Many young people do not have a clear notion of how yesterday, today and tomorrow are linked. They have a vague notion of weekdays and months but if they are going to participate in the modern world of technology, they must have orientation to both space and time.

Moreover, through the Open Universities and distance learning initiatives, mechanisms are in place to upgrade skills at regular intervals and develop new competencies. People's needs of lifelong learning are constantly expanding. The Open University System was initiated in the country to augment opportunities for higher education as an instrument of democratising education and also to make it a lifelong process. The first Open University in the country was established by the state government of Andhra Pradesh in 1982. In 1985, the central government established the Indira Gandhi National Open University (IGNOU).

The Legal Foundations of NFE Policies

The Indian Constitution in its 86th Amendment Act, 2002 stipulates: Right to Education, "The State shall provide free and compulsory education to all children of the age of six to fourteen years in such manner as the State may, by law, determine."

However, the most important official confirmation of the need for expanding adult education services in India came in the form of the National Policy Resolution of 1968. The first important initiative in adult education—the National Adult Education Program (NAEP) -- was not established until 1978. It defined education as literacy, functionality, and conscientisation, and although its structures were eventually established, they did not always function effectively. In 1980, the program was renamed (it was now simply called the AEP – Adult Education Programme) and expanded from a 10-month to a 3-year program with emphasis on health, family planning, and functional programmes. Unfortunately, the AEP was not extremely successful either. The main thrust of the new National Program of Adult Education (established in 1986) is like its predecessors in that its main thrust is efficiency rather than equity and its general mode is technocratic.

The 1986 education policy envisages a national system which will take determined action to bring about universal primary education and promote the spread of adult literacy, thereby helping to reduce inequalities. The education system will be based on a national curricular framework which contains a common core as well as components specific to each region. The core will cut across subject areas and will be designed to promote such values as India's common cultural heritage, egalitarianism, democracy and secularism, equality of the sexes, protection of the environment, observance of the small family norm, and the scientific approach. Pace-setting schools called Navodaya Vidyalayas will provide quality education to particularly gifted children, irrespective of their families' means, and will promote excellence as well as equity and social justice. The 1986 policy also emphasizes the need to raise the level of investment in education from about 4 per cent of national income in 1986 to 6 per cent by 1990 and even higher thereafter (A new policy for education – India; UNESCO Courier, February 1989, by Anil Bordia).

It has to be noted that education in India is on the concurrent list, that is, it is the joint responsibility of both the Centre and the States. This leads to a considerable amount of confusion and indeed passing the buck in the actualisation of responsibilities in imparting education. While India is a signatory to the EFA processes, in terms of legislations, the education processes are governed by Government Orders (GOs) passed from time to time. The framework does not seem to be justifiable in the sense that the state cannot be taken to court for non-implementation of the education policies.

Governance & Finance

The major implementing bodies of the NFE come under the Ministry of Human Resource Development (MHRD). The MoLE (Ministry of Labour and Employment) is accountable for some modular vocational training courses. Moreover, according to various officials, there are some 17 Ministries and Departments, which claim to provide NFE vocational training through various schemes and programmes. Information on this is not readily available.

Supervision

In terms of supervision of NFE, the National Policy on Education, 1986, instructs the need for a substantial strengthening of the supervisory and administrative apparatus of NFE. Rather than depending on the urban-oriented bureaucratic model, emphasis is laid on taking up well designed projects of approximately 100 NFE centres, in a compact and contiguous area. Supervisors should be selected from the local community and if possible, an experienced and committed NFE Instructor.

These persons should be intensively trained and wherever possible, there should be the involvement of an organisation of continuing education programme. Village Education Committees should be set up as envisaged in NPE/POA (National Policy on Education / Programme of Action) to involve the local community in the programme and also to make the NFE centre in-charge accountable to it.

The broad aim of this scheme is to effectively involve voluntary agencies, public trusts, non-profit making companies, social activist groups and the rest, in the implementation of NFE programme.

Voluntary Organisations in Non-formal Education

A major problem in the promotion of non-formal education is its lack of recognition in comparison with formal, academic education. As a result, the importance of non-formal education is not fully recognised and the opportunities to use it are not fully realised. The financial means required for non-formal education are not sufficiently allocated given the increasing demands placed on finite resources and time . While formal education can be quantified and described, this is more difficult in the case of non-formal education, which largely escapes structure and is difficult to assess quantitatively and qualitatively. Hence, funding is a problem. National education planners should reconsider their policy and practice in order to promote non-formal education as a means of increasing skills and knowledge. Non-formal education has a long history and in many countries it is seen as an important way for people to learn and develop to participate in society. However, formal education institutions have systemically developed a monopoly on the provision of education, especially in the last century, due to their power to certify learning outcomes and due to the structure and visibility that they can give to the learning process.

One of the most important challenges that education policy makers will have to face in the coming years will be to find ways to increase recognition of the value of non-formal education among young people. Non-formal education is essential for the personal development and life-long learning of individuals. The inadequacy of civics' courses in further and higher education institutions to ensure active citizenship among young people is also symptomatic of the need for complementary non-formal education methodologies where the skills and competences necessary to be an active citizen in society are acquired. In recent years employers are increasingly looking for people who have obtained not only academic qualifications but who can also demonstrate that they have a wider range of practical skills that cannot all be learned in formal education. These 'soft skills' cannot easily be 'taught' in formal education because they are learned through 'hands-on' practical experience and thus are much more effectively gained in non-formal environments. Youth organisations are very important providers of non-formal education but young people are not always aware of the fact that they are acquiring a wide range of skills through their participation in youth activities. Youth organisations can reach out to young people from a wide variety of backgrounds in the local context, and encourage them to learn and gain skills through their participation in non-formal education. Young people feel less intimidated in non-formal learning environments. Due to the fact that participation is voluntary, they often find learning more enjoyable. Non-formal education can provide an alternative learning pathway to those whose 'needs and wants' are not met in the classroom. In addition, 'young people who have left school early or who are in precarious situations in society could benefit from non-formal education as a second chance that could have a strong impact in their lives'.

Organisation at the Central, State, Regional and Micro Levels

Change is a natural phenomena and is inevitable, where as, its nature and the pace at which it occurs, varies within the 'time and space' matrix. Efficacy and survival of any system therefore, depends on how well it responds to the imperatives of change. This probably is true more in the field of education, wherein, the frontiers of knowledge keep on expanding at such a rapid rate, that the earlier methods and methodologies tend to become obsolete.

In today's world means and resources to seek knowledge are so enormous and diverse, that the process of learning has become deinstitutionalised. The pattern of education and its delivery mechanism, Changes in higher education, keeping India in view, have traditionally been slow, interms of its pattern and delivery, mainly because of its elitist nature and the ivory tower existence of its institutions. After world war IInd, higher education, world over, has undergone transformation from elitist systems to mass focused systems. As a consequence, there have been remarkable developments in individualising mass-learning. At the global level, higher education is undergoing a paradigm shift from an instruction-centred college / university model, to a learner-centred integrated network model which is based on access to learning resources and student initiative (ICDE, 1996).

In India, at present there are 60 Distance Learning Institutions (DLIs), including 9 open Universities. Indira Gandhi National open University (IGNOU), has emerged as one of the India's pioneering and biggest open university and the second biggest in the world after Central Radio and Television University, China, Established in 1985. The aim was to provide cost-effective, quality education to large sections of population including those living in remote and far-flung areas. It was also intended to provide ample opportunities to those, who for one reason or the other, could not seek or improve their educational standards. Therefore, IGNOU, stated imparting education to the professional managers, primary and secondary school teachers, computer professionals, construction-workers, medical and health personnel, Panchayat (local bodies) members, host of NGO activists. IGNOU is endeavouring to reach out to all sections and stratas of masses, who otherwise, would have remained deprived of higher education.

Issues and Challenges

Most of the programmes offered by IGNOU fall within the spectrum of non-formal education and are very popular, as these are intended for self-enrichment and professional upgradation. However, IGNOU's reach-out policy in spreading mass education through distance mode must also reorient itself to the local conditions. This is warranted to ensure that the impact and achievements are sustainable in local level in different parts of country. Issues which have emerged in respect to IGNOU functioning in J&K State, need to refocus its delivery system, to popularize mass education both in terms of qualitative and quantitative aspects. Some of such issues which have come to surface are:

- The growth in enrolment has not been uniform across all programmes and at different study centres.

Enrolment of a small number of students with some of the study centres has rendered them virtually non-functional.

- The present study centre network is urban based, leaving small towns and rural areas out of reach and focus.
- Locational access to study centres and their timings, have in many cases, made it difficult or impossible for students to attend counselling sessions regularly to seek clarification and advise with regard to courses and specialisations to be chosen. In view of the above whether study centre approach alone can take education to the doorsteps of the students in the state is a questionable proposition.

In the light of the issues discussed above, the challenges for IGNOU in effective management of its non-formal education programmes are:

- There is an urgent need to create awareness amongst study centre spread over different locations about the programmes being offered by IGNOU.
- Net working of various study centres has to be integrated with the rural areas of the region, in which they operate. It is expected to enhance the accessibility of the distant learners seeking education through IGNOU.
- IGNOU has to match and balanced various educational packages with the expectations and felt needs of the prospective learners.

IGNOU Programme and J&K

J&K State is situated in extreme northern part of India, boarding Pakistan, Afganistan and china as border countries with unique features in terms of geographical conditions, population, literacy, economy and other prevailing conditions (extreme weather conditions and cross-border sponsored terrorism). State has witnessed a phenomenal growth in student enrolment because of free education policy of the state government. Since 1986, IGNOU has also been imparting education in the state. As such, it is an opportune time to introspect the delivery system adopted by IGNOU in J&K to assess its success matrix of educational programmes, in terms of their effectiveness and impact as also evaluate its delivery system. Has the objective of educating all sections of the society, living even in the remotest corners and backward regions been accomplished as to nullify, the imbalances in the development of education in the state.

Though there has been increase in enrolment as also academic programmes and courses, being offered by IGNOU have multiplied in J&K State. However, nature of facilities and support system required to sustain such academic endeavours have to match up such an expansion.

As such for state like J&K, keeping in view its socio-economic conditions IGNOU programmes must focus on the following:

- Empowering Women Through Distance Education
- Panchayati Raj Project
- District Primary Education Project
- Human Rights Project
- Community Awareness in Disaster Preparedness
- Education and Training of Rural Youth Through Distance Education Mode
- Project for Providing Vocational Training to Tannery Workers.
- HIV and Family Education
- Commonwealth Youth in Development
- Commonwealth of Learning Literacy Project
- Mapping Experiences in The Education of Adolescent Girls
- Certificate Programme for In-service ANMS/FWHS
- Certificate Course for Professional Development of Adult Education Functionaries
- Awareness and Preparedness Among Rural Parents for Effective Primary Schooling
- Computer Literacy for School Dropouts.

Management of Teacher Resources

Adult learners are themselves tremendous resources for learning because they have varied and wide experiences. They enrol in the learning centre with expectations of immediate benefit. Adults learn best when they learn by doing. Adults learn when they are in a group, which provides potential for learning from one another (peer learning).

Adults learn from each other's experiences. In adult learning, success reinforces learning.

The Experience-based method is founded on participatory adult learning principles. The adult learner needs to acquire new knowledge and skills by the end of the training session. This new knowledge and skills must be immediately applicable. The possibility to transfer the knowledge from the training to the surrounding community is an important source of adherence. The adult's appreciation of her or his own progression is a permanent source of motivation.

Role-playing games may be proposed by the facilitator or the learners and may complement another activity. In the role-playing game, the participants take on (according to their own ideas) the roles of people who must engage in verbal and non-verbal (body and face gesture, tone of voice) exchange. A theme is launched to start the game. The "actors" are free to interpret their role and to create the dialogue as they wish. Role-playing games allow for free expression and teach the learners to use their imagination in their verbal and non-verbal exchanges. It is the ideal situation for practicing expression techniques and developing communication related skills.

In this example we can see that role-playing games require a situation or a reason for action that is used to start the game and arouse creativity. The learners who are not actively involved in the role-playing should be encouraged by the facilitator to observe and take notes. Otherwise, the game becomes nothing more than a performance. At the end of the game, the facilitator should interrogate the learners, comment on certain strengths and weaknesses and draw lessons from roles played (for example, what kind of behaviour one should adopt regarding tobacco or family planning). As facilitators we must know how to conduct teaching and learning sessions for adults. Principles of adult learning differ from those used in children's education. Here are examples which we must consider when conducting teaching and learning sessions:

Participation and involvement are essential components of adult learning. Participation calls for involvement. Adult learning focuses on both individual and group needs. The content of adult learning should arise from the concerns of the adult learners and be centred on the learner. The overall aim of adult education is to enhance the learners' capacity to participate more actively in the economic, political and social life around them as well as to improve their lives thanks to greater awareness, creativity and emphasising their potential. Adult education should be negotiated with the learners and based on the needs they express. Based on these principles, a methodology for raising awareness and enhancing the abilities of the learners should be used by the facilitator. This will allow her/him to provide a training that takes into consideration all desired aspects of knowledge, skills and attitudes:

Awareness: Awareness can be created through dialogue among participants and the facilitator during which problems and concerns are discussed and analysed; the solutions are then proposed.

Knowledge: Knowledge can be obtained through information input in the form of conferences, discussion groups, the intervention of specialists and through reading. It should be noted that all information should be relevant and accurate.

Skills: Learning new skills or reinforcing existing skills requires: A detailed explanation of the process by the facilitator. Repeating the explanation of the process while emphasising the key operational points. Allowing the learners to explain and then repeat the process themselves.

Afterwards, the facilitator explains to them the key operational points. The practical nature of literacy and non-formal education requires the use of active methods (active learning). In this respect, the training process varies with each discipline. However, the following steps can generally be carried out during a teaching or learning activity:

1. The facilitator must explain the purpose of the class as thoroughly and accurately as possible, illustrating it with one or several concrete examples relevant to each learner.
2. A discussion regarding the related subject is introduced. Discussion allows for the correction of potential misunderstandings and the adjustment of information for each learner.
3. The facilitator evaluates individual learning by means of questions or exercises whose successful completion depends on the understanding of the information that has been given.
4. The facilitator plans lessons in the community for applying what the participants have learned in class.

In lesson planning, especially in adult learning, the facilitator must prepare herself/himself beforehand:

Advanced lesson planning.

Information search, concrete examples and learning aids about the subject.

Mobilisation of a resource person to lead the class if necessary.

Choice of a specific participatory approach.

Define the different steps of the lesson.

Afterwards, the facilitator can elaborate the planning sheet by drawing inspiration from the participatory methods learned, taking into consideration the importance of the following steps:

1. The introduction of the objectives of the session, the participants' expectations and the working rules.
2. Referring to the participants' real-life situations regarding the subject.
3. Assessing the learners' knowledge about the subject followed by a contribution of additional information.
4. Applying the acquired knowledge through exercises that could be connected to reading, writing or arithmetic.

5. Taking time to think about the knowledge learned and its application to real situations experienced by the learners in their environment.
6. Assessing the learners' knowledge, emphasising self-evaluation.

Management of Reading Materials

Designing educational programmes for street and working children is a critical area of curriculum concern in India. Based on the philosophy and focus of various organisations, several strategies have been evolved at Non-Government Organisations (NGOs) and at -government levels.

Under the project, 'Development of Learner-specific Skill-based Materials for Street and Working Children', drafts of five instructional packages were developed for five categories of street and working children, namely, children engaged in (i) agricultural activities, (ii) children working in repair workshops (cycle, scooter, car, etc.), (iii) children employed by roadside dhabas, tea shops and restaurants, (iv) ragpickers, and (v) girls working in several types of home-crafts.

Four primers and 72 lessons were developed. The lessons were sequentially arranged in five packages. These materials were developed on the basis of (i) identification of vocabularies of five groups of children prepared through frequent interactions, (ii) analysis and review of day-to-day life situations and environmental set-up of the concerned groups, (iii) competencies identified under MLLs at primary level, (iv) designing potential strategies for presentation of the content areas with specific focus on children's concerns and MLLs.

The lessons were developed in a variety of format and style: name, story, poem, songs, dialogue, travelogue, narration, games, pictorial frame for generating discussions, cards and posters.

There is emphasis on the joyful learning. The learning situations provide ample scope for critical analysis of problems faced by these children. The materials developed as integrated packages are currently being field-tested.

MLL-based Pictorial Materials in Environmental Studies

The NCERT has evolved a design for development of MLL-based 12 teaching-learning materials catering to four semesters of primary level NFE programme under the series Milkar Seekhein. 'A workshop was organised for finalisation of one book in Environmental Studies following the pictorial frame. The book focuses on developing pre- learning basic skills (e.g. observation, differentiation and classification of objects in environment and in work places) among learners.

Local -specific Materials

Under the series Milkar Seekhein, four more titles are under print. The material is based on popular folk stories, children's games, riddles, poems, songs, proverbs and jokes.

Supplementary Materials in Mathematics at Primary Level for Motivational and Joyful Learning Under this programme, levels of children of the third and the fourth semesters in NFE were identified with regard to their power of understanding mathematical terms, concepts, principles, processes and language on the basis of personal interaction with them. Two NFE Centres and two formal primary schools in Delhi were selected for this purpose.

A regional workshop (covering southern region) was' organised for developing exhaustive supplementary materials. Similar materials have been planned to be prepared through regional workshops.

Budgeting of Organisation and Financing of Programmes

Budgetary Provision during X Plan

The system for allocation of funds for literacy and continuing education in India is a part of the allocations for School Education and Literacy. At the Union or Central Government level, there is no other Ministry, which makes a separate allocation for literacy in respect of nonliterate adults. During IX Five Year Plan (1997-98 to 2001-02) the approved outlay for literacy and continuing education programmes was Rs. 630.39 crore. An enhanced allocation amount of Rs 650.97 crores was made out of which an expenditure of Rs 521.19 crore was incurred. During the X Five Year Plan (2002-03 to 2006-07), an allocation of Rs.1241.50 crores was received for Adult Education. The expenditure incurred was Rs. 1148.04, as given in table 1 below.

Table 1: Year wise Allocation and Expenditure under the IX Five Year Plan

Year	*Allocation*	*Expenditure*
2002-03	233.00	216.29
2003-04	233.00	232.50
2004-05	250.00	236.47
2005-06	290.00	249.30
2006-07	235.50	213.48
Total	1241.50	1148.04

As has been the practice, the allocation of funds was clearly earmarked for different components of adult education, as below (Table 2).

Table 2: X Five Year Plan Outlays for Adult Education Programmes

S. No.	*Name of Scheme*	*X Plan Outlay (Rs. in Crores)*
1.	Literacy Campaigns	95.00
2.	Continuing Education	826.00
3.	Jan Shikshan Sansthan	130.00
4.	Support of NGOs	110.00
5.	NLMA	10.00
6.	Directorate of Adult Education	70.00
7.	Population Education	8.00
8.	National Institute of Open Schooling	1.00
	Total	1250.00

As evident from the table 2, the allocation for CE programme was the highest, viz., Rs.826 crores, followed by the allocations for Jan Shikshan Sansthans- Rs. 130 crores and support to NGOs- Rs.110 crores, most of which were the allocations for the SRCs

Contributions from other Sectors/Ministries for Literacy and CEP The target group of that National Literacy Mission addresses are also the same addressed by many other social welfare and development Ministries/departments and its agencies. Their contributions range from earmarking of funds, as part of their own programmes, for awareness and knowledge dissemination, life and livelihood skills imparting/training, releasing their professional/technical personnel to work for literacy and continuing education programmes, but paid by parent department. These agencies include university and college and school teachers both under State and Central Governments purview, professionals from banks and other departments/professional and research institutions, being released to work on secondment basis. The institutional facilities and resource persons provided for training of literacy personnel at national and state levels constitute another instance of the contribution of other Ministries/departments and their agencies. The most important dimension relates to the extension activities to make clientele aware and give them the knowledge, and skills to avail their schemes. Some of these Ministries included Rural Development, Panchayati Raj, Health, Social Justice, Tribal Development, Minorities, Women and Child Development, Agriculture, etc. Such a kind of involvement has been enjoined in education policy and NLM programmes and its implementation guidelines.

ALE in Decentralised/local Bodies' Budget

The Constitutional Amendments (73 and 74) decentralized a large number of social sector, infrastructure and basic amenities related subjects to the elected local self-government bodies, both in urban and rural areas, known as the Nagar Palikas and Panchayats. Adult education, like formal school education, is one of them. But the extent of devolution of resources to panchayats varies from state to state. States such as Karnataka, Kerala, West Bengal, etc., do not only devolve funds directly to panchayats in respect of literacy and continuing education programmes but also accord a great deal of priority for the panchayats and urban local bodies to effectively utilize the funds.

Other Investments including Foreign Bilateral/multilateral Agencies

In the field of adult literacy and continuing education, there has not been any significant external funding, while in respect of primary education, there has been substantial external funding from many bilateral and multilateral agencies. UNESCO has been involved in encouraging and giving awards for innovations and best practices in programmes as well as by institutions engaged in ALE. It has also been involved in promoting research and documentation of innovations and best practices. UNICEF has undertaken a pilot project last year in four states viz., Jharkhand, Chhattisgarh, Madhya Pradesh and Rajasthan to involve college students enrolled in the National Cadet Corps in literacy programme in collaboration with the respective ZSS.

The recently held UNESCO Regional Conference in Support of Global Literacy at New Delhi on 29-30, 2007, and attended by delegates from 14 countries of South, South-West and Central Asian countries recommended that: International partners and donors should give high priority to adult literacy, and support programmes, capacity development, monitoring, evaluation and research; and, as an EFA financing and support mechanism, the EFA Fast Track Initiative should raise awareness of the possibility of using it to support adult literacy and increase its funding in this area.

Support to Literacy and Continuing Education Programmes

From Private/corporate Sector

Literacy and Continuing Education in India has predominantly been a government responsibility except for a very limited scale of NGOs involvement. There has been no tradition of private and corporate sector involvement in literacy programmes, as can be seen in the case of formal education system from pre-primary to higher and professional levels. Of late, there have been a few cases of corporates entering the adult literacy sector using ICT especially computers for literacy. Computer Based Literacy Programme has been undertaken in many states on an experimental basis by the Tata Consultancy Services.

In the State of Rajasthan, especially in Chittorgarh District, there are cases of Public Private Partnerships wherein corporates are engaged jointly with the ZSS in promoting literacy linked livelihood project on a pilot basis covering every single illiterate in the selected villages. There are also instances of corporates undertaking ICT capacity building of literacy and continuing education grassroots workers – Animators (Preraks) of the CE centres and Nodal CECs and also for imparting computer literacy to the neoliterates. Instances such as these are still limited and financially very miniscule in relation to the national budget for the literacy programmes.

Civil Society and Individuals' Support for Literacy and Continuing Education Programmes Civil society support to adult literacy programmes in India could be said to have been one of the most distinguished facets of the whole venture. This has been more so at the level of basic literacy – TLC phase. It is reckoned that the NLM mobilized and brought under the literacy fold nearly 150 million non-literates. They were taught by 12-15 million literacy Volunteers. At least another 2 million academic Resource Persons provided training and other academic and managerial support on voluntary basis. Even at a conservative estimate of Rs. 1000 per Volunteer, and reckoning the average TLC duration to be 10 months (i.e., Rs. 10,000 per Volunteer), the cost to the government on 12 million Volunteers alone would have been Rs. 12,000 crores, if payment were made.

The civil society generosity during the Environment Building (EB) phase, especially for the performances of the cultural troupes, used to be in myriad forms – ranging from welcome arrangement, including arcs and gates, garlands, food for members of cultural troupes and its other staff, electricity, lights and sound system, stage arrangements and the like.

Even on an average of Rs. 10,000 per performance and @ 200 villages per district, the cost of EB to the community in 600 districts would have been Rs. 120 crores. This is just for one cultural performance. There were many literacy meetings, rallies, conventions, cultural performances during the TLC, PLP and CE phases. The money value of community involvement must have been manifold more, leave alone the actual expenses they shouldered. Literacy activists used to vouch for the fact that the civil society generosity was greater among the poorer sections than among the better off sections.

Literacy Volunteers in most cases have been the youth – school/college students, and school/college pass outs or dropouts. Learners'/Individuals' contribution to literacy programmes in Indian context could more appropriately be counted as the family and civil society contribution. The socio-economic profile of the learners, almost as a rule, is one of deprivation. Not only they give their time for literacy and participation in literacy-related functions and events organized. But when the organizers approach the community for contribution, it is the learners whom they approach with greater liberty and expectation. And it is the learners who contribute whatever they could – some times in kind, in the form of time and labour, etc.

The Preraks, who manage the CE Centres almost on full time basis, receive only a nominal/token honorarium. Their counterparts in formal primary education level receive 3-4 times more. Thus, the money value of the Preraks' contribution to continuing education centres too is a significant parameter.

Direct and Indirect Financial Incentives in Support of Literacy and CEP

One of the central features of the mass literacy campaigns, called TLCs in India, has been the principle of voluntarism. No payment of any kind was ever provided to the literacy Volunteers. This was also the case in respect of the learners. The system under the CE Programme has been different. As the Preraks were expected to man the CECs for at least 6 hours a day, an honorarium @ Rs. 500 since 1997 and Rs. 750 from 2007 has been given. Of late, however, many state governments started experimenting payment to the literacy instructors as well. The first case has been Madhya Pradesh in the late 1990s, wherein a Guruji (teacher) identified by a group of learners, register themselves as a society called Padna Badna Samiti (Study and Progress Society).

Upon their registration with Block Development Officer, learning materials were supplied to them besides training to the Gurujis. The Guruji would receive Rs. 100 per person made literate at the end of the literacy campaign, as ascertained by actual testing by an external evaluation agency.

The second State to tryout this model has been Rajasthan. The consideration is that the literacy instructors are engaged in literacy camps which are day long engagements for more than a month.

The learners are also supplied with tea and snacks during the camp. In Karnataka, literacy instructors give nearly 3 hours a day for teaching literacy and they get Rs. 20 a day. The learners get Rs. 10 a day for their participation in the literacy camp. Karnataka also uses the students of IX and XI Standard in the Each One Teach Two programme where a student has to teach two non-literate adults, mainly their own kith and kin or neighbours and receive 10 and 20 marks respectively in their annual examinations.

Benchmarks in regard to Financing Literacy and Continuing

There has been a policy consensus that 6% of GDP must be diverted to education. But there has been no separate benchmark in respect of resource allocation to adult literacy programmes. The notion about realistic benchmark within adult education circles could be seen generally in the recommendations of the Working Groups for Adult Education for the Five Year Plans. The Working Group on Adult Education for the Eleventh Five Year Plan suggested Rs. 34,000 crores against which only Rs. 6000 crores has been allotted for adult literacy and continuing education programmes in the Eleventh Plan..

Management

Monitoring: Monitoring of literacy campaigns is one of the important activities of the Directorate of Adult Education. In order to ensure reliability as well as steady flow of information in literacy campaigns, the State Directorate of Adult Education (SDAEs) have been asked to monitor literacy campaigns. The Directorate has taken steps to strengthen the monitoring system by involving State Directorates in regular monitoring of the progress of literacy campaigns in each of the districts. Detailed guidelines were evolved and issued by the Directorate for strengthening of monitoring system under these guidelines. SDAEs are required to hold monthly meeting in which the presence of Secretary, Zilla Saksharata Samitis, Director, SRC and other resources persons has been made mandatory. The State Directorates are now required to consolidate the district reports at the state level and forward the same to the Central Directorate of Adult Education, which is to examine critically these reports and submit feedback to the State Directorate. The Status Reports of Literacy and Post Literacy Campaigns are brought out at the end of each quarter.

Evaluation

With a view to ensuring effective implementation of the literacy campaigns the NLM has now introduced more meaningful and rigorous evaluation system. Each literacy campaign is now required to take up concurrent evaluation of the ongoing programme through an outside agency nominated by the State Directorates of Adult Education. The State Directorates have been asked to empanel agencies for undertaking concurrent evaluation. Concurrent evaluation aims at quick mid-term appraisal of a project to assess the strengths and weaknesses of an ongoing programme and to identify correctives for improvement of the programme.

Guidelines on Concurrent Evaluation are evolved and circulated to all literacy campaign districts and State Directorates. The NLM had planned for a comprehensive and systematic M&E, anticipating data flows from learners groups on the ground on to the district headquarters, to the states and then to the Centre. Internal monthly monitoring was also expected to be complemented with formal internal evaluations when required. External spot checks were also part of the monitoring plans. The hope was to collect policy oriented feedback that could be collated for use at 6-month intervals. Concurrent Monitoring as well as Quick Appraisals were to be conducted at all the various levels and locations of the overall system. Data in the Monitoring system was to be used to develop program evaluations in all the aspects of formative evaluation, evaluation of instruction, and outcome evaluation. In addition to in-house monitoring and evaluations, large-scope evaluations of TLC's were mandated that were to be paid for by the central government. At least three evaluations had to be conducted in each TLC: (1) a quick appraisals at the beginning; (2) a mid-term evaluation; and (3) an end-term evaluation. The list of questions that evaluations should find answers to were also established. The state governments had to contract these evaluations with outside experts--in university departments, specialized institutes, or NGO's who have acquired a reputation for doing good evaluation work, and were on the approved list. Normative frames for methodology, for testing achievement, for definition of success are also provided.

In addition, an official of the Ministry of Human Resource Development (Department of Education and literacy) of the rank of a Deputy Secretary (Teacher Education) has been assigned to oversee all the matters pertaining to the scheme of Teacher Education and of monitoring the TE scheme in the country as a whole. By 2002, some 14 years after its launch, the NLM, using goal-oriented, area-specific and time-bound strategies, had covered 574 of the nation's 598 districts. As many as 302 districts were already offering continuing education programs. Total enrolment had touched 125 million adults, with some 12 million volunteers leading learners groups. As many as 71.45 million had become literate.

Research and Training

The National Institute of Education Planning and Administration (NIEPA), under the MHRD is the government body conducting research and training in the NFE sector. The

Institute comprises of the Department of school and Non-formal Education, whose prime focus is on the critical issues of school education, non-formal and adult literacy providing strong empirical base in order to contribute more meaningful inputs for developing and improving education. The Department maintains close linkages with government, non-government and international agencies with the objective of restructuring educational system at subnational, national and international levels. Apart from NIEPA, civil society organisations like ASPBAE and Nirantar are actively involved in training and research in the NFE sector.

Organisation of Literacy and Continuing Education within Government

With respect to legislative and policy environment relating to literacy and continuing education in India, and the nodal agency (ies) for its implementation, it would be pertinent to remember the Constitutional set up and governance system in India. India is a federal set up with the Union or Central Government at the national level and State Governments (under 35 States and Union Territories). Education under Indian Constitution is a Concurrent subject and both the Union and State Governments have the right and obligation to promote education – both formal (from the pre-primary to higher education, including all branches and specializations) and non-formal education. On the pattern of the national Five Year Plans, the State Governments too formulate their five year plans, conforming largely to the broad strategies, approaches and priorities spelt out in the national five year plan document.

The same applies to education policies and legislations as well. In respect of literacy, the National Literacy Mission as an arm of the Central Government formulates the policies and strategies on the lines of the NPE 1986 and 1992 and its POA, as well as in conformity with the successive Five Year Plan approaches and priorities with respect to the EFA goals and targets. Within this overall national EFA and adult literacy perspectives, the State governments also align their EFA and adult literacy plans and strategies.

Adult Education People on the Move

If the goal of total literacy in India has slipped out of the realm of the impossible and entered the realm of the achievable, a large part of the credit accrues to the Total Literacy Campaigns (TLCs). The National Literacy Mission (NLM) was set up in 1988 with the goal of making 80 million people, in the age group 15-35, literate by 1995. The Total Literacy Campaigns have been the dominant strategy for achieving this goal.

The Mission has now been given a more ambitious goal of covering 100 million non literates by the year 1999. Children in the age group 9-14 are also included under this scheme where there are no NFE Centres. So far, the TLCs have been extended to 430 districts in the country of which 195 have entered the post literacy phase in 22 states and UTs. An estimated 90 million learners have been enrolled in the programme and 64 million have been made literate.

* The Total Literacy Campaigns have been extended to 430 districts in the country.
* 195 districts of these have entered the post literacy phase.
* An estimated 90 million learners have been enrolled in the programme and 64 million converted into literates.

This trailblazing experiment in literacy has aroused wide interest amongst the international community and has become the role model for many Asian and south Asian countries. At the national level, the current thrust is to consolidate the gains of literacy and to concentrate efforts in the four major states in the Hindi heartland whore the bulk of the illiterate population resides.

The literacy campaigns are area-specific, time-bound, delivered through voluntarism, cost-effective and outcome-oriented, and are implemented by Zilla Saksharata Samitis (District Literacy Societies) usually headed by District Collectors who are the chief executives of their districts.

The campaigns are initiated with appropriate environment building activity coupled with a door-to-door literacy survey during which potential learners and volunteers ate identified.

Suitable primers are developed and primer-specific training is provided to the required personnel. The environment-building activity as well as monitoring and internal evaluation are continued through the teaching/learning activity which accounts for a total of 200 hours.

Continuing Education for Neo-literates

The National Literacy Mission (NLM), besides emphasising other aspects of the programme, lays special emphasis on post literacy and continuing education for neo-literates so that they can be prevented from relapsing into illiteracy. Keeping this in view, the Scheme of Post Literacy and Continuing Education was launched in March 1988 to institutionalise this concept through establishment of 'Jan Shikshan Nilayams' (JSNs) all over the country in a phased manner. The basic objective of the scheme is to provide opportunities of continuing education to neo-literates to facilitate retention of their literacy skills, enable the learners to continue their learning beyond elementary literacy and to create a scope for application of their learning skills for improvement of their living conditions. Currently 195 post-literacy programmes are in progress in the country.

Continuing education is also an indispensable aspect of the strategy of human resource development and of the goal of creation of a learning society. The Scheme of Continuing Education for Neo-literates aims to provide an institutionalised mechanism of continuing education through Continuing Education Centres (CECs) to enable the neo-literates to retain, improve and apply their basic knowledge and skills for satisfaction of their needs and to facilitate continued learning through a self directed process for improvement of the quality of their lives. Under the Scheme the main thrust is given to setting up of CECs to serve as Library, Reading Room, Learning Centre, Training Centre, Information Centre, Charcha Mandal, Developmental Centre, Cultural Centre, Sports Centre and other individual interest promotion programmes centre. CECs are set up in a cluster of 8 to 10 with one of them being designated as the nodal CEC. Ideally, there is one CEC for one village to serve a population of 1500 to 2000 which includes 500 neo-literates or other targeted beneficiaries like the dropouts of primary School. In terms of content, continuing education has been classified broadly into four categories:

* Equivalency Programmes (EPs): designed as alternative education programmes equivalent to existing formal general or vocational education.
* Income Generating Programmes (IGPS): help participants acquire or upgrade vocational skills enabling them to take up income generating activities.
* Quality of Life Improvement Programmes (QLIP) these aim to equip the learners and the community with that essential knowledge, attitude, value and skills both as individuals and members of the community.
* Individual's Interest Promotion Programmes (IIPP) these provide opportunity for individuals to participate in and learn about their own chosen social, cultural, spiritual, health, physical and artistic interests.

Management of Non-formal Education Programme at the Micro Level

Micro planning is a process of designing "a family-wise and child-wise plan of action" by which "every child regularly attends school or NFE centre, continues his/her education at the place suitable to him/her, and completes at least 8 years of schooling or its equivalent at the non-formal centre." A revenue village would be ideal for specific planning; however, micro planning for UEE may be carried out at the Block, Taluk, District levels. Within this area the steps by which this micro level planning will be operationalised are:

i) The Village Education Committee and similar participatory structures at Block, Taluk and District levels would play an important role in operationalising micro planning.

ii) Mobilizing community participation through environment building activities such as jathas, street plays, folk songs, etc.

iii) Ascertaining educational requirements of the areas through a family-wise survey to be conducted with the help of the community.

iv) Bringing to school all children who can be enrolled, and providing NFE centres or other innovative and supportive channels for those who cannot go to school.

v) Ensuring that all children, specially girls and SC/ST children, regularly and actually participate in elementary education.

vi) Planning for the improvement of schools or NFE centres so that effective learning takes place.

vii) Reorienting and strengthening local level administrative and resource support systems.

viii) Decentralizing educational administration.

ix) Integrating all the schemes being implemented in the area which would contribute to the improvement of school system (e.g. Operation Blackboard, JRY, ICDS, Social Forestry, Health Check-up etc.).

In most of the total literacy campaign (TLC) districts, a positive environment has already been created for taking up Micro planning Projects. Many District Literacy Societies who have launched the TLCs have shown keen interest in elementary education and some of them have submitted project proposals under Micro planning to the MHRD. The initiative shown by these societies needs to be encouraged. DIETS/SCERTS and voluntary agencies will also be involved in the implementation of this programme. Micro planning can be effective only when there is total integration of efforts and resources – human and financial from all quarters. While centrally sponsored schemes, OB, JRY, NFE, etc. will provide the major share of funds for improving school facilities and access, the State Governments will provide resources for opening new schools. Additional resources required for survey, environment building, training of VEC members, etc. will be provided by the Centre under this scheme.

Micro planning will be made operational in about 20 project areas on an experimental basis during 1992-93. Based on the experience gained during the course of implementation it will be expanded to cover about 100 districts during the 8th Plan. In due course the entire country will be covered, thus ensuring universal access and enrolment, and universal retention.

Need for Micro Level Programme

There is no doubt that one of the important aims of development in the developing countries of Asia and the Pacific has been the removal of poverty amongst the masses. It is now accepted that in poor countries production and planning need to be specifically geared to the satisfaction of basic human needs.

In fact, the United Nations Development Programme in its Human Development Report (1997) provided HPI (Human Poverty Index) values for several countries in the Asia-Pacific region which clearly indicate the existence of large numbers of people below the poverty line. Income-generating programmes (IGPs) have a major role to play in alleviating poverty in these countries.

In India, the need for poverty alleviation has been recognized almost since the nation's independence 50 years ago. While initially it was expected that the overall economic development strategies incorporated in the Government's five-year development plans would also reduce poverty among the masses, later on (perhaps in the 1960s) programmes specifically designed and addressed to the cause of poverty alleviation among the rural poor became indispensable.

In the last four decades a number of such programmes have been and still are being implemented in this country. Simultaneously, the control of population growth through family welfare programmes and the eradication of illiteracy through special literacy drives were conceived and implemented as important planks of human development. Thus Family Welfare Programmes (FWP) and Universalisation of Primary Education (UPE) have been important aspects of development planning in India.

However, for a multiplicity of reasons, not the least important of which has been inefficient implementation, the expected results from family welfare and universal primary education programmes have not come about. To be sure, there have been marked increases in literacy levels, and also, at least in some selected areas of the country, an appreciable reduction in TFR (Total Fertility Rate) in the last two decades. Along with the extension of formal schooling facilities to the far corners of the country, non-formal education (NFE) programmes have been vigorously implemented over the last two decades as part of India's commitment to the Education for All (EFA) initiative sponsored by UNESCO.

While it may be difficult to link NFE directly with poverty alleviation programmes, basic education does form the basis for skill development and the empowerment of the deprived which in turn enables the poor to participate in IGPs for poverty alleviation. In India, both governmental as well as non-governmental/ voluntary organizations are implementing NFE programmes. Not all of these organizations are directly involved in IGPs as well, but many of them have also taken up such programmes along with their other activities directed towards EFA.

NFE and IGPs

The NFE programmes are being implemented by the Central and State Governments as well as non-governmental organizations (NGOs) to fulfil the national commitment to Universal Primary Education (UPE) and Education For All (EFA), as set out in the National Education Policy of 1986. NFE is commonly defined as any organized education activity outside the established formal system – whether operating separately or as an important feature of some broader activity – that is intended to serve identifiable learning clienteles and learning objectives.

Shri. J. P. Naik, the doyen of the Indian education system, has discussed in great detail the three channels of learning, viz., incidental, non-formal and formal. According to Naik, the non-formal education channels cover both liberal arts and vocational education; they are traditional as well as modern; they have continued to play an important role in the education and socialization of individuals, both before and after the birth of formal education. NFE addresses all three educational objectives of imparting knowledge, teaching skills and promoting values, although in the traditional forms it was most commonly used for teaching skills (J. P. Naik: Some Perspectives on Non-formal Education, 1977).

APPEAL uses the term "non-formal" for courses and programmes offered outside the formal system. The formal system covers programmes offered by established education institutions such as schools, technical colleges and universities. Thus the term "non-formal education" is expected to cover all organized courses of studies outside the formal system, irrespective of whether these are for general, liberal arts, vocational or technical education, and also regardless of the level of education (APPEAL, UNESCO, PROAP, ATLP – CE, vol. I, 1999).

In recent years, however, non-formal education has come to be identified in India with the primary level education provided outside the formal system. It is also sometimes referred to as the "equivalency programme" because students (children ages 9-14) are provided a condensed course and prepared for Standards IV or V of the formal school in a shortened period of two or three years. The children who missed the bus in the first instance for one reason or the other are thus able to join the formal mainstream later on. For the purposes of this research study, we endorse the concept of NFE as elaborated by Naik and endorsed by UNESCO. To reiterate, NFE is the channel which covers both liberal arts and vocational education outside the formal mode. Moreover, vocational training programmes (or IGPs) may be independent of liberal arts education at the elementary level.

We must emphasize that the eradication of illiteracy from a nation that is set to become the most populated in the world within only a few decades has had to be necessarily accorded the top billing in national priorities. However, this does not mean that the skills development and empowerment of the rural poor have been neglected. With the emergence of millions of neo-literates due to successful total literacy campaigns, the need to train these individuals in the skills needed for raising their incomes has become all the more pressing. Several governmental, non-governmental and voluntary organizations have taken upon themselves the task of training neo-literate as well as illiterate adults in income generating skills and activities. There is no central or even state-level direction in regard to the type and content of these training programmes aimed at promoting income generation in the rural areas. These organizations are locally based, and build up their programmes and activities around local needs. Many of them are devoted to the empowerment of rural women so as to make them active partners, along with men, in earning for their families.

Assessing Facilities Available at the Micro Level

The concept of basic human needs has recently gained favour in the thinking of experts concerned with new strategies of development for poor countries. These thinkers are unanimous in their agreement that production and planning must be specifically geared to the satisfaction of these needs. Poverty is the condition where human beings are not able to meet the basic needs of life. One way to determine the number of people in this condition is to use the concept of the "poverty line." There are several indicators we can use to determine where to draw this line:

- per capita income
- household consumption
- per capita consumption of specific items such as cereals
- proportion of expenditure on food items
- calorie intake
- basic metabolic rate and other medical indicators

There is no single method combining all these indicators to obtain figures on the number of people living below the poverty line. Thus there are wide variations in estimates of the percentage of people living in poverty. In India, for example, these estimates range from about 25 per cent to a little more than 50 per cent of the population. Further attempts to define poverty in relation to area or region, caste and community, education and occupation, or the ruralurban divide have only added to the confusion.

The United Nations Development Programme (Human Development Report, 1997), using a few important variables (people expected to die before age 40, illiterate adults, people without access to health services, unsafe drinking water, underweight children, etc.), has calculated a human poverty index (HPI) for developing countries in the Asia-Pacific region. The HPI for India is 36.7 per cent, compared to Singapore (6.6), Thailand (11.7), China (17.5), Pakistan (46.8) and Cambodia (52.5). Using this index and other poverty indices, we can assume that almost 40 per cent of India's population live below the poverty line. In other words, these people are unable to satisfy basic human needs.

Treatment of Immediate and Long Term Problems

According to the UNDP report a little more than a quarter of the total population of the Asia-Pacific region are poor. They are mostly illiterate, with low incomes. There is an uneven distribution of poor people within a country, with a high concentration in rural areas. The poor are exposed to many risks and hazards due to their living conditions and means of livelihood. The appalling living conditions of the poor, especially in regard to inadequate ventilation, unsafe drinking water and poor sanitation, expose them to constant disease.

The poor are generally without land and capital, and have no way to acquire the skills needed for remunerative labour. Because of social and legal discrimination, women and girls are more commonly the victims of poverty. They have to accept without question their subordinate status in the home and in society. Children from poor families suffer both physically and psychologically. Malnutrition forces them to start life with poor health, impaired development and reduced resistance to disease. The poor are also found in urban areas also, although in relatively fewer numbers in some countries. The urban poor are mostly squatters residing in slums or destitute families and individuals living in the open air. They lack access to basic services and are exposed to health hazards and crime. They are compelled to earn a living as casual wage workers, street-side vendors, rickshaw pullers, beggars or prostitutes. The hallmarks of the poor, especially the rural poor, are illiteracy, malnutrition, poor health, and economic, social and cultural exploitation by the more powerful groups in society.

Social and Educational Factors Affecting Micro Level Management

There is now enough empirical evidence (if any was really needed) to indicate that a large proportion of the Indian population is not in a position to meet basic needs as defined in terms of employment, consumption, health, nutrition, life expectancy, child mortality, literacy, opportunities for schooling, and access to public goods or property. As a long-term measure for the eradication of poverty and improving the quality of life, broad-based literacy and basic education for all is the main foundation and an essential precondition. Thus, in the developing countries, raising literacy and education levels should be viewed as the principal instrument of poverty eradication. Although mainstream economists may insist that poverty will be addressed by the regular growth processes of the economy, many of them also agree that economic growth alone cannot alleviate poverty without structural changes in favour of the poor. There is also a growing realization that market mechanisms are neither efficient nor reliable instruments for allocating resources when the income distribution is highly distorted as is the case in India (and other densely populated countries of South Asia, like Pakistan and Bangladesh). The need for a direct attack on poverty in these countries cannot be over-emphasized.

In India poverty eradication is one of the major objectives of planned development. The magnitude of the problem is still quite staggering. Thirty-six per cent of the Indian population were below the poverty line in 1993-94, the latest year for which data are available, and the absolute number of poor was 320 million, of which 244 million (37 per cent of the rural population) lived in rural areas. The main determinants of poverty are 1) a lack of income and purchasing power due to lack of productive employment and considerable underemployment (not to lack of employment per se); 2) a continuous increase in the price of food, especially food grains which account for 70-80 per cent of consumption; and 3) inadequate social infrastructure, which affects the quality of life of the people and their employability.

It is recognized that a dramatic increase in incomes is by itself not enough to improve the quality of life of the poor. Unless all citizens, especially the poor, have certain basic minimum services, their living conditions cannot improve. These minimum services include, among other things, literacy, education, primary health care, safe drinking water and nutritional security. The Government of India has identified seven basic minimum services: safe drinking water, primary health care facilities, universal primary education, nutrition for school and preschool children, shelter for the poor, accessible roads for all communities, and a public distribution system with a focus on the poor. The Ninth Plan (1997-2002) places special emphasis on these seven basic minimum services and their provision in partnership with State Governments and local government institutions.

Direct poverty alleviation programmes on an expanded scale are also an important feature of the Ninth Plan. These programmes are oriented towards strengthening the productive potential of the economy and providing more opportunities for involving the poor in the economic process. Broadly, there are schemes for generating incomes through supplementary employment, for improving the welfare of the poor in rural and urban areas and for a targeted public distribution system to ensure that the poor have access to food grains at prices they can afford. These programmes are based on approaches and methods that involve the poor themselves in the process of poverty eradication and economic growth. Local government institutions, voluntary organizations and community based self-help groups are closely involved in these programmes.

Utilization of Financial and Human Resources—Needed Organisational Setup

The poverty alleviation programmes serve as the basis for a direct attack on poverty. These programmes essentially aim at generating incremental incomes for the poor. This means a direct transfer of additional purchasing power into the hands of people living below the poverty line. It is also an attempt to alleviate the problem of almost negligible "trickle down" from economic growth to the bottom rungs of society because of structural constraints. India has implemented a number of income and employment generating programmes for poverty alleviation in the last three decades.

A. Self-Employment Programmes

1. Integrated Rural Development Programme (IRDP)
2. Training of Rural Youth for Self-Employment (TRYSEM)
3. Supply of Improved Toolkits to Rural Artisans (SITRA).

B. Rural Wage Employment Programmes

1. Rural Manpower Programme (RMP)
2. Crash Scheme for Rural Employment (CSRE)
3. National Rural Employment Programme (NREP)
4. Rural Labourers Employment Guarantee Programme (RLEGP)
5. Jawahar Rozgar Yojana (JRY) (a rural works programme introduced in 1989-1990, which later incorporated the NREP and RLEGP).

C. Special Area Development Programmes

1. Drought Prone Areas Programme (DPEP)
2. Desert Development Programme (DDP)
3. Hill Area Development Programme (HADP).

D. Development of Women and Children in Rural Areas (DWCRA)

Treatment of Immediate and Long Term Problems: The "Adivasi Sahaj Shikshan Pariwar" is located in the village of Maswan, a tribal community in the Thane district of Maharashtra state. The majority of the population are Malhar Koli, a prominent ethnic minority in the district. Kunabi and Agari are other ethnic groups found in this area. Twenty-five years ago, most of the tribal area of Thane district was unknown to the rest of the world. Not only government agencies but also social services organizations failed to take any notice of this area. The people here were deprived of all civic amenities, affected by ignorance, poverty, malnutrition, disease and unemployment. Starvation and the untimely death of family members had become routine occurrences in their day-to-day lives. Only a few primary schools existed there. Even those people who lived nearby were unwilling to send their children to school. One of the most important reasons was poverty. Although education was free, parents could not afford to send their children to school because they would lose the earnings of these children, who collected firewood or edible items from the forest for sale in the village markets. Another compelling reason was the need for older children, especially girls, to look after the younger siblings and do the household chores like fetching water, cooking and tending cattle.

A social worker and ardent follower of Jayaprakash Narayan, the doyen of Indian socialists, made up her mind to work for the uplift of these tribal people. In 1978, which was declared the International Year of the Child, the Samajawadi Mahila Sabha decided to undertake a project on tribal children's education. The Sabha initially surveyed 320 families in and around Maswan to find out the reasons for people's indifference to education. The results indicated that these children were not attending school because 1) they did not have sufficient clothes to wear due to poverty; 2) they were receiving one meal a day by working as caregivers to younger children; 3) they were forced to stay at home to look after their younger siblings because both parents were absent; and 4) they could not understand the language of the textbooks due to the differences between this language and the tribal dialect. As a result, they had difficulties in comprehension and could not generate any interest in studying.

On 1 April 1978, the first tribal welfare centre was established at Maswan. As the life style of the tribal people differed from that of urbanites, formal methods of teaching could scarcely be successful. On the advice of Shri J. P. Naik, the leading Indian educator, centre staff decided to adopt Non-formal methods of teaching. Staff members visited almost every hut in the village and were thus able to recruit some 70 to 80 children to attend classes. People from surrounding villages developed an interest in this experiment and requested such centres in their *padas* or hamlets. Within a year, eleven such centres had started. Each centre is a small institution carrying out multifarious activities related to education, health and nutrition, skill development for income generation, and social welfare. In May 1980, an independent trust was established, which was registered under the Societies Registration Act with the name "Adivasi Sahaj Shikshan Pariwar" (ASSP).

Support

The ASSP's main objective is tribal welfare. This means involvement in activities that lead to empowerment and improvement in the living standards of the ethnic minorities living in this area. A Board of Trustees and an Executive Committee supervise the activities of the ASSP. It gets its funding and donations from the following institutes and organizations:

- Central Social Welfare Board, New Delhi
- Department of Human Resources, New Delhi
- State Children's Welfare Society, Mumbai
- Khadi Gramodyog Mandal, Mumbai
- German Agro Action, Germany
- Gandhi Smarak Nidhi, New Delhi
- Samajawadi Mahila Sabha
- Rashtra Seva Dal
- Bhoomi Sena
- National Institute of Rural Development
- Yusuf Meharally Centre
- Palghar Taluka Panchayat Samiti
- Indian Institute of Education
- Lesley Swahey Centre.

Infrastructure Facilities

The ASSP owns approximately four acres of land at Maswan. Facilities at present consist of a bakery, hostel, dispensary and accommodations for staff. The ASSP provides a hostel for 25 to 30 girls attending secondary school, although the Social

Welfare Department gives grants only for 24. The ASSP also has a small library with a good collection of books. Teachers as well as children use this resource to good advantage. At Dhuktan, a neighbouring village, the ASSP has bought 1.5 acres of land for paddy cultivation. The institute also owns five acres of land at Koknare, another village close by. Of the eleven centres, five of them are established on the institute's own land. For transport, the ASSP has two jeeps, one of which is used as a mobile dispensary.

Programmes and Activities

This project, which initially focused on the education of tribal children, has over the last twenty years gradually diversified and expanded its activities into various areas of human welfare. The ASSP now aims at the overall development of ethnic minority communities in the vicinity of Maswan, with the main emphasis on education and health and targeting children and tribal women in particular.

Non-formal Education Programmes: At present, the ASSP operates eleven centres, with Maswan as the central office. Initially each centre served three groups separately. There was a *sahaj shikshan* or non-formal education class (6 to 14 years), a nursery (3 to 5 years) and a creche for children under 3. But at present only two activities, nurseries and crèches, are continuing at most of the centres. Gradually the number of children in the first group kept on decreasing. In fact, the decline of the Non-formal education classes is one of the significant achievements of the ASSP, because as parents became more aware of the importance of education, they started enrolling their children in formal schools. At present, most children above 6 years of age are enrolled in the regular primary school. At each centre, a trained teacher, an assistant teacher and two "ayahs" (nannies) are appointed. These teachers and ayahs participate in a number of workshops, short-term courses and camps. The removal of poverty has been by far the most important developmental strategy adopted by the developing countries in their post-liberation phase. There is a unanimous opinion that in the poor countries production planning needs to be specifically geared to the satisfaction of basic human needs. In India, the need for poverty alleviation has been recognized almost since its independence from colonial rule 50 years ago. In the last four decades, programmes specifically designed and addressed to the cause of poverty alleviation amongst the poor have been implemented throughout the country. Simultaneously, the control of population through family welfare programmes and the eradication of illiteracy through special literacy drives were conceived and implemented as important planks of human development. The last two decades have witnessed considerable improvement in the literacy levels and also appreciable reduction in the total fertility rate. Non-formal Education (NFE) programmes have been vigorously implemented to attract those who never went to school or who dropped out for various reasons, not the least important being dire poverty. While NFE may not be directly linked with poverty alleviation programmes, it is clear that basic education forms the basis for skill development and empowerment of the deprived which in turn enables the poor to participate in poverty alleviation programmes.

The Effects of Programmes for Poverty Alleviation, Literacy and Family Welfare When we think of alleviating the poverty of the rural masses, we think of various ways of transferring purchasing power into the hands of the poorest among the poor, of meeting their basic needs through social investments and also putting a check on their growing numbers. In India, poverty alleviation programmes are given high priority in the national development plans and hence large-scale funding is provided for large-scale wage employment programmes undertaken in rural areas, and for programmes that provide financial and infrastructural assistance for incremental income earning through self-employment in agriculture and allied activities, industries, services and business. In addition, there are training programmes in production skills for rural as well as urban youth who are illiterate, neo-literate or school dropouts.

A special scheme for women and children in rural areas is also being implemented. Similarly, special development programmes are dedicated to improving the lives of people residing in drought-prone, desert and remote hill areas. It is generally accepted that the operation of these programmes over the last 3-4 decades has resulted in lowering the poverty level. About 30 years ago, almost 55 per cent of the population was estimated to be below the poverty line. According to official data, the percentage dropped to 36 in 1993-94 and to 26 in 2001. As indicated in the first section of this report, the UNDP human poverty index for 1995-96 gives the figure of 36.7 per cent for India. There may be variations in the estimates by different sources, but it is generally believed that the number of people living below the poverty line has steadily come down in the last two decades. The extent to which the poverty alleviation programmes mentioned above have contributed to this decrease is, however, difficult to assess quantitatively.

The importance of NFE in this country where almost half of the world's illiterates live was widely recognized in the 1960s. However, actual NFE projects got under way only in the late 1970s. The NFE programmes were implemented by a large number of NGOs and voluntary associations that were locally based and enjoyed the confidence of local communities. Such an atmosphere was necessary in the rural areas, especially for increasing the enrolment of girls. The newly introduced Sarva Shiksha Abhiyan (SSA), Educational Guarantee Scheme (EGS) and the Alternative and Innovative Education (AIE) programme also aimed to provide basic education to rural children, especially in the most remote and poorly served districts.

Literacy has progressed well in the decade after India signed the Jomthien declaration. NFE was reinforced and strengthened to reach all corners of the country. The literacy rate rose by 13 percentage points between 1991 and 2001 (from 52 to 65 per cent). Interestingly, for the first time the rate of increase in literacy was higher for females (14.9 percentage points) than males (11.7 percentage points). The male-female gap in literacy rate has also come down from 24.8 (1991) to 21.7 (2001). NFE is believed to have helped increase female literacy, as this is a mode far better suited to rural girls than formal full-time schooling. However, there is hardly any scope for complacency when we learn that, according to the latest official statistics, 29 per cent of the children of school-going age

(6-14 years) were not attending school in the year 2000. Almost 60 per cent of these children were girls. The national rate of population growth has come down from 24.8 per cent in 1971 to 21.3 per cent in 2001, in spite of the increased number of couples in the reproductive age groups. The demographic transition phase characterized by a drop in the death rate accompanied by a fall in the birth rate seems to manifest itsel in India even if rather late. However, the rate of populatio growth is still high, being more than 2 per cent per annum which is a stumbling block to the quick alleviation of povert in this country.

Utilization of Financial and Human Resources-Need Organisational Set up There is a large number of young m and women in the countryside who are literate (or nev literate), willing to learn new skills and who can work themselves. What is more important to know is that th number has steadily grown over the last 2-3 decades and t they cannot be gainfully employed in the traditional fa enterprises. The fragmentation of land holdings, an influ factory produced goods into rural areas, and the increasing of labour-saving equipment and machinery in the r al vocati and professions have resulted in unemployment al frustrat among the rural youth. With both formal n-formal mo of education reaching even the smalle anges, the levelf literacy have increased.

an increasing numr ducation in Mahar

A noteworthy developme ucted. But parent of village girls are now tside the home fo state, where this s or service centres reluctant to allo ey can use only a or to set u ung women in rura to lea receive no encourager all of the programmes in n interviewed by researc ers of age, were literate (be stages or students at N rn any skills that generating self-employment enterprises. There is no relationship between the traditional family occupations and the new skills learnt. The emphasis is on self-reliance rather than wage employment. Men prefer to learn technical skills (mechanical, electrical, electronic, workshop technology, etc.) while women prefer activities like tailoring, knitting, embroidery, baking, and pathology lab work. In urban areas, the demand is for skills leading to small-scale production of domestic consumer goods. Computer literacy courses have recently been introduced and are in great demand by young women and men, in both urban and rural areas.

All of the vocational training programmes are conducted according to the principles and methods of NFE. There is generally no insistence on any minimum level of educational qualifications, although trainees are expected to be able to read and write. There is a great deal of flexibility when it comes to course content, course duration and the scheduling of classes. Much emphasis is placed on practical work, learning through doing or working. Hands-onexperience is given greater importance than theoretical teaching. Capital shortages and the inability to find new markets for goods and services in the rural areas, which are being increasingly invaded by the urban sector, are the main problems faced by these trained young men and women. Nevertheless, the increasing demand for these non-formal [illegible] vocational training clearly shows that such training is be[illegible] [illegible]many. Several success stories were noted during the [illegible] study. Some individuals claimed that because of the [illegible] hands-on experience, their earning pote[illegible] [illegible] three or four times.

We can say by way of a final conclusio[illegible] [illegible] a cost-effective mode of vocational education [illegible] model, contributing to the potential of individua[illegible] their own incomes and improve their standard of [illegible] to create a new culture of rural entrepreneurship [illegible] dependent on the declining traditional occupatio[illegible]

UNIT-V

Agencies of Non-formal Education

Agencies of Non-formal Education—Role of University and Voluntary Agencies

India's open universities, adult education programs, and widespread distance education cater to the needs of a diverse population. The Department of Education, since 1980, has been sponsoring Non-formal education (NFE) for children of ages 6 to 14, especially those marginalized from the formal system for various reasons, especially poverty. In 2001, some 740 voluntary agencies were implementing NFE programs in 25 states. Another 85 agencies sanctioned 9,485 NFE centres during 2000.

The National Open School (NOS) was established in November 1989 as an autonomous registered society to examine and certify students up through pre-degree courses. NOS provides the following programs: (a) foundation course, (b) secondary education course, (c) senior secondary education course, (d) open vocational education program, (e) life enrichment program, and (f) basic education for Universal Elementary Education (UEE). NOS provides individualized support through a network of study centres. Also called Accredited Institutions, the 972 study centres serve about 400,000 students all over the country. The aforementioned Indira Gandhi National Open University (IGNOU) also provides distance education.

Traditional societies have thrived on their Non-formal systems of education. "Ancient records of the Indian tradition testify to the search for the Rishis and sages for higher knowledge (*para vidya*), and their discoveries have been continuously transmitted to posterity and kept alive through its history, marked by periods of expansion, specialization, decline and renewal" (1998). Long before the bureaucratized western structures of schooling mushroomed in the "less developed" nations, India's Non-formal education was enshrined in its familial and cultural units.

Students and educators in India thus usually share a common history and a legacy of collective wisdom. This learning process reinforces the curricular thrusts in structured settings. To isolate the two systems from each other is to fracture the whole learning process. There are fields—fine arts, medicine, astronomy, and numerous other skills—where knowledge has been transmitted from one generation to another within familial ties without any formal structures. One can argue that India's cultural continuity is indebted to this informal system of education. Community services have been existing in India since the inception of Gram Panchayats, but the term Community Information Service (CIS) is of recent origin, and may have its roots in the West. It has been emerging as a fact of public library system in the developing countries; with Britain and America taking the lead in this regard.

The term Community Information (CI) was coined to describe the services as these were neighbourhood based, sewing as signposts to charities and services available within the welfare system. The Library Association (London) defines Community Information Services (CISs) as "services which assist individuals and groups with daily problem-solving and with participation in the democratic process. The services concentrate on the needs of those who do not have ready access to other sources of assistance and on the most important problems that people have to face, problems to do with their homes, their jobs and their rights". According to A Bunch, who first attempted synthesisntion of Cl has the following two common aspects:

1. Providing information in the community to help people with daily problem solving or in raising the quality of their lives.
2. Concerned with a specific clientele, namely, those who belong to the lower socioeconomic groups or are disadvantaged through an inability to obtain, understand, or act on information that affects \heir lives.

JC Donohue, one of the earliest creators of CIS, stated that the following two types of information should be provided by CISs:

1. Survival information such as that related to health, housing, income, legal protection, economic opportunities, political rights, etc. (Information and Referral).
2. Citizen action information, needed for effective participation as individual or as members of a group in the social, political, legal, and economic process (Public Policy Information).

The public libraries which are working with a statutory provision should take a lead in India. The Government of India appointed a Committee under the Chairmanship of Prof. DP Chattopadhyaya (Chairman, RRRLF) to prepare a draft of National Policy on Library and Information System (NAPLIS).

The draft of NAPLIS, submitted to the Government of India in March 1986, has strongly emphasised on, the need for provision of information services to citizens. It included the following under the heading Objectives of National Policy. Library and information sources are vital for all sectors of national activity. The availability of information, expeditiously and pinpointedfy, supports all decision-making processes at all levels. Relevant information accelerates the pace of national development. An informed citizen is an asset to a democratic system of government and the proper utilisation of information can improve the quality of citizens. Further, it stated that one of the main aims of the national library and information policy should be to foster, promote and sustain, by all appropriate means, the organisation, availability and use of information in all sectors of national activity. It is heartening to note that Prof. Chattopadhyaya Committee had stated that the main thrust in the area of public library system should go to the rural public library. It said that a village or a village cluster with an adequate population should have a community library which will also serve as an information centre. Resources of different agencies engaged in the work of public health, adult education, local self-government and such others may be pooled to build up the composite centre.

In March 1986, the Government of India appointed another committee calkd Empowered Committee under the Chairmanship of Prof. DP Chattopadhyaya to suggest what recommendations of NAPLIS report should be adopted. The Empowered Committee in its report, submitted in March 1988, underlined the importance of CISs. It said, "NAPLIS h a recommended that the main thrust should go to the rural public library which should be developed like a community library and information centre". It will serve all sections of the community: the adult and the children, the literate and the illitrate, through reading materials and audio-visual packages. Such a rural library or community centre library should be developed by pooling the resources of different Central Government and State Government agencies engaged in rural developmental activities. The Empowered Committee feels that this kind of rural library service should be made available in each village under the Minimum Needs Programme by 2000 AD.

It appears that some of the above recommendations are in the process in the Department of Culture, Human Resources Development, Government of India. A developing country like India may concentrate its services to a few thrust areas in the initial stages. Some of the suggested areas are:

- Health-immunisation, hospitals, specialists, admission procedures, first aid, grandma's remedies;
- Education-courses, colleges, teachers, admissions procedures;
- Employment-both local and out-station, including self-employment;

- Agriculture—new farming methods, seeds, insecticides, fertilisers, etc.;
- Village industries-assistance for setting up, financial sources, technical know-how;
- Utilisation of local resources-human and material;
- Transport—bus, rail, etc.;
- Daily necessities-strong supplying provisions and foodgrains at reasonable rates;
- Sources of finance-banks, governments subsidies, etc.;
- Redressal of grievances of villagers-contact points, government agencies/departments;
- Government welfare schemes-rural development, weaker sections, etc.;
- Consumer services;
- Housing; and
- Schemes mainly intended for most backward areas.

So, the Government should direct the universities to include CIS in their curriculum, arrange orientation programmes for the inservice candidates and also insist upon public libraries, Nehru Ywak Kendras and Chaitanya Kendras started under adult and continuing education programmes to start CIS in their organisations. An attempt was made to collect four authoritative papers from the experts working in CIS area. These papers give theoretical foundation of CIS and highlight new vistas in modernising the services with a network, and even marketing the CIS. It is hoped that the use of this material will be highly benefited in revamping the libraries with novel and needy community information service.

Scheme of Assistance to Voluntary

Voluntary agencies are given financial assistance for undertaking pro-Agencies working in the Field of jects of -tional literacy, post-literacy, publications and Resource -dult Education, organisation of workshops and uring 1983-84, 350 voluntary agencies in 16 ries have been approved for undertaking Centres for functional literacy and post-literacy work. These agencies will cover nearly 4.90 lakhs people. Grants amounting to Rs. 288 lakhs have been sanctioned by the Minister to these voluntary agencies for this purpose.

Departments of NFE at the National Universities

The University Grants Commission (UGC) has played a key role in shaping the character of University Adult Education in India since the launching of the National Adult Education Programme in 1978. During the last two decades, the UGC has not only formulated a number of guidelines on adult continuing education programmes, but has also provided one hundred per cent funding support to universities to implement the programmes. Today as many as 93 universities have set up Adult Education Departments and they have implemented a variety of programmes.

National Framework for the Training of NFBE Educators and Trainers

The history of adult education in India shows that due emphasis and importance has been given to training strategies, programmes and policies. With the launching of the NLM, Project Formulation Guidelines were issued. These guidelines were supposed to be implemented in operationalising the Literacy and Adult Education Programme throughout the country. At the National Level Training Programmes are designed by the NLM, Directorate of AE, and Management institutions. At the State Level the Programmes are designed and organized by the State Resource Centres (SRCs), State Literacy Mission Authorities (SLMA) and other educational institutions. At the District Level the training programmes are designed and organized by SRCs, the District Institutions for Educational Training (DIET).

The Zilla Saksharata Samities (ZSS), Jan Shikshan Sansthans (JSS) and the NGOS, while at the Community Level the training programme is run by the ZSS, the JSS, NGOs, the Block Resource Centres (BRC) and the Literacy Resource Centres (LRC). To conduct training programmes at different levels a pyramidal approach is adapted, with the Core Group the Resource Persons, Master Trainers and lastly

Implementers. The training of core group and key resource persons is conducted by SRC. The Resource persons train the master trainers and the master trainers train the Implementers. The funds are provided to district agencies by National Literacy Mission (NLM) through the State Literacy Mission Authority (SLMA).

The training Programme available for NFE facilitators have facility for Pre Service (basic role and responsibilities), In service (when new issues are introduce to programme) and Short Course which is need based. The programmes are organized in the following methods: the SRC training group travels to the districts for training, the Core group Conducts District Resource Persons (RP) training, the RPs go to Block for Master Trainers (MT) training, and the MTs go to the Panchayats for Volunteers (VTs) training. For occasional courses, they go up to the district/ block or to the State level also. The main contents of the training programme are to explain the participants the Concept of Continuing Education programme and its importance; the establishment of CE Centres (CEC) and Nodal CECs; the management of CEC and Nodal CEC; the programmes organized at these CECs; the roles and duties of a facilitator and the strengthening of the CEC and launching innovative programmes and skill development programmes The participants of the training programmes are selected at District/Block/Panchayat level by the ZSS (District Literacy Committees) while for the Core group and the other special training; SRC gives the criteria for selection of trainees. The SRC assesses the usefulness and impact of the training programmes through its Research and Development Cell. The State also assesses by monitoring and external evaluation.

Information about Major types of NFBE Activities

There are many, many providers of NFE programmes in India. Apart from the NGO initiatives, including the famous ones like the BGVS and Nirantar, there are Central Government and State Government Initiatives too. It really would not be an exaggeration to say that almost every ministry except the Defence, Home and External Affairs runs some kind of programme or the other. This is apart from the TLC initiative under the NLM. The medium of instruction is the State vernacular that is in the dominant language of the state. Thus in Uttar Pradesh, Bihar or Jharkhand, it is Hindi and field observations show that this creates problems for, say, the ethnic indigenous groups like the tribals. Also, the official language of the state is the standard colloquial one and often not followed by the speakers of particular dialects.

The teaching-learning methods of the programmes are generally hard to come by. For most programmes, (the exception being the TLCs of the 1990s) there are hardly any comprehensive evaluation reports available in the public domain on these aspects. Sometimes it is even difficult to pin-point who runs a particular programme. The NIOS and the NCVT (National Council of Vocational Training) schemes are run by the government approved centres (ITIs) as well as NGOs like Don Bosco.

The picture gets more complicated as one tries to compile an indicative list of programmes that are supposed to provide basic literacy plus, that is try to impart life skills and/or economic development (income-augmenting) skills. The bigger picture that has to be kept in mind is that of the low literacy rates (65.4 percent overall, 75.4 percent male and 54.1 percent female in 2001) as well as the elementary school (class 1-5) dropout rate (31.4 percent in 2003-4) in India.

Also, insofar as skill training (that is imparting literacies apart from basic literacy and numeracy) is concerned, it has to be kept in mind that "the actual number of persons expected to enter the labour force is about 12.3 million persons per annum…the number of those entering with some degree of formal training is about 1.5 millions" (Mitra, A p.159, "Decent Work in the Informal Sector: South India" in Madhu Singh (ed) 2005, Meeting Basic Needs in the Informal Sector, Springer, The Netherlands).

The numbers of those who are possibly provided for, the government and NGO initiatives put together just don't match the high demand. Against this background, the rest of this section gives a glimpse of some of the major NFE initiatives in the country.

NGOs: Partners for Change

Non-Governmental Organisations (NGOs) have emerged as important players in the area of social development in the country in recent years. They are important stakeholders, in social development programmes and their participation is crucial. They are also a repository of knowledge of grassroots realities because of their proximity to the people. NGOs associated with the various educational projects such as DPEP, Shiksha Karmi Project and Lok Jumbish have been instrumental in mobilising community resources in terms of participation which contributed also directly towards the success of the various projects. Without this level of partnership with experienced and committed NGOs, the level of mobilisation would not have been what it is today.

NGOs hove helped in:

- facilitating formation of the VECs;
- assisting in training and evaluation;
- assisting resource units in the modification of curriculum for local relevance;
- providing training in local communication skills to educators;
- review and participate in evaluation activities on a continuing basis.

The Participation of NGOs together with community support has helped to improve the physical conditions, environment of primary schools as well as promotion of girls' education. Many NGOs also act as local resource base for the various projects currently being undertaken in the country today.

All said and done, it is felt that more effective involvement of the NGOs in primary education is needed. The NGO sector has tremendous potential to contribute in moving towards the goal of universal primary education. As of now, nearly 700 NGOs are actively engaged in rendering cooperation and resource support to various ongoing educational projects with assistance from the government. New initiatives need to be taken to harness the NGO sector more directly into the primary education development programmes even while continuing with the existing programmes NGO involvement through the central scheme of Innovative and Experimental Programmes.

Other Non-formal and Alternative Initiatives

There are many other innovative and non-traditional approaches that are being tried out in India today to meet the diverse needs for educating children. These initiatives are the responses of the Central and state governments, educational institutions and voluntary organisations to varying expectations rooted in different region-specific traits.

Some of these are: PROPEL, M.V. Foundation, Digantar (Jaipur), SWRC (Tilonia), Rishi Valley Education Centre, IPER (Calcutta), Butterflies (New Delhi), Insan, Eklavya. A few more initiatives have been outlined below.

The Bodh Shikshan Samiti, based in Jaipur, represents an innovative approach to the education of non-school going children in slum areas. The agency manages 5 centres comprising 600 children and 25 teachers. The centres function at different hours depending upon the convenience of the children and their families. There is no fixed curriculum and the children pursue learning at their own pace; the centre also provides for amicable interaction among the students. The association has also established centres for women.

The lessons learnt through the experience of running the centres are vital for the future functioning of the Samiti. Some facts that have come to light are:

- Before the implementation of any plan of action, an extensive contact with each segment of the community is essential. An identification of what the community needs and its potentialities is important.
- Involvement of the parents is a strong factor for the motivation of the child towards learning.
- Alongwith the professional competence of the teachers, their degree of motivation and commitment is also essential for the success of the programme.
- There is a need to understand the nature of opposition from vested interests and fight it.

One major aspect that the innovative approach of the Bodh Shikshan Samiti needs to integrate in itself is the facilitation of the children's entry, at various points, into the formal education system. The need is to generate flexibility and competence in the formal system to meet the educational needs of communities with differing capacities and socioeconomic situations.

National Bal Bhavan: The enhancement of creativity among children from the weaker sections through activities of their choice, in a free and congenial environment, was the basis on which the Bal Bhavan Society (now the National Bal Bhavan) was formed in 1956. An autonomous body funded by the Department of Education, the activities of the National Bal Bhavan include: creative art performing arts, environment, astronomy, photography, integrated physical and science-related activities, in a joy manner. The role of the Bal Bhavan movement as an out of school support programme to the educational curriculum has been particularly recognised in the area of curriculum-based joyful activity.

The National Bal Bhavan has a membership of over 100,000. In addition to that, 52 Bal Bhavan centres in Delhi, 67 in the states and UTs, and 2 Jawahar Bal Bhavans in Srinagar and Mandi have been established for those children who cannot afford to participate in the activities of the national headquarter. These centres are provided general guidance, training facilities and transfer of information by the National Bal Bhavan.

The National Bal Bhavan has spent Rs.590,000, for the benefit of 312,000 children during the last five years (1992-97).

The focus areas for the future are: strengthening the National Bal Bhavan; strengthening the State Bal Bhavans and Jawahar Bal Bhavans; and opening new State Bal Bhavans.

Community Centres—Libraries

The notion of non-formal education has been a significant feature of policy debates around education in southern countries for three decades. It has drawn attention to the importance and potential of education, learning and training that takes place outside recognized educational institutions. There are questions about usefulness of the notion when looking at the process of education. It has also gone in and out of fashion. Fordham (1993) comments that if we try to correlate the flourishing of non-formal education and political change then the 1970s can certainly be described as the decade of non-formal education (Rubenson 1982). Similarly the 1980s saw the neglect of non-formal education and Fordham suggests that this was in tune with the politics of the decade, accompanied by greater inequalities both within and between countries. Given the extent to which notions of lifelong learning and associated ideas have gained ground in recent years it will be interesting to see how the language of policy debates will change over the next few years. Libraries are educational centres. A library is a collection of sources, resources, and services, and the structure in which it is housed: it is organized for use and maintained by a public body, an institution, or a private individual. In the more traditional sense, a library is a collection of books. The term can mean the collection, the building that houses such a collection, or both.

Vidyapeeths

Vidyapeeths Play a vital role in providing Non-formal adult and continuing education to the urban community. 53 Shramik Vidyapeeths have been set up by 1995-96 and are likely to be expanded in the future.

The basic idea behind the multidimensional or polyvalent approach to the education of the urban working community in this Programme, is to meet the various interrelated needs of target groups with specifically tailored programmes. The aim is to provide knowledge and import skills simultaneously and in an integrated manner.

The prime concern of the Shramik Vidyapeeth is to improve the socioeconomic status of the poorest of the poor beneficiaries by providing income generation skills. The programmes have been widely recognised as a potent means for promoting continuing education and developing the attitude for lifelong learning.

During 1995-96, the SVPs conducted 10,119 programmes and benefited 376,802 persons. The participation of women in programmes has been as high as 63.21 % of total participants. Nearly 88% of the participants were in the age group of 15-35. 84% belonged to the income group with an income of less than Rs. 155 per month spread over a period of six months. An external evaluation is made at the conclusion of the teaching.

After completion of the TLC, Post Literacy Campaigns (PLCs) are launched to mop up the leftover illiterates to consolidate the gains of literacy acquired during TLC, and to enable the neo-literates to develop abilities for self-learning.

Implementation of TLCs in various parts of the country has evoked an enthusiastic response from the weaker sections of the society, especially the Scheduled Castes and Scheduled Tribes. Experience has also shown that more than 60% of the learners attending classes are women. The Indian experience highlights the fact that literacy campaigns tend to evoke a positive attitude towards primary education and generate a demand from the beneficiaries for basic education for their children. In addition, this attitudinal change also enhances the participation and retention of children in schools.

Development and Empowerment of Women

The Quarry Initiative in Pudukkottai: At about the same time as the TLC was sanctioned, the Pudukkotta district administration had taken an important initiative, viz., leasing the stone quarries under the DWCRA scheme to women quarry workers. For quarry DWCRA members, the literacy campaign provided a key input into strengthening group solidarity and also enabled them to establish wider contacts with dedicated activists of the literacy campaign. Poverty, low levels of literacy and little social clout made these quarry workers easy targets for the unscrupulous quarry contractors. Hard labour, caste discrimination, low wages, and uncertain employment characterized the working conditions of some 40,000 quarry workers in Pudukkottai district. Economically and socially oppressed, these quarry workers were in virtual bondage to the contractors of quarries. Entire families worked in the quarries eking out a meager living. Women earn red about Rs. 5-7 per day, the mean around Rs. 15. The contractors made huge profits as there was a ready market for the materials mined. The profits accrued to the contractor mainly because of his ability to take the quarries on auction and not because he exercised much entrepreneurial or managerial ability. The process was clearly exploitative.

Vesting the lease rights of quarries with the labourers themselves could break the age-old bondedness of the labourers to the contractors. A conscious decision was taken by the district administration to give the un-auctioned quarries on lease to especially groups of women workers, as it was feared that many of the men were addicted to drink and could be pressured into submitting to heir old masters. A new experiment of social change was thus attempted by giving groups of women labourers the lease rights of the quarries they had worked in. Vesting the rights of mining quarries with the women labourers was to throw a challenge to decades of domination exercised by entrenched, vested interests that were not willing to surrender to easily. The initial breakthrough was possible because of the strong interest shown by the district administration. The process became sustainable, however, due to changes brought about in the social milieu by the TLC and the women leaders and activists who emerged during the process of the campaign. Economically, the DWCRA quarry workers are better off than every before. While the economic transformation of the lives of the quarry workers has been remarkable, the change that the process had wrought in the psyche of these people has been even more so. Vasantha had learnt to cycle at the Kudimiyamalai training camp and she now goes whizzing past the erstwhile contractors, unmindful of their disapproval. She and her companions have done what would earlier have brought swift retribution.

Literacy Houses—Bengal Social Service League (BSSL)

BSSL is a secular voluntary organisation founded in 1915. (Rabindranath Tagore was its president from 1917, for a number of years). Today, one of the major institutions engaged in adult education in India. It's main objective is to spread adult education; combine literacy with basic health and nutrition; spread awareness on harmful social practices like casteism and communal prejudice.

Programmes

Adult Education-in 1978, BSSL was given the status of a State Resource Centre (SRC) for Adult Education in West Bengal. In 1990, the Total Literacy Campaign (TLC) was launched all over the country and West Bengal took up adult education using the learning material prepared by SRC for learners in the age group of 9-14 and 15-45 years. Over 1,00,000 volunteers are engaged in training the population, even those administering the programmes being volunteers. An estimated 75 lakh learners have attained basic literacy levels with the help of teaching and learning materials prepared by the SRC. In support of this large adult education programme, BSSL has a number of support activities-trains resource persons who in turn train volunteer teachers for the TLC; prepares special primers for groups like marginal farmers, landless labourers, women, tribal people and people living in slum areas of industrial cities; organises conferences, workshops and seminars; undertakes research and field studies. BSSL has received many national and international awards.

Indian Adult Education

Objectives

To improve the educational opportunities for Indian adults who lack the level of literacy skills necessary for effective citizenship and productive employment and to encourage the establishment of adult education programs.

Types of Assistance

Direct Payments for Specified Use.

Uses and Use Restrictions

All funds must be for direct services. Funds may not be used for administration.

National Literacy Co-ordination Committee

By Laws:

- The affairs of the corporation shall strictly be governed by its National Coordinating Committee (sometimes referred to as NCC), which shall consist of not more than fifteen and not less than three Coordinators.
- Coordinators other than the President shall continue to serve until their death, resignation, or removal by the President, with or without cause, or until the expiration of the term for which elected or appointed.
- The National Coordinating Committee, shall appoint all the Coordinators from a list submitted by the Executive Committee and designate National Convenor, National Coconvenor, National Public Relations Coordinator and National Finance Coordinator.
- The NCC would diligently strive to distribute the membership of the Executive Committee across several Chapters of the India Literacy Project, and in particular at least shall designate the National Convenor and the Finance Coordinators from different approved Chapters in existence.
- Any vacancies of Coordinators arising out of death, resignation or any other reason shall be filled by the Executive Committee subject to the approval of the NCC.
- Unless sooner terminated, Coordinators other than the President shall serve for a term of two years or as designated by the President.
- Any Coordinator, except the President, may be terminated, with or without cause, by a two-thirds affirmative vote of the National Coordinating Committee.

Kerala Grandhsala Sangham and their Literacy Programmes

Library Movement: First library came into existence in Kerala was the Trivandrum Public Library. During the first quarter of the 20th century more libraries started as part of an organised movement when the All-Travancore Grandhasala Sangham came into being in 1949. Later its name was changed to Kerala Grandhasala Sangham. Adult and Non-formal Education activities in Kerala started in an organised manner with the setting up of Kerala Grandha Sala Sangham (KGS) with 47 rural libraries. Shri. P. N. Panicker, the driving spirit behind the concept, succeeded in bringing 6000 libraries into this network. These libraries functioned as good community centres where useful discussions, seminars and symposia were held for the common public. Grandhasala Sangham won the prestigious 'Krupsakaya Award' from UNESCO in 1975 as an endorsement of its good work. In 1979 Government of India sanctioned 40 literacy Centres in two districts (20 in each district) as per a Project submitted by KGS.

The history of the library movement is closely related to the growth of the publishing industry. As already mentioned printing, installation of presses, and publishing of books started in Kerala during the latter half of the 19th century. In the early decades of the 20th century, publishing houses, mainly those dealing with the literary works of eminent Malayalam scholars, came into being. The establishment of Sahithya Pravarthaka Sahakarana Sangham (SPCS) in 1949 revolutionised the publishing industry in Kerala. In the first 18 years SPCS published more than 2000 books, i.e. at an average of more than 100 books a year. This put an end to the scarcity of books in Malayalam. Cooperation between the library movement and SPCS opened a new chapter in the history of printing, publishing, and sales of Malayalam books.

Till then, the major public libraries in Kerala had been dealing more with English books than Malayalam books. Rural libraries in Malabar were a different phenomenon politically and socially. As they were the centres of political activities, the British rulers in Malabar had always shown a negative approach to libraries. Assistance from the government was not therefore available to these libraries as was the case in Travancore and Cochin. With Independence, conditions underwent a sea-change. For the first time in India, a Library Act came into existence in 1948 in Malabar. Following this enactment Malabar local library authorities were formed with district education officers as secretaries. After 1959, local library authorities were formed in Kannur, Calicut, and Palakkad districts. A number of libraries were formed on their initiative. With the formation of Kerala State in 1956, Travancore-Cochin Grandha Sala Sangham was renamed the Kerala Grandha Sala Sangham. And its activities spread to the Malabar region also. Thanoor Sanchara Grandha Sala in Malappuram was the first library, which joined the Kerala Grandha Sala Sangham. This was in 1957. At that time there were around 500 libraries in Malabar apart from those libraries under LLAs.

Seva Mandir

Seva Mandir is a non-governmental organization (NGO) working for the development of the rural and tribal population in Udaipur and Rajsamand districts of southern Rajasthan. The work area encompasses 626 villages and 56 urban settlements. In total the organization reaches out to around 70,000 households, influencing the lives of approximately 360,000 persons.

Seva Mandir's mission is to make real the idea of a society consisting of free and equal citizens who are able to come together and solve the problems that affect them in their particular contexts. The commitment is to work for a paradigm of development and governance that is democratic and polyarchic.

Seva Mandir seeks to institutionalize the idea that development and governance are not only to be left to the state and its formal bodies such as the legislature and the bureaucracy, but that the citizens and their associations should also engage separately and jointly with the state. The mission, briefly, is to construct the conditions in which citizens of plural backgrounds and perspectives can come together and work to benefit and empower the least advantaged in society.

In an effort to achieve its mission, Seva Mandir works through a three-pronged focus on the following distinct, yet interlinked areas

- Creation of platforms for people to come together and participate in development processes.
- Equipping village groups and leaders with skills and resources to respond to their own needs.
- Ensuring that members of village communities are able to interact with, and access benefits from panchayati raj institutions and other government and non-government agencies.

Objective

Seva Mandir focuses on:

- Enhancing people's capabilities for self-development by working for improved literacy levels, better health status and sensitization against oppressive gender relations.
- Creating sustainable improvements in the livelihoods base by revitalizing the natural resource base of communities.
- Strengthening village institutions by creating an alternative paradigm of power structures and community interactions that reinforce the positive forces of cooperation, transparency, equity, justice and responsible citizenship.

Organisation Structure

Organogram of Seva Mandir: The management structure is organized along a matrix integrating sectoral thrust areas with field programmes. In order to carry out development interventions effectively, Seva Mandir's organizational structure is spread across different levels. A cluster of 10–15 villages together make a zone. At the zone level, zonal workers are assisted by livelihood and capabilities workers as well as by a cadre of village-level volunteers.

About 5–7 zones are integrated at the block level. A block has a team leader, who coordinates the different activities at this level. The other team members at the block include sector in-charges for natural resource development, women and child development, education, and health.

While the demand for these programmes is generated at the village level, these programmes require substantial technical and social inputs in order to be effective. There is also a pool of facilities at the centre, which is utilized by the entire organization. This pool includes services of accounts and administration, as well as competent sector specialists. Seva Mandir has 284 full-time staff members, who are engaged in the task of implementing its various developmental works.

Adult Education Facilities of Universities Department of Continuing Education and Correspondence Courses

As one traces the recommendations of the various Commissions and the UGC guidelines issued from time to time for Adult, Continuing Education & Extension, it is evident that one of the goals of the UGC is to transform the university system into an active instrument for social change through the institutionalization of Extension as the Third Dimension and by ensuring that the university system is adult learner friendly and pro-life long learning.

It is commonly known that through the dimension of teaching, there is dissemination of knowledge, through research new knowledge is generated and through the dimension of extension there is application of knowledge in real life situations, which leads to the further generation of new knowledge.

It was way back in 1960 that the Kothari Commission first articulated the concept of Extension and the TRINITY of Teaching, Research & Extension. The Commission stated that Extension was essential for:

- making education relevant to real life situations
- for preventing the alienation of the educand from society
- for developing in the educand a sense of responsibility towards society
- for deepening the teacher's knowledge through a wider exposure to real life situations

In 1977 the University Grants Commission first incorporated Extension into its Policy Statement for Higher Education when it stated that. If the University system has to discharge adequately its responsibilities to the entire education system and to the society as a whole it must assume extension as the third important responsibility and give it the same status as teaching and research. This is a new and extremely significant area which should be developed on the basis of high priority. The acceptance of Extension as the Third Dimension equal in importance to teaching and research was in the context of a growing realisation that the universities and colleges having institutional resources-knowledge, manpower and physical-have an obligation to develop sensitivities to involve the development of the community with particular reference to the overall and diverse learning needs of all the segments of the people of the community.

Aim/Objectives

Aim: The Third Dimension was to aim at promoting a meaningful and sustained rapport between the Universities and the community.

Objectives: Firstly its objective was to extend knowledge and other institutional resources to the community and vice-versa and secondly its objective was to gain insights from a contact between knowledge resources and socio-cultural realities with a view to reflecting these in the entire curricular system of higher education including teaching and research. It was to be a two-way process between the experts and the people, an intellectual intervention in the community's living problems which need to be overcome through an educational process. It was to be that education which helped students to face life and its challenges and which created an ambience for a learning society.

Efforts by UGC

The opportunity to introduce the Extension Dimension in Universities was taken when the National Adult Education Programme (NAEP) was announced by the Government of India in 1978. Then Centres/Departments for Adult and Continuing Education were set up in Universities. Thereafter, the Adult Education Programme as Point 16 of the 20-Point Programme of the Government of India was introduced

(1983-1989) followed by the Area Based Approach Programme (1989-1992) and the Total Literacy Campaign (1992-1997) of the National Literacy Mission. In the Ninth Plan the UGC continued the Adult and Continuing Education Programme in a manner that facilitated the Centres \ Departments of Adult and Continuing Education and Extension to cast their own Plan of Action for the Extension Dimension specific to their own University.

In all, the programmes introduced by the UGC from time to time, the main focus has been on Adult Literacy, Post-literacy and field outreach programmes. Attention was given in the Ninth Plan to Adult and Continuing Education for university groups, groups that had passed the university system but had a need to return and to groups which did not have access to the university system.

In the Ninth Plan, the UGC has implemented the schemes under its Non-formal Education Bureau. As evidenced from the UGC's vision and strategy for the X Plan, the scheme will continue to be operationalised by UGC under the Non-formal Education Bureau. In order to ensure continuity, the UGC has already released grants to Departments for the years 2002-2003 and 2003-04.

Current Scenario

Now as the guidelines for the Tenth Plan period are being cast it is essential that the current situation, internationally and nationally, be considered. It is well known that the impact of globalisation has placed new demands on the education system. Transformation with rapid change is taking place everywhere. The student and youth have to be prepared by the university to adopt change and learn new skills in accordance with the new demands of the world of work. In other words, the university system has to prepare the student to be a life long learner. Then only will the student be able to sustain his knowledge and skills at an international bench mark level ?

Further private universities are being setup and international universities will soon be entering the country. Also, Information & Communication Technology (ICT) is being more frequently used in the field of learning. On-line learning and e-learning will soon become a regular feature of university courses. It is, therefore, essential that the university system and specially the Departments of Adult and Continuing Education & Extension begin to interact and collaborate with the private sector. Secondly, e-learning and the on-line mode for the conduct of courses be utilized for continuing education to cater to the needs of various sections of society including professionals.

While universities have to enhance student employability skills through a formal system, on the other hand, the non-formal stream of education is being developed by the Ministry of Human Resource Development for reaching education to the unreached. There is a rapid growth of the National Institute of Open Schooling and State Open Schools and improvisation of quality teaching through the development of a momentum in Sarva Shiksha Abhiyan (SSA) under the Education for All programme. Universities also have to integrate formal and non-formal education by opening their doors to adult learners for life long learning programmes and by making the University an adult learner friendly institution. (Refer-Cape Town Statement on Characteristic Elements of a Life long Learning Higher Education Institution, January 2001). The Departments, will, therefore, have to play a more dynamic role and move from the periphery to the centre stage of the university system and to ensure this the Advisory Committees overseeing the work of the Department need to play a more pro-active role. The Departments also have to play a major role in the development of the human resource expertise in the subject of Adult, Continuing Education, Extension & Field Outreach. At present, there are 73 Departments/Centres working in the country. As visualized earlier in the Ninth Plan, all Universities are to establish a Department for institutionalizing extension and for meeting the current demands of adult and continuing education in their respective areas of operation.

Thrusts

The thrusts for the Tenth Plan Period are therefore projected taking the current scenario into account. These thrusts are:-

- the acceptance of the philosophy of continuing education as a part of total education programme of the institution;
- integration between formal and non-formal education and out of school learning processes;
- reaching out to the larger sections of adults through the university system and specially deprived groups for the purpose of equalization of educational opportunities;
- enrichment of the learning process of faculty and students through exposure to community needs, problems, issues and reaching out to socio-economic and cultural groups;
- attending to major issues relating to the National Literacy Mission, bonded labour, child-labour, street children, health conditions and issues on drugs and AIDS / HIV, nutrition, sanitation, environmental issues, gender issues with stress on gender equity, human rights education, consumer rights issues, communal harmony and cultural integration, self-employment generation and use of technology appropriate to the society;
- development of the discipline of Andragogy / Adult and Continuing Education & Extension;
- research for the development of theory and conduct of action research/operational research;
- introduction of courses offered on campus, off campus, on-line and through e-learning;
- development of courses linked specifically to business and industry which would include work ethics, work culture and preparation for the changing world of work;
- development of a range of credit courses at the undergraduate and postgraduate levels leading to an Associate degree in Continuing Education and Extension and Field Outreach to focus on continuing education programmes at the grassroot level through the CECs of the National Literacy Mission and through the National Institute of Open Schooling and State Open Schools;

- communal harmony and peace education;
- human rights and rights of vulnerable groups;
- environmental issues;
- panchayats and development issues;
- health education for the community and through the Health Care Centre of the university;
- women's empowerment and
- social issues and gender issues
- initiating change in the policies and procedures of the university so as to make the university courses more accessible to the adult learner and
- establishing a new relationship with government organizations NGOs, Civil Societies, NGO networks and other professional bodies to address social issues.

Target Groups

The major target groups for the Tenth Plan period shall be:-

- Groups / students in the colleges and university system;
- Groups who have passed out of the university system and need to return for upgradation or for the acquisition of new skills. These could include groups from industry and services;
- Groups who are already in service or the underemployed or the unemployed who need to enhance their employability;
- Groups which would normally not be enterants into the university system;
- Women, SC/ST, disadvantaged groups, street children, bonded labour, child workers, etc.;
- Neo-literates, CE learners, Out of school youth and Senior citizens;

Programs and Activities

It is suggested that the following programs be conducted in order to cater to the needs of the different target groups. Departments can formulate the proposals by keeping the following programs in mind. Developing the discipline of Andragogy / Adult Education and Continuing Education through academic programs and courses such as:

- Foundation Courses;
- Certificate and Diploma Courses;
- Undergraduate, postgraduate, M.Phil, Ph.D., optional/ regular courses;
- Courses integrated with different degrees such as B.Ed., M.Ed. and professional degrees;
- Projects related to continuing education and extension and field outreach in-built into a discipline of studies and
- Conduct of inter-disciplinary research in Adult, Continuing Education & Extension.

Vocational Career Oriented Courses/Programs

Courses and programs for people at different socio-economic and educational levels for the acquisition of marketable vocational skills according to the needs and demands of urban and rural, local, national and international markets;

- Continuing education courses for the students and out of school youth;
- Courses related to the electronic media, multi media, computer applications, etc. to receive special focus;
- Apprenticeship, internship, training programs with industry and business;
- Courses specially focusing on the demands of the changing world of work;
- Para-professional courses for knowledge and skill updates and
- Career guidance for the university and college students

Associate Degree / Diploma in Continuing Education

Development of a credit system for courses in adult & continuing education leading to an Associate Degree / Diploma in adult & continuing education for the benefit of students who are pursuing courses on the campus.

Need for Open University System

Programmes for developing the potentialities of students and out of school youth, particularly of the girl students and women and Training of elected representatives of local, self-government, self-help groups and persons from community based organizations, NGOs, under-privileged and resource-deprived communities.

Quality of Life Improvement Programs: Conduct of courses and awareness programs for facilitating improvement in the quality of life of the people.

Individual Interest Promotion Programs: Courses and programs catering to individual interests of adults for promoting personal development.

Social and Citizenship Role Awareness Programs: For increasing knowledge, awareness and functional skills of the student youth and out of school youth in areas such as environment food, shelter, health, family welfare, etc. which affect them

Resource Support Programs: Programmes to support and evaluate TLC, PLP, CE, Sarva Shiksha Abhiyan, women's empowerment, etc. in collaboration with or for the NLM, State Literacy Mission (SLM) Zilla Sakisharta Samiti (ZSS), Centres for Women's Studies, Population Education Centres, Open Universities, People's Organizations, Community Based Organizations, Civil Societies and others. Special programs for indigenous populations, aboriginals, slum dwellers, tribals and other vulnerable sections of society.

Equivalency Programs : Parallel programs offered by the Non-formal Education Sector of the Ministry of Human Resource Development of the State and Centre, Open Schools, Institutes, etc. may be facilitated, developed and expanded.

Academic Credit: The work of the students involved in adult education, continuing education, extension and field outreach work should be considered for academic credit in addition to or as a part of their regular course of studies. For determining academic credits, standards may be evolved and adopted.

To illustrate:

- Projects related to extension/field outreach within a discipline at the undergraduate or postgraduate level;
- Field work in respect of a subject of study;
- Participation in literacy, post-literacy, continuing education, population education and non-formal education programs;
- Participation in programs for enhancing employability and technology skills;
- Any other activity approved for the purpose by the University Authority with the approval of the Commission.
- Each University will have to determine the measures of weightage and the evaluation process for the award of an academic credit.

Role and Functions of the Department

Teaching, Training and Research : Teaching courses in Adult and Continuing Education and Extension & Field Outreach:

- Conducting need-based continuing education courses, including online courses on credit or non-credit basis;
- Conducting Orientation and Refresher courses for university and college teachers with the Academic Staff College;
- Undertaking research in the subject;
- To assist in the development of a curriculum for multi-disciplinary programs;
- To assist in the development of a library in the subject and
- Training for human resource or skill development for the different target groups

Catalyst Role:

- Acting as a focal agency in the university system for all Extension and Field Outreach Programs with the involvement of university departments and colleges;

- Serving as a Technical Resource Centre for university's community-based activities and
- Assessing the needs of the university students and out of university learner for continuing education programs and career guidance

Collaborative and Networking Role

The department shall undertake collaborative programs and network with:

- business and industry;
- university departments;
- N.L.M.A;
- NGOs, Civil Society, development and government agencies and others and
- International organizations / universities and agencies, such as, UNESCO, UNICEF, UNDPA, International Council for Adult Education, Asia South Pacific Bureau for Adult Education and similar organizations

Documentation and Dissemination

Publication of News Letters, journal, magazine, e-journal, creation of an interactive website, preparation of materials, dissemination of materials and information, etc.

Monitoring and Evaluation

- Of activities and field programs of the department and of the colleges
- Facilitating Academic Departments to provide for Extension work through Offerings, Projects, Research, Field Activities etc.

Organizational Aspects

(A) Status of Departments of Adult and Continuing Education, Extension work & Field Outreach

The IX Plan guidelines have clearly stated the need for the Universities to accord a statutory status to the Departments of Adult, Continuing Education & Extension with amendments, if necessary, in the University Act and Statutes. It was also stated that the Department will have the same status as that of any other teaching department of the university with the core faculty eligible for representation on all the University bodies, like Syndicate / Executive / Management Council, Senate, Academic Council, Standing Committee on Academic Affairs, Board of Studies etc. corresponding to other University teachers. During the X Plan period, the Universities must take suitable action in this regard if such action has not been taken so far. The release of grants for the X Plan will be based on the fulfilment of this condition. In the absence of assurance from the State Govt., no vacant sanctioned post was filled.

The Department of Adult, Continuing Education and Extension & Field Outreach should be headed by Professor / Director / Head of the University Department as per the nomenclature in the University for the same position with major responsibilities similar to that of the head of any other teaching department.

The University, in accordance with the status of the Department, shall give academic freedom to this Department for the planning and conduct of innovative programmes in Teaching, Research, Extension & Field Outreach. The faculty of the Department is also eligible for the Unassigned Grant of the UGC available to the university and for the research and other grants of the various UGC schemes for teachers.

Departments already in existence shall be eligible for Special Assistance Programs (SAP) and other such special assistance schemes of the UGC and other national / international agencies

(B) Nomenclature of the Departments

Those Departments which are already known as Departments of Adult, Continuing Education & Extension or any other name approved by the university, may retain the nomenclature. In case of new Departments, they should adopt the nomenclature Departments of Adult, Continuing Education and Extension & Field Outreach (ACEEFO). For the purpose of these guidelines the Departments are referred to as Departments of Adult, Continuing Education, Extension & Field Outreach (ACEE & FO).

(C) Structure

At the UGC level: The Commission may constitute Expert Committee(s) to examine proposals from universities for financial support under the scheme for fresh induction, advise on policy matters, monitor and review of the Departments completing its tenure, implementation and utilization. The Committee will also be responsible for finalizing consolidated activitywise and programmewise annual and action plan for the X Plan, reviewing performance reports from the Departments for further action.

Advisory Committee: Since the university is the focus of continuing and extension education and outreach activities, it is necessary to have an Advisory Committee of Adult and Continuing Education and Extension & Field Outreach to oversee various academic and extension field outreach programmes of the university. The Advisory Committee will have members as representatives from a) the Syndicate / Executive Council / Management Council, b) UGC representative from the concerned Bureau, c) representative of NLMA/SLMA, d) Heads of University Departments / Principals (for Colleges) in concerned areas, e). two three experts in the field, f). Government Departments and g) NGOs. The membership of the committee may be between 10-12. The Head of Department of Adult and Continuing Education and Extension & Field Outreach will be its Member-Secretary. The Advisory Committee must meet at least twice a year, advise and take steps on courses, curriculum, prepare the annual programme of activities, look into proper utilization of grants, monitor and review the implementation of the programme with the help of Implementation Committee.

Implementation Committee: In order to facilitate the functioning of the Department, an Implementation Committee, consisting of 4/6 members of the Advisory Committee including 1/2 local members in the areas may be constituted with the Director as the Convenor. The Implementation Committee must meet once in 2 to 3 months. This Committee may also recommend to introduce certificate and other short-term courses, suggest course guest faculty, determine eligibility of students, lay down fee structure and evaluate the programmes.

The Board: To advise the Department in academic matters including research in the area of ACEE & FO and monitor academic activities, an Academic Board will be constituted as per the university procedure in the form of a Regular Board of Studies

(D) Faculty and Staff: Head / Director of the Department of Adult Continuing Education, Extension Education & Field Outreach

Each Department will have a Head/Director. The Department will be headed by a Professor / Director, directly responsible to the Vice-Chancellor to whom he / she will report. The Professor / Director of the Department may be selected on part time basis from the disciplines/department of Adult Education / Social Sciences / Education / Humanities / Management with experience in teaching, research, extension work and field outreach.

The duties of the Professor / Director will be similar to those of Heads of other teaching departments. However, he/she will have the additional responsibility of implementing the UGC guidelines for the scheme. Since extension has to be the focus of the university, the Professor/ Director of the Department should possess considerable leadership qualities in continuing and extension education, field outreach programmes.

Faculty: The faculty for the Department of Adult & Continuing Education may be engaged on contract basis or on per lecture basis as per the rates approved by the Commission. All these appointments be within the approved budget.

Secretarial and Non-teaching Technical Staff

The Department will have Secretarial and Non-teaching Technical Staff whose service conditions shall be the same as are applicable to other non-academic staff of the university and they will be eligible to all benefits like pension/CPG/GPF, medical aid, etc.

Field Investigator/Project Assistant

In the Tenth Plan period the Department will be permitted to appoint from the salary component of the UGC grant, additional manpower of 3 to 5 Field Investigators/Project Assistants to implement its programs.

Qualifications and Experience

Graduates or Post Graduates with at least one year's office/ field experience in Adult and Continuing Education & Extension and not more than 35 years of age and Graduates/Post Graduates with a diploma in Adult and Continuing Education & Extension and related fields will be given preference. However, the age of such candidates will not be more than 35 years.

Selection Procedure and Appointment

The advertisement, selection and appointment shall be made by the Department itself after obtaining the University permission. The appointment shall be on a contract basis for the Tenth Plan period only. The candidate will have no claim or right for re-appointment or permanency;

Role and Functions

The Field Investigator/Project Assistant shall carry out academic, administrative and supporting field activities as directed by Head/Director of the Department.

Compensation/Salary

Field Investigator/Project Assistant shall be entitled to a consolidated amount of

- Graduate-minimum of Rs. 4000/- per month and Rs. 500/- Fixed Travel Allowance and
- Post-Graduate minimum of Rs. 6000/- per month and Rs. 500/- Fixed Travel Allowance.

Supervision

His/Her work will be supervised/monitorised by the Head/ Director of the Department.

Project Staff on Hiring

No regular or contract staff is permissible under the scheme other than mentioned above. The miscellaneous work of the Department may be got done by outsourcing on hiring basis.

Nodal Universities

The UGC has identified Nodal Universities and also defined their service areas. The Nodal University is a link between the UGC and the universities in the service area. During the Tenth Plan the Nodal Agency System will be continued. However, the Nodal Agencies will be reviewed in the Tenth Plan by the UGC Committee of Experts. New Nodal Agencies may also be considered based on the performance and requirements In addition to the normal responsibilities expected of a Department, each University, being a nodal University, will have the following functions and roles:

(A) Co-ordinating role —

- New initiatives, specially in designing courses;
- Disseminating information on innovative programs and
- Motivating universities in the service area for strengthening the programme by organizing orientation/ training programs.

(B) Documentation and Dissemination of information —

- Documentation Building Archives;
- Updated reference lists of available material for dissemination Books, Journals and Audio-visual materials;
- Use of new technology like Internet, Publishing Newsletter, creating websites and
- Publications

(C) Networking at different levels with —

- Government programmes;
- Ministries connected with outreach work;
- Official bodies;
- Other universities, professional bodies / training centres and
- Non-governmental Organisations and their networks, Civil Societies

(D) Advocacy—

- Liasioning with UGC, State Government, Vice-Chancellors Committees, State Council for Higher

Education, Universities, drawing attention to critical issues;

- Each Nodal University will convene two meetings of the Departments in its Service Area every year. The meetings are conducted at different universities in the service area by rotation. At least, at one of the meetings every year, a UGC officer be invited for interaction, who should report his / her observations to the UGC Committee of Experts. The departments will be responsible for submitting the annual report and review proforma to their respective Nodal Agency. The Nodal Agency shall be responsible for preparing a comprehensive report of the Departments in its service area and submit the same to UGC;
- The UGC shall convene a meeting of the Directors of Nodal Agencies, atleast once a year and
- The Nodal University is expected to be dynamic, rather than routine, if it must fulfil its role and responsibility effectively. For this p urpose, the Nodal University must prepare an annual work plan through which it can appraise its performance.

Functions of NIOS

The National Institute of Open Schooling has a pivotal role to play in the promotion and development of Open Schooling in the country. In a diverse country like India, it is not possible for the NOS alone to cater to the regional requirements. The NIOS has therefore evolved alternate models of State Open Schools and State Centres for Open Schooling. The NIOS has also been providing professional and technical support to States in order to set up and develop State Open Schools, particularly with regional medium.

In order to systematise the interaction between the NIOS and the State Open Schools and other agencies, it was considered appropriate to establish a forum under the NIOS in the form of a Consortium. The National Consortium for Open Schooling (NCOS) was therefore launched in September, 1997, with a view to facilitate better cooperation, collaboration and expansion of activities in the Open Learning System. The major objectives of NCOS are:

- Sharing of resources, expertise and experiences.
- Professional, technical and academic support in setting up of the SOSs/SCOS.
- Designing need specific curriculum, developing/ translating self-instructional material in the local medium.
- Human resource development.
- Development of prototype materials and other pedagogical inputs.
- Pace setting and maintenance of database on OLS.
- Organizing national and international conferences/ seminars on Open Schooling.
- Research and Development.

State Open Schools have been set up in Haryana, Madhya Pradesh, Punjab, Tamil Nadu, West Bengal, Karnataka, Kerala and Jammu & Kashmir with NOS collaboration and assistance. Other States like Andhra Pradesh and Rajasthan have set up their own State Open Schools. State Centres for Open Schooling has been established at Himachal Pradesh.

Exploratory meetings for setting up of Open Schooling have been held in the States of Orissa, Maharashtra, and Uttar Pradesh. Apart from this, advocacy programmes for promotion of Open Schooling are held from time to time in which all State Open Schools and participants from other states are invited to work out the strategy for strengthening the Open Schooling System in India. Positive response have been received from Maharashtra, Uttar Pradesh, Orissa and Chhattisgarh who have showed their willingness to set up State Open Schools. NIOS is to expedite the process with these states.

During the Tenth Five Year Plan Period, more State Open Schools/State Centres are expected to come up. These schools may offer Secondary, Senior Secondary, Vocational and Basic Education Programmes as per the needs of each state thereby making attempts to cater to regional variations.

Management of Voluntary Organisation—Concept of a Social Worker and Social Work

Social work is both a profession and social science. It involves the application of social theory and research methods to study and improve the lives of people, groups, and societies. It incorporates and uses other social sciences as a means to improve the human condition and positively change society's response to chronic problems.

Social work is a profession committed to the pursuit of social justice, to the enhancement of the quality of life, and to the development of the full potential of each individual, group and community in the society. It seeks to simultaneously address and resolve social issues at every level of society and economic status, but especially among the poor and sick. Social workers are concerned with social problems, their causes, their solutions and their human impacts. They work with individuals, families, groups, organizations and communities.

Social work and human history go together. Social work was always in human societies although it began to be a defined pursuit and profession in the 19th century. This definition was in response to societal problems that resulted from the Industrial Revolution and an increased interest in applying scientific theory to various aspects of study. Eventually an increasing number of educational institutions began to offer social work programmes.

The settlement movement's emphasis on advocacy and case work became part of social work practice. During the 20th century, the profession began to rely more on research and evidenced-based practice as it attempted to improve its professionalism.

Today social workers are employed in a myriad of pursuits and settings. Professional social workers are generally considered those who hold a professional degree in social work and often also have a license or are professionally registered. Social workers have organized themselves into local, national, and international professional bodies to further the aims of the profession.

History

Social work has its roots in the struggle of society to ameliorate poverty and the resultant problems. Therefore, social work is intricately linked with the idea of charity work; but must be understood in broader terms. The concept of charity goes back to ancient times, and the practice of providing for the poor has roots in all major world religions.

The practice and profession of modern social work has a relatively recent scientific origin, originating in the 19th Century. The movement began primarily in the United States and England. After the end of feudalism, the poor were seen as a more direct threat to the social order, and so the state formed an organized system to care for them. The development of the profession was linked closely with public health and psychiatry, and over the 20th century expanded to include radical and feminist philosophies.

Social Workers

Definition: A social worker is a helping professional who is distinguished from other human service professionals by a focus on both the individual and his or her environment. Generally, social workers have at least a bachelor's degree from an accredited education program and in most states they must be licensed, certified, or registered. A Master's in Social Work is required for those who provide psychotherapy or work in specific settings such as hospitals or nursing homes.

Description: Social workers comprise a profession that had its beginnings in 1889 when Jane Addams founded Hull House and the American settlement house movement in Chicago's West Side. The ethics and values that informed her work became the basis for the social work profession. They include respect for the dignity of human beings, especially those who are vulnerable, an understanding that people are influenced by their environment, and a desire to work for social change that rectifies gross or unjust differences.

The social work profession is broader than most disciplines with regard to the range and types of problems addressed, the settings in which the work takes place, the levels of practice, interventions used, and populations served. It has been observed that social work is defined in its own place in the larger social environment, continuously evolving to respond to and address a changing world. Although several definitions of social work have been provided throughout its history, common to all definitions is the focus on both the individual and the environment, distinguishing it from other helping professions.

Social workers may be engaged in a variety of occupations ranging from hospitals, schools, clinics, police departments, public agencies, court systems to private practices or businesses. They provide the majority of mental health care to persons of all ages in this country, and in rural areas they are often the sole providers of services.

In general, they assist people to obtain tangible services, help communities or groups provide or improve social and health services, provide counselling and psychotherapy with individuals, families, and groups, and participate in policy change through legislative processes. The practice of social work requires knowledge of human development and behaviour, of social, economic and cultural institutions, and of the interaction of all these factors.

Concept of Volunteer and Voluntary Work—Concept of Co-operation

Across the world, in developed and developing countries the concept of volunteering is gaining more acceptance and participation of people irrespective of their age, social status, religion, gender and racial affiliation. It not been seen a "rich thing" or what people can earn from monetary as a case of perceptions from some quarters. The concept of volunteering is not singular to any country or economic stance as it occurs in largely every societies or communities. Volunteering know no boundaries and works with any socio-cultural terrain of societies. It is arguably correct to imply that the development of a simple community start with volunteering, members of the community dedicating a special time for the wellbeing of the entire community to undertake tasks and assignments, also the emergence and history of foundations, service organisations, charities and non-governmental organisations as volunteering enshrine in its roots. Volunteering has its part in the lives of people, businesses, societies and nations as it is contributing immensely for better understanding and cooperation amongst persons, groups and societies.

The activities of volunteers and volunteering did not get unnoticed, as there are several national, regional and international bodies on volunteering, prominent among them are the united nations volunteering service, peace corps, red cross and crescents, national volunteers networks and organisations.

Definition of Volunteer

- One who enters into, or offers for, any service of his own free will.
- One who enters into service voluntarily, but who, when in service, is subject to discipline and regulations like other soldiers; — opposed to conscript; specifically, a voluntary member of the organized militia of a country as distinguished from the standing army.
- A grantee in a voluntary conveyance; one to whom a conveyance is made without valuable consideration; a party, other than a wife or child of the grantor, to whom, or for whose benefit, a voluntary conveyance is made.

The Definition of Volunteer Work: "Performance of activities, voluntarily and unpaid, for the benefit of others or society, set up by an organisation."

This means:

- no form of compensation whatsoever
- No mandatory commitments such as internships
- volunteer work is different from practising a hobby or helping relatives or friends
- volunteers are always individuals, as opposed to an organization or a company
- volunteer work is never meant with commercial goals in mind.

How Voluntary Organizations are Formed—How do They Function—Comparative Studies of Voluntary Organizations in Different States

Involuntary resettlement is an issue that currently is high on the development agenda. In India, fifty million people are estimated to have been displaced in last five decades by the construction of dams, power plants, highways and such other infrastructure development projects. Subsequently no more than one-fourth of them could be assisted to regain their livelihoods. (Roy: 1999) The majority, reduced to poverty from the loss of land and other means of making a living, continue to face an uncertain future.

Development-Induced Resettlement

Development is undertaken to generate benefits for the society at large, but the process has often led to forced relocation of thousands of people, uprooting their communities and shredding to pieces their essential social fabric. It is now being increasingly acknowledged that the key problem with projects requiring resettlement is that the costs are unequally shared. Those who bear the cost may not be those who enjoy the fruits of development, and those enjoying the fruits of development may not be those who bear the costs. For example, electricity generated in the Singrauli region is available in homes in New Delhi and other north Indian cities hundreds of miles away, but the people in that region who gave up their lands for the erection of power plants often have no access to it. (Mathur: 1999) Conflicts between wider societal interests and interests of the people adversely affected by development projects are therefore increasingly coming into the open.

The NGO intervention in development induced resettlement issues has taken place in two ways. (Pandey: 1996) Many NGOs have been denouncing development projects which displace people in large numbers. They are active in mobilising project affected people against their impoverishment due to developmental activities. With support from academia, media, environmentalists, human rights activists and others concerned, these NGOs have successfully built up strong protest movements against mega-projects. (Udall: 1995) Their role has been significant in highlighting the plight of the uprooted people and in lobbying for a fair deal for those who happen to lose from the development process. There are, then, NGOs who actively work with government agencies in the planning and implementation of resettlement operations. Their primary goal is to see that the hardships of project affected people are mitigated as much as possible

Resettlement is clearly a contentious issue. NGOs have not remained undivided on this issue either. Some NGOs, perceiving development as some kind of a sinister device to promote interests of the rich and the powerful at the expense of the poor and the weak, are opposed to the current development paradigm itself which often gives rise to problems of resettling the displaced people. They see no use in continuing with this destructive process in the name of development, and would want it to come to a halt to save people from preventable disruption to their lives. In their view, governments and the donor agencies which assist them in their development plans alone are accountable form disruption to lives of the affected groups.

They are also getting wide support in their struggle against development projects. By putting pressure on international development agencies and aid establishments in donor countries, they sometimes even succeed in stopping the flow of funds for projects that they regard as harmful. However, not all NGOs react to the resettlement problems created by development projects in a similar hostile manner. Those on the other side of the fence, too, are critical of the mindless pursuit of development that instead of improving the quality of life only adds to the woes of large numbers, but they are not in favour of abandoning development altogether. They recognise that without planned development no government can hope to meet the rising expectations of its peoples for better living conditions. What they definitely want, however, is that the previous neglect of the displaced people should be replaced with policies and programmes that assure them a future better than their past, not promise them a return merely to their 'good old days.'

The fact is that the NGOs are not a homogeneous group, all united in the way they perceive the resettlement problem and the manner in which they wish to deal with it. Perhaps nothing illustrates better the sharp differences in the NGO community than the situation of NGO movements in this area. (Dhagamwar; 1997) While some NGOs are supportive of the resettlement plans and are willing to lend their helping hand to such initiatives, there are others whose confrontational stance in effect tends to obstruct the resettlement process.

NGOs in Development Agencies

Development agencies are now increasingly turning to voluntary organizations (commonly known in India as NGOs, a short form for non-governmental organisations) to seek their help in dealing with the problems of involuntary resettlement. In recent years a number of NGOs have, in fact, been contracted to carry out resettlement operations by several major public sector organisations, especially those being funded by the World Bank and other external donor agencies. The Coal India Limited (CIL) and the National Thermal Power Corporation (NTPC) are among the major Government of India undertakings that took an early lead in using the NGO resources in their resettlement activities, especially their expertise in generating new income opportunities for the displaced people. Many other organisations are now following their example. Indeed, the last few years have been a boom time for voluntary organisations working in the area of involuntary resettlement.

Only a decade ago this level of NGO involvement in resettlement activities would have been inconceivable. For long NGOs have been generally viewed as trouble-makers by government agencies. Partly their campaigns against development projects, often conducted with international support, strengthened such negative perceptions about them.

Government agencies in the face of protests have been even forced to roll back their development plans in some cases. Donor agencies too have not acted differently in such situations. One well known case is the campaign launched by the Narmada Bachao Andolan (NBA) which resulted in the withdrawal of the

World Bank funding support for the Sardar Sarovar Project. (Dreze, et al: 1997) The Koel Karo Jan Sanghatan (KKJS) also successfully challenged the might of the state and saved 150000 tribal lives in 256 villages from displacement. Their sustained pressure forced the government to cancel the laying of the foundation stone of the project on 5 July 1996 the Prime Minister. (Sekhsaria: 1996)

What has, then, brought about this turnaround in the outlook of development agencies? The pressure of external donor agencies is not the whole answer. Other factors have been at work too. The fact is that government agencies themselves have now become more aware of their limitations in managing resettlement. This is a task that requires live contact with the people to be resettled on an almost daily basis, and NGOs known for their closeness to the people definitely appear better suited for it. A major factor that has changed the attitude is, however, the impressive track record of many

NGOs in the fight against poverty. Here development agencies see for NGOs with their participatory approaches a useful role in a difficult task facing them-the challenge of reconstructing livelihoods of the affected people, and seeing that at least they do not end up worse off than before due to development activities, as has so often happened in the past.

The Myths about NGOs

Many myths have grown about NGOs. The common perception is that NGOs are by their very nature participatory, democratic, transparent and flexible, while government carries the baggage tack of red-tapism and rigidity. The NGO views about themselves seem to have perpetrated many of these myths. NGOs tend to view themselves as pursuing a participatory approach that is uniquely their own, giving them particular strengths which the government agencies are believed to lack. It is because of these distinct advantages they possess that, in comparison with government agencies, NGOs are better able to: (1) reach the poor; (2) obtain true, meaningful participation of intended beneficiaries; (3) be flexible and responsive in their work; (4) strengthen local level institutions;

(5) achieve outcomes at less cost; (6) experiment with alternative ideas and practices; (7) utilise indigenous knowledge and other local resources. (Fowler 1990:11)

How far this depiction of their self-image is a true account of the NGO strengths remains debatable. Experience has shown that there is a great variation among NGOs themselves and within government. Government is not a monolith. Some government programmes function with remarkable sensitivity, transparency and accountability and the instances of rigidity in NGO operations are not unknown. (Ramachandran: 1996) As participants at a Royal Tropical Institute seminar held in Amsterdam observed: "The stereotyped way of thinking often enncountered-that NGOs 'can do' and government departments 'cannot'-is an oversimplification'. (Jaeger:1986)

Corruption, manipulation, power and control are not the exclusive preserve of government institutions. NGOs are not free from it. Given shrinking employment opportunities, people register charitable or service organisations as a means of livelihood. (Ramachandran: 1996) Many political leaders and retired civil servants also set up their own NGOs to make money for themselves, using their contacts for easy access to government funds without being pestered with awkward questions. It is public knowledge that many NGOs function as family establishments with the majority of governing board members and organisational leaders drawn from one family. The organisation's assets are also treated as family property with unwritten inheritance rights.

On the basis of their studies, Gazelius and Millwood (1988) are unable to confirm that NGO-supported participatory projects are more effective than government-supported ones. While it is true that the examples of NGO experiences are in general more positive with respect to participation, this does not mean that NGOs are always more disposed towards and effective in participatory development. In a number of cases NGOs have been rather paternalistic in their approach. (Uphoff 1989:9) Commenting on the anti-dam movement launched by the Narmada Bachao Andolan (NBA), Singh (1997) stated: "It has been less successful in developing a truly democratic representation of the people's interests, and of the diversity of these interests. The oustees have never really been their own spokespersons, nor have they been incorporated in the top leadership of the NBA. In fact, as the momentum of the movement grew, the functioning of the NBA became somewhat less democratic and participatory."

The NGO claims of giving voice to the people are being increasingly questioned. As people become better aware of their own situation they are able to see things for themselves. They are becoming critical of the NGOs that claim to speak on their behalf. In some cases people have even begun campaigns against such NGOs. As recently reported in the press, the people affected by the Maheshwar Hydel project in Madhya Pradesh went even as far as submitting a memorandum to the National Human Rights Commission accusing the widely respected Narmada Bachao Andolan (NBA) of violating human rights and their right to development. They stated in the memorandum that though they were in favour of speedy implementation of the Maheshwar project, the antidevelopment forces led by NBA activists were creating hurdles in completion of the project. The affected people alleged that NBA was intimidating the government officials and their activists were bringing anti-social elements from outside to create law and order problems. (The Hindu: 1999 April and The Observer 1998)

As Dhillon (1997) observed, the concept of voluntary work appears to have changed with NGOs becoming a source of income and employment generation for people sitting in plush, air-conditioned offices in the capital or other major cities, hopping from country to country for conferences around the globe, and doing 'advocacy work'-a fancy term for churning out reports that put you to sleep by the time you reach page three. NGOs are in the throes of a credibility crisis; a crisis brought about by racketeers in their midst. Examples of their misdemeanours now abound. The Council for Advancement of People's Action and Rural Technology (CAPART), a Government of India organization that supports the projects and activities of NGOs, recently blacklisted 400 such organisations. The

Central Social Welfare Board (CSWB), which funds NGOs on behalf of the Department of Women and Child Development, has a long blacklist of 3,000 NGOs.

Growing Disenchantment

NGOs can play a useful role, providing much needed support to development agencies responsible for resettlement management. However many NGOs, those based in the capital and other big cities in particular, tend to steer away from resettlement work. Apart from the remoteness of rural areas, what seems to hold them back is the difficult nature of this task. Success in resettlement operations is often hard to achieve. In case of failure, they may lose credibility. They find it more rewarding networking with their counterparts in capitals of the developed world. There is a growing feeling among development agencies that NGOs are generally reluctant to come forward to do field jobs (income generation job for people being involuntarily resettled, for example). Instead their preference is to stay back in their offices and do research and such desk jobs.

Many NGOs simply lack the experience necessary to perform their job. Galab and Reddy (1998) report one scheme of income generation for displaced people from the Singoor project which did not work due to the NGO's lack of familiarity with local traditions and conditions. Despite reluctance of the people, this NGO went forward with its plan to distribute the high milk yielding Jersey cows, little aware of the fact that these people had neither experience of nor inclination for rearing cows. The NGO did not even bother to check the local demand for milk. As people could not take due care of cows or feed them properly, many cows died. A few that survived the neglect became unproductive.

Often, NGOs arrive on the scene with the project. They would not be around if there were no project. Many NGOs have sprung up from almost nowhere simply because there is money in resettlement. They are game for anything that promises to be lucrative. "NGOs are getting into event management, media management and business planning for better returns. Today, heading an NGO is almost like running a business. These organisations sell everything-gender sensitisation, sanitation, AIDs awareness, palliative care, education, policy research, legal advice, water management, tree plantation and housing". (Kaul: 2000)

A major criticism against the NGOs is their reliance on government funding support. NGOs are becoming mere contractors for government agencies, middlemen who take money for a job and do it indifferently. As Slim remarked: "Increasingly dependent on government funding, it is becoming commonplace to question the appropriateness of the 'N' in the NGO acronym". (Slim:1997) The fact that many of the NGOs active in protest movements receive foreign support, and often use their external networks to influence policies, also lends them to be dubbed as anti-national. The cash compensation is never adequate to enable the displaced to rebuild their livelihoods, yet NGOs in the Singrauli region have often negotiated with the NTPC for just cash payment. For NGOs this is an attractive proposition. It is the easiest way to organise the affected people and to win a quick victory (though the cash may prove inadequate in the long-run). (Perera:2000)

Once established at any project site, NGOs seem to be in no hurry to work themselves out of job. On one pretext or the other, they tend not to phase out, ensuring that local capacity building does not take place. They conveniently forget that "the goal should be to decrease dependency of relocatees on all outside organisations, not simply replace dependency on government agencies with dependency on NGOs" (Koenig and Diarra: 2000) Far from turning communities into self-reliant entities, they themselves are becoming dependent on them for 'doing development' in perpetuity. While nobody suggests the withdrawal without first preparing people to take full charge of their affairs, but the reluctance to hand over local affairs to people's own local organisations is not desirable.

It is the anti-development slant of some NGOs that has provoked the most criticism. In pursuing anti-development goals they seem to follow no holds barred approach. As Singh (1997) reported, the campaigning against the construction of

Sardar Sarovar dam on Narmada river the Narmadan Bachao Andolan (NBA) went as far as preventing all project officials and other government officers from entering the project area villages. This put the tribal people of the valley in a position of total dependence on the NBA for information and leadership. The people earlier deprived of basic information about the prospect of displacement now received incomplete information on resettlement opportunities, and-more importantly perhaps-on possibilities of negotiation for improved resettlement. Gill (1995) goes as far as to speak of the 'reign of terror' unleashed by the NBA on government officials as well as on those oustees who preferred to negotiate with the government in the light of a revised resettlement policy. He questions the NBA claim that the oustees are against the dam per se, and determined to oppose displacement no matter what the government offers them. He also cites the cases where oustees have had to resist the NBA's pressure tactics in order to establish contact with the government to discuss resettlement. He also criticises NBA's disinformation activities.

Limitations of NGOs

While NGOs have played an important role in resettlement, often their outreach has remained limited. People served are usually a fraction of the affected population. When asked about the role of NGOs in their communities, most people rank the contribution of the NGOs to their development as secondary to the government efforts. Even in areas where they operate, the people are often unaware of their existence. One major limitation is that NGOs often do not exist in project areas where their need is the greatest. On the other hand, in some other areas they are heavily concentrated.

In the Singrauli region efforts of the NTPC to involve NGOs in resettlement activities proved largely unsuccessful. NTPC then set up their own NGO called 'Chetna', managed by their staff in its spare time. NGOs tend to get rooted at one place; they find expanding their operations in other places a bit problematic. For example, an NGO that has done successful work in resettlement in Bombay may not necessarily be equally effective in Calcutta. The NGOs in Calcutta too may not much welcome an outside NGO on their home turf. A number of NGOs have chosen a confrontational stance. They see no use in any collaborative relationship with government agencies. The presence of NGOs with an adversarial outlook proves a hindrance to agencies providing resettlement assistance to those affected by development projects. Such NGOs tend to keep away from government agencies, and this prevents a potentially productive relationship from developing. NGOs are willing to work with government agencies under contract, but quibble over the use of term 'contractor' to describe their legal status. Although contracting is one of the important functions of NGOs, the term 'contractor' evokes a negative perception of their role. (Partly this may be due to the fact that the expression 'contractor' is not felicitious in India).

The management capacity is often a limitation, hindering overall effectiveness. Often NGOs are without adequately equipped staff to deal with day-to-day problems of management and accounting. With a tight budget they operate on a voluntary basis. Recognising the limitations of the NGO approach, Morse and Berger (1992) observed: "But there is a limit to what non-government organizations can achieve. They may be effective at the level of community mobilization and policy design; they may have the ability and experience to shape policies in a way that no one else could; and they may be able to help the process of implementation. But their resources do not allow them to achieve all this for thousands of families spread across several hundred villages...Nor should they be expected even to attempt so vast an undertaking".

The NGO Viewpoint

NGOs too have a long list of complaints against the way resettlement is managed by development agencies. They think that when they are asked to do resettlement, it is to ask them to do work that can hardly be successful, the failure for which NGOs will then have to take responsibility. A related complaint is that usually they are brought into the picture too late, and are then expected to produce results magically. In the Singoor Project where NGOs were associated with income generating schemes for the displaced people, NGO experience with government agencies has not been a very happy one. (Galab and Reddy: 1998) NGOs have faced certain difficulties in the implementation process vis-a-vis the role of resettlement and rehabilitation authorities. While NGOs were given a relatively free hand in the preparation of plans, the same kind of autonomy was not witnessed during the implementation phase. This often resulted in some friction between NGOs and the authorities. In some villages, this resulted in inordinate delays. The required level of cooperation from officials (particularly those at the grassroots) was lacking and this had considerable repercussions.

Although purchasing committees were constituted comprising beneficiaries, officials and NGO representatives, the officials on may occasions rejected the choice of beneficiaries related to the purchase of the asset. On many occasions purchases were cancelled due to such problems. In animal husbandry schemes, it was felt that the places of purchase were thrust upon beneficiaries. Project affected families were taken to places as far as 500 kilometres away, suffering much hardship. True, some were involved in fictitious purchases in the early stages of the scheme's implementation. But shifting purchases to such far off destinations was unwarranted. NGOs did not have much say to change the course of events. However, the involvement of NGOs improved the process substantially.

Had the authorities given NGOs more discretion the economic rehabilitation programme would have been much more effective, benefiting larger numbers. It would have considerably mitigated the hardships faced by the project affected families. NGOs are not oblivious to some of their own weaknesses and are, in fact, quite concerned about the rapid loss of their popularity. Their protests against development projects do not seem to evoke the kind of response which they should. Analysing the reasons why "these protests do not enjoy adequate hearing space or acquire the necessary momentum and political clout is that they have, in the main, been marked by weaknesses and schisms in the mobilisation of different players. For instance, in the case of the Narmada Valley Project, differences between those who were arguing for appropriate relief and rehabilitation for the displaced and those who articulated a blanket 'no dam' position: between those who favoured a greater mobilisation of the project affected people and those who sought to lobby and influence the concerned officialdom, did not help in conveying a sense of cohesion. It also helped the Government to play off one set of activists against another. Secondly, all such movements have so far been led by NGOs, which to put it mildly, have enjoyed an antagonistic relationship with political parties."

Government-NGO Relationship

The friction between project officials and NGOs contracted to work for the project is not uncommon. In some cases this results in project authorities terminating the contract, and NGOs retaliating with withdrawal from the project in the middle of the implementation process. For government personnel the reasons of dissatisfaction with NGOs are many. They are city based with no knowledge of local conditions where they are supposed to work. In fact, NGOs rarely move into the project area, preferring to operate from their offices in the city. Their presence in the project is minimal. Usually a few poorly paid, inadequately qualified staff are assigned to the project area. The staff turnover is too rapid to provide any continuity in service to the people. The potential for government-NGO collaboration in resettlement is enormous. Much however remains to be done. The collaboration has not proceeded on a completely smooth course, but both governments and NGOs are rapidly learning the ways to pool their skills, and to organise their action plans in ways that prove beneficial to those most in need. (Bhat: 1992) So far the results of this collaboration have been mixed. While NGOs have been helpful in managing relocation, the main resettlement task, namely the restoration or improvement of incomes and livelihoods, is proving to be an uphill one. As Morsea and Berger (1992) noted "it is one thing to persuade people to move, and provide them with a house and some land at a resettlement site; it is another thing to ensure their long-term rehabilitation".

Government agencies have necessarily to choose NGOs that have the right credentials. Such NGOs are still small in number. Often NGOs with expertise in generating new income and employment opportunities for the displaced people are also unwilling to come forward. Resettlement has nowhere been an east task, and the risk of failure which may boomerang on their credibility has held back many NGOs. The choice before development agencies interested in working with NGOs is thus very limited. On their part, the government agencies, too, are unhesitatingly seeking NGO assistance in the planning and implementation of resettlement operations. Closeness to people gives NGOs a distinct advantage in assisting them. Barring those who on ideological considerations wish to steer away from government programmes, NGOs are now increasingly coming forward to work with development agencies. They are also recognising the need to have good working relationship with project authorities. (Das:198) Although there is still a long way to go, the results of this cooperative activity are beginning to bear fruit. In Gujarat the resettlement process has been greatly facilitated by NGOs. Morse and Berger (1992) noted that the identification of land, its purchase and selection by oustees, and many other aspects of the relocation process were greatly assisted by the collaboration between non-government organizations and Nigam officials.

The NGO Contribution

The role of NGOs in planning and implementing of resettlement is now being more fully acknowledged. Morse and Berger (1992) consider commendable the role played by NGOs in relocating people affected by the Sardar Sarovar Narmada Project in Gujarat. In their estimate without Arch Vahini and Anand Niketan the resettlement process would have been little short of disastrous. Moreover, the Sardar Sarovar Narmada Project experience has clearly demonstrated the important role that NGOs played in forcing the government and funding agencies to incorporate the human and environmental dimensions into developmental projects.

The NGO presence in many project areas has made people more vocal in demanding their rightful claims. As (Marsden: 1998) pointed out, "the emergence of large number of organisations of civil society has meant that poor performance is increasingly visible, and more easily translates into pressures for action and change. It is no longer easy for powerful organisations to ride roughshod over the interests of the weak and marginalised, or to impose solutions which have not been publicly debated and agreed to by all the major stakeholders. This imposes increased costs on projects, which means that it is no longer possible to conduct business in the same way; dealing successfully with R&R involves the development of a different cost-benefit analysis, a different configuration of interest groups, and the establishment of new alliances."

In India, NGOs have played an important role in formulation of the national policy on resettlement which, however, is still at a draft stage. (Fernandes: 1998) In addition, NGOs also provide important lobbying functions, to ensure greater compliance with newer and stronger policy guidelines, at local and international levels through emerging global linkage.

Where there are no NGOs, the displaced people are often unable to get resettlement assistance to which they are entitled. Parasuraman (1999) found the absence of NGOs in the Upper Krishna project to be an important factor contributing to the failure of resettlement programme. "The absence of advocacy groups had serious negative consequences for the welfare of the displaced people. The multiplicity of castes, the numerical predominance of backward castes and the strong economic differences within and between the caste groups effectively prevented the people from organizing themselves to bargain for better R&R provisions. At the same time, the intervention of advocacy groups from outside the affected villages was also absent. (Parasuraman: 1999/178) Mathur and Marsden: (1998) sum up the NGO contribution to resettlement as follows: "If involuntary resettlement today figures prominently on the development agenda, much credit for it must go to the voluntary organisations. Their persistent campaigns, giving a voice to the people marginalized by development projects, have done a lot to bring about a perceptible change in the way the resettlement task is now visualised."

Bibliography

Aggarwal, Santosh : *Three Language Formula: An Educational Problem*, New Delhi, Sian, 1991.

Ainley, P.: *Degrees of Difference*, London, Lawrence and Wishart, 1994.

Almond, B.: *Applied Philosophy: Morals and Metaphysics in Contemporary Debate*, London, Routledge, 1991.

Belanger, P. and Valdivielso, S.: *The Emergence of Learning Societies,* NY, Pergamon, 1997.

Bottery, M. : *The Ethics of Educational Management: Personal, Social and Political Perspectives on School Organization*, London, Cassell, 1992.

Collins, M.: *Adult Education as Vocation: A Critical Role for the Adult Educator,* London, Routledge, 1991.

Coombs, P. And Ahmed, M.: *Attacking Rural Poverty. How Non-formal Education can help*, Baltimore, John Hopkins Press, 1974.

Elliott, J. : *Action Research for Educational Change*, Milton Keynes, Open University, 1991.

Evers, C. & Lakomski, G. : *Knowing Educational Administration*, Oxford, Pergamon, 1991.

Galbraith, M.W. : *Education Through Community Organizations*, San Francisco, Jossey-Bass, 1990.

Giroux, H. : *Critical Theory and Educational Practice*, Geelong, Australia, Deakin University, 1983.

Goodlad, John I. : *Educational Renewal: Better Teachers, Better Schools*, San Francisco, Jossey-Bass, 1994.

Grace, G. : *School Leadership: Beyond Educational Management*, London, Falmer, 1995.

Jeffs, T. and Smith, M. : *Using Informal Education*, Milton Keynes, Open University Press, 1990.

Kennedy, K.J. : *Citizenship Education and the Modern State*, Washington, D.C: Falmer Press, 1997.

Lovett, T. : *Adult Education, Community Development and the Working Class*, London, Ward Lock, 1975.

McConnell, C. : *Community Education: The Making of an Empowering Profession*, Edinburgh, Scottish Community Education Council, 1996.

McGivney, V. : *Informal Learning in the Community, A Trigger for Change and Development*, Leicester, NIACE, 1999.

Mocker, D. and Spear, G.: *Lifelong Learning: Formal, Nonformal, Informal, and Self-directed*, Columbus, OH, 1982.

Nuna, S.C. : *Education and Development*, NIEPA, New Delhi, 1987.

Potter D. : *Information Technology and Higher Education: A Twenty Year View*, Unpublished Paper, 1996.

Premi, M.K. : *Educational Planning in India*, New Delhi, Sterling, 1972.

Simkins, T. : *Non-formal Education and Development*, Manchester, Manchester University, 1977.

Smith, M.K. : *Local Education, Community, Conversation, Action*, Buckingham, Open University Press, 1994.

Sommerlad, L.: *Informal Learning & Widening Participation: Literature Review*, London, Tavistock Institute, 1999.

Torres, C. A.: *The Politics of Nonformal Education in Latin America*, New York, Praeger, 1990.

Warner D. and Palfreyman D. : *Higher Education Management: The Key Elements*, London, The Society for Research into Higher Education and Open University Press, 1996.

Werner, E.E. and Smith, R.S.: *Vulnerable But Invincible: A Study of Resilient Children*, New York, McGraw-Hill, 1982.

Wiggins, Grant : *Educative Assessment: Designing Assessments to inform and Improve Student Performance*, San Francisco, Jossey-Bass, 1998.

Index

□□□